A BRIEF

HISTORY OF

MOTION

Tom Standage

A BRIEF

HISTORY OF

MOTION

From the Wheel,
to the Car, to What Comes Next

BLOOMSBURY PUBLISHING

NEW YORK · LONDON · OXFORD · NEW DELHI · SYDNEY

BLOOMSBURY PUBLISHING
Bloomsbury Publishing Inc.
1385 Broadway, New York, NY 10018, USA

BLOOMSBURY, BLOOMSBURY PUBLISHING, and the Diana logo are trademarks
of Bloomsbury Publishing Plc

First published in the United States 2021

LIBRARY OF CONGRESS CATALOGING-IN-PUBLICATION DATA IS AVAILABLE

ISBN: HB: 978-1-63557-361-9; eBook: 978-1-63557-362-6

2 4 6 8 10 9 7 5 3 1

Typeset by Westchester Publishing Services
Printed and bound in the U.S.A. by Berryville Graphics Inc., Berryville, Virginia

To find out more about our authors and books visit www.bloomsbury.com and sign up
for our newsletters.

Bloomsbury books may be purchased for business or promotional use. For information
on bulk purchases please contact Macmillan Corporate and Premium Sales Department at
specialmarkets@macmillan.com.

To Kirstin, my lifelong co-driver, with thanks for all the adventures

CONTENTS

INTRODUCTION

Many of our technology-related problems arise because of the unforeseen consequences when apparently benign technologies are employed on a massive scale.

—MELVIN KRANZBERG, AMERICAN HISTORIAN (1917–95)

The story of the dawn of the automotive era traditionally goes something like this.

In the 1890s the biggest cities of the Western world faced a mounting problem. Horse-drawn vehicles had been in use for thousands of years, and it was hard to imagine life without them. But as the number of such vehicles increased during the nineteenth century, the drawbacks of using horses in densely populated cities were becoming ever more apparent. In particular, the accumulation of horse manure on the streets, and the associated stench, were impossible to miss. By the 1890s around 300,000 horses were working on the streets of London, and more than 150,000 in New York City. Each of these horses produced an average of twenty-two pounds (ten kilograms) of manure a day, plus a quart (about a liter) of urine. Collecting and removing thousands of tons of waste from stables and streets proved increasingly difficult.

The problem had literally been building up for decades. A newspaper editor in New York City declared in 1857 that "with the exception of a very few thoroughfares, all the streets are one mass of reeking, disgusting filth, which in some places is piled to such a height as to render them almost impassable to vehicles." Residents of other American cities voiced similar complaints, describing the streets as "too foul to serve as the sties for the hogs," "filthy in the extreme," and "extremely unhealthy." As well as filling the air with a terrible stench, the abundance of horse manure turned streets into muddy cesspools whenever it rained. An eyewitness account from London in the 1890s describes the "mud" (the accepted euphemism among prudish Victorians) that often flooded the Strand, one of the city's main thoroughfares, as having the consistency of thick pea soup. Passing vehicles "would fling sheets of such soup—where not intercepted by trousers or skirts—completely across the pavement," spattering and staining nearby houses and shop fronts.

Crossing sweepers would help the well-to-do across the road in larger cities, ensuring for a small fee that the path was clear of fresh horse droppings. But any street that was not constantly cleared, noted an American writer in 1899, "is literally carpeted with a warm, brown matting of comminuted horse-dropping, smelling to heaven and destined in no inconsiderable part to be scattered in fine dust in all directions," as it was ground down by iron-shod wheels and hooves. Manure collected from the streets was piled up at dumps dotted around major towns and cities. Huge piles of manure also built up next to stables and provided an attractive environment for flies. Health officials in Rochester, New York, calculated that if the manure produced by the fifteen thousand horses in the city each year was piled up, it would cover an acre of ground to a height of 175 feet and breed 16 billion flies. And Rochester was a small city by comparison with Chicago, which had five times as many horses, or New York City, which had ten times as many.

All of this was bad for public health. The board of health's statisticians in New York City found higher levels of infectious disease "in dwellings and schools within fifty feet of stables than in remoter locations," the *New York Times* reported in 1894. According to one turn-of-the-century calculation, twenty thousand New Yorkers died annually from "maladies that fly in the dust," clear evidence of the dangers posed to health by reliance on horses. To make matters worse, horses were frequently overworked, and when they dropped dead, their bodies were often left rotting on the streets for several days before being dismembered and removed, posing a further health risk. By the 1880s, fifteen thousand dead horses were being removed from the streets of New York City each year.

Paradoxically, the advent of the steam locomotive and the construction of intercity railway links, starting in the 1830s, had helped make the problem worse. Faster and more efficient transport between cities increased the demand for rapid transport of people and goods within them, which required a greater number of horse-drawn vehicles. "Our dependence on the horse has grown almost *pari passu* [step for step] with our dependence on steam," noted one observer in 1872. The result was more horses, more manure—and steadily worsening congestion. One observer in 1870 wrote that Broadway in Manhattan was "almost impassable" at some times of the day. By 1890, "streets in the lower part of the city are completely blocked three or four days out of the week," observed *Scientific American*. And when the traffic did move, it was deafening, as metal horseshoes and iron-rimmed wheels clattered over uneven surfaces. In the 1890s conversation was barely possible on New York City streets because of the sound of traffic. Straw was sometimes strewn on roads outside hospitals, and some private houses, to reduce the din.

Pollution, congestion, and noise were merely the most obvious manifestations of a deeper dependency. An outbreak of equine influenza in North America in October 1872 incapacitated all horses and mules for several weeks, providing a stark reminder of society's reliance on animal power. The *New York Times* noted "the disappearance of trucks, drays, express-wagons and general vehicles" from the streets. "The present epidemic has brought us face to face with the startling fact that the sudden loss of horse labor would totally disorganize our industry and commerce," noted the *Nation*. Horses and stables, the newspaper observed, "are wheels in our great social machine, the stoppage of which means injury to all classes and conditions of persons, injury to commerce, to agriculture, to trade, to social life."

Yet societies on both sides of the Atlantic continued to become steadily more dependent on horses. Between 1870 and 1900, the number of horses in American cities grew fourfold, while the human population merely doubled. By the turn of the century there was one horse for every ten people in Britain, and one for every four in the United States. Providing hay and oats for horses required vast areas of farmland, reducing the space available to grow food for people. Feeding America's 20 million horses required one third of its total crop area, while Britain's 3.5 million horses had long been reliant on imported fodder.

Horses had become both indispensable and unsustainable. To advocates of a newly emerging technology, the solution seemed obvious: get rid of horses and replace them with self-propelling motor vehicles, known at the time as horseless carriages. Today we call them cars.

In recent years this episode (sometimes referred to as "the great horse-manure crisis," though nobody called it that at the time) has been cited as evidence of the power of innovation, and an example of how simple technological fixes to seemingly intractable problems will show up just when they are needed—so there is no need to worry about climate change, for instance. Yet it should instead be seen as a cautionary tale in the other direction: that what looks like a quick fix today may well end up having far-reaching and unintended consequences tomorrow. The switch from horses to cars was not the neat and timely technological solution that it might seem, because cars changed the world in all kinds of unanticipated ways—from the geography of cities to the geopolitics of oil—and created many problems of their own.

Today it is the motor vehicle, rather than the horse, that seems unsustainable. The *Horseless Age*, a magazine founded in 1895 to champion the new technology, proudly declared that "in cities and in towns the noise and clatter of the streets will be reduced," because of cars' rubber tires—yet it is still difficult today to hear yourself think on Broadway. The average speed of cars in central London today is 8 mph, the same as it was for a horse-drawn carriage in the 1890s, belying predictions that cars, taking up less space on the road, would reduce congestion. Road accidents are a major cause of death and injury worldwide. Huge areas of land are devoted to parking, even as cars sit unused, on average, 95 percent of the time—making cities as much dormitories for cars as habitats for people. "On sanitary grounds too the banishing of horses from our city streets will be a blessing," the *Horseless Age* declared. But although the pollution produced by cars is harder to see than horse manure, it is just as dangerous to human health (in the form of poisonous fumes and particulates) and to the planet (in the form of climate-changing greenhouse gases).

These modern problems show the story of the adoption of the automobile in a new light. They also give it new relevance, because a little over a century later, we once again find ourselves grappling with the question of the sustainability of the dominant means of urban transport. As in the 1890s, we are approaching a fork in the road. But this time around, history can help us choose which path to take.

Just as it was once difficult to envisage how society would function without horses, it is hard to imagine how the modern world would function without so many motor vehicles. But a pandemic disease has once again emptied the streets in cities around the world, providing a glimpse of what it would look like to turn away from the car. And just as in the 1890s, there is both growing recognition of the need for change—driven by concerns over environmental impact, safety, and congestion—and a multitude of newly emerged alternatives vying for consideration.

Back then horseless carriages existed in a wide variety of shapes and sizes and were variously propelled by internal combustion engines, electric motors, or steam power. It was not immediately clear what sort of vehicle would prevail, or even what to call it. Horseless carriages were also, like the horse-drawn variety, assumed to be something only the rich would be able to afford. But for the less wealthy, hailing a cab would at least get cheaper, because removing horses would reduce operating costs. An article published in June 1899 in the *Los Angeles Times*, under the headline "Coming of the Auto," provided a primer on these "odd-looking, rapidly-moving, ingeniously-constructed vehicles" for the city's residents. It predicted that within a year, "the automobile, with all its comfort, simplicity, cheapness and speed, will soon be as familiar a sight to the residents of Los Angeles as they now are to the citizens of New York, London and Paris." The article explained that "electric automobiles are now considered the best for city use." The introduction of electric vehicles to Los Angeles would offer citizens "a cheaper cab service than they now enjoy . . . by reason of the excessively cheap cost of maintaining electric cabs as compared with maintaining the horses and cabs of a horse-cab service." Anyone who has been to Los Angeles will have noticed that things turned out rather differently, however: most people do not get around the city by hailing electric cabs when needed.

Everything was up for grabs in the 1890s, but although change seemed inevitable, nobody knew what the world would look like after the passing of the horse. Today there is once again a sense of change, opportunity, and uncertainty, as a result of a sudden proliferation of new forms of transport. Electric cars, having failed to take off in the early twentieth century, are in ascendance a century later. Switching the world's cars over to electric propulsion would go a long way to reducing their environmental impact, though traffic and safety concerns would remain. Meanwhile, smartphone apps have made public-transport services simpler to navigate. Ride-hailing apps can summon a taxi with a few taps. App-based car-rental and car-sharing services provide access to a vehicle for a few hours or days. Bikes and scooters can be found on street corners in many cities for rental by the minute. And even more radical approaches are coming over the horizon. Proponents of autonomous or self-driving cars predict that summoning a robotaxi when needed will eventually be cheaper than car ownership, and that such vehicles could reduce traffic congestion and road deaths. More ambitious still are the start-ups working on flying cars—giant aerial drones that are large enough to carry people.

Revisiting the history of the car, and how it changed the world, can provide a roadmap to help make sense of these new transport options, by showing how social, political, and technological forces interact to produce both expected and unexpected outcomes. That is the tale this book will tell, putting the rise of the car, and the future of urban transport, into a broader historical context. Although it starts in the ancient Near East and then moves to Europe, it is a heavily America-centric story, because of America's outsize role in the development of global car customs and culture, from Stop signs to shopping malls. Along the way, this book will examine the various ways in which the modern world has been shaped by the car, many of which are so familiar we no longer notice them. Why does red mean stop and green mean go? Why do some countries drive on the left, and some on the right? How did cars redefine dating, eating, and shopping? The answers to these questions are more than just trivia.

They serve as a reminder that seemingly unimportant decisions can have consequences decades or even centuries later—something that is worth bearing in mind when making choices about the future. Many modern habits, behaviors, and attitudes toward cars were shaped in a brief period in the first half of the twentieth century and have persisted to this day. But we have forgotten their origins and no longer question them; we just assume that is the way things must be.

Today's car-centric civilization is the result of a succession of choices, extending back through millennia. Many of those choices could easily have gone a different way, and they now make change difficult—a phenomenon known as path dependency. But by understanding those choices, and the context in which they were made, it is possible to draw lessons from eras past that can be applied today.

So buckle up for a road trip through five thousand years of history, from the wheel, to the car, to what comes next—a brief history of motion. Considering the consequences of the car offers us a road map for dealing with the unforeseen impacts of new forms of transport. By learning from the past, we are more likely to ask the right questions and make informed choices in the future. And as we start to unpick the car from the fabric of modern life, it is helpful to see where and how it was woven in.

A BRIEF

HISTORY OF

MOTION

1

Wheels in the Ancient World

Men's fortunes are on a wheel, which in its turning suffers not the same man to prosper forever.

—HERODOTUS

A HISTORICAL TURNING POINT

It all starts with the wheel. Today, in a world that has literally been built to accommodate wheeled vehicles, it is difficult to imagine life without them. The story of how such vehicles transformed the world begins around 3500 B.C.E., with the invention of the wheel. It is an idea whose power seems obvious in retrospect. Yet the notion that the wheel is the greatest invention in history is recent. Only in the past century or two, in a world that runs on wheels, has its usefulness become universally apparent. Wheeled vehicles faced a surprising amount of resistance. Enthusiasm for them went through many ups and downs over thousands of years. And many cultures, despite knowledge of the wheel, declined to use it at all.

The wheel was long assumed to have been invented in Mesopotamia, the region between the Tigris and Euphrates rivers that roughly corresponds with modern Iraq. Known as the cradle of Western civilization, this was where cities and writing first emerged, around 3200–3000 B.C.E., so it was not unreasonable to conclude that wheels originated there, too. And there is evidence for wheels in Mesopotamia during this period, in the form of pictograms on clay tablets that seem to show wheeled wagons, though they could also be sledges on rollers. Free-spinning (but horizontal) potter's wheels were in use in the region by this time, so vertically mounted wheels would not have been a big leap. Archaeologists concluded that the idea must quickly have spread from its presumed Mesopotamian birthplace, because evidence for wheeled vehicles also appears roughly simultaneously in northern and eastern Europe.

Yet in recent decades carbon-dating evidence has lent support to a competing view: that the wheel emerged in Europe first. The earliest-known wheeled object is a clay model of a bull, mounted on four wheels, found in the Carpathian Mountains of western Ukraine and carbon-dated to 3950–3650 B.C.E., hundreds of years before any sign of wheeled vehicles in Mesopotamia. A representation of a four-wheeled vehicle, scratched onto a pot found in Bronocice in southern Poland, just north of the Carpathian Mountains, has been carbon-dated to 3630–3380 B.C.E. Parallel ruts observed at Flintbek in northern Germany, dated to 3400 B.C.E., suggest that a wheeled vehicle was used to move soil during the construction of a long barrow; the uneven shape of the ruts indicates that they were made by wheels, rather than the runners of a sledge. And the oldest actual wheel ever found, the so-called Ljubljana Marshes Wheel, dates to around 3200 B.C.E. and was discovered in modern-day Slovenia.

People living in the Carpathian region would have had both the means and the motivation to create wheeled vehicles during this period, which is known as the Copper Age. As the name suggests, this was when metalworking first began, allowing tools to be made from copper rather than stone. (Bronze, an alloy of copper and tin, was subsequently found to be stronger than copper alone, ushering in the Bronze Age.) The Carpathian Mountains are rich in copper ore, but producing an ingot of the metal still required the processing of large amounts of ore, which had to be dug out of the mountains by hand. Shifting heavy loads of ore would

The earliest wheels, such as the Ljubljana Marshes Wheel (dated to around 3200 B.C.E.) were made of planks fastened together using battens.

have been laborious, even with the aid of wicker backpacks, or large baskets dragged on sledges or on top of wooden rollers.

So an enterprising copper miner might first have had the idea of attaching four wooden wheels to the base of a wicker basket, to make what is now known as a mine cart, which could then be pushed or pulled by hand. Cutting up wood to make wheels and axles would have been quite possible using copper woodworking tools such as chisels and adzes—items that copper miners would have had access to. Contrary to popular belief, the earliest wooden wheels would not have been made by cutting circular slices from large logs; that would have required metal saws, which are a later invention, and single-piece wheels made by slicing logs are small (making them less able to traverse uneven ground) and weak. Instead, logs were repeatedly split from end to end using hammers and wedges, and wheels were cut from the resulting planks. By fixing two or more planks together, wheels with a larger diameter than that of the tree from which the planks were cut could be made. (The Ljubljana Marshes Wheel, for example, is made from two planks fastened together using wooden strips, called battens.)

The idea that the first wheeled vehicles were hand-pulled Carpathian mine carts, proposed by the historian Richard Bulliet in 2016, would explain why so much of the early evidence for wheels is found in and around the region. More than 150 clay drinking vessels with four wheels, dating from 3500–3000 B.C.E., have been found on the southern flanks of the Carpathian Mountains. They have been discovered in settlements and graves, which suggests that they were not mere toys, but were models of larger vehicles that played an important role in the local culture. Many of them have patterns on their sides that are suggestive of wickerwork. But even if these were indeed the first wheeled vehicles, the idea almost immediately led to the creation of four-wheeled wooden wagons pulled by cattle. The wagon drawn on the Bronocice pot shows the pole and

A representation of a four-wheeled vehicle is scratched onto this pot, found in Bronocice in southern Poland and dated to around 3500 B.C.E.

yoke that would have allowed it to be pulled by two oxen. These were the first vehicles capable of carrying heavy loads, or people. Whether the first wheels and wagons originated in Europe, in Mesopotamia, or in the area in between—the Pontic steppe around the north of the Black Sea—the notion of the four-wheeled wagon quickly spread along the trade routes that connected them. By 3000 B.C.E. such wagons could be found in all three regions, though they were being put to rather different uses.

REINVENTING THE WHEEL

In Europe wagons seem to have been used primarily for agriculture. It seems unlikely that they were used to transport loads over long distances—something that requires relatively flat, open country or well-maintained trackways. Early wagons lacked steering, which made them difficult to maneuver, and they also required care and maintenance. Repairing a broken wheel or axle would have required woodworking tools and would have been difficult to do while out and about. So early wagons would probably have had quite a limited operating range. In Europe, their use may have been restricted to short local trips within a particular farm or community, for example to transport manure into the fields and carry harvests and firewood into villages.

On the plains around the north and east of the Black Sea, however, the herders of the Pontic steppe found quite a different use for these vehicles: as mobile homes. Using wagons to carry food, supplies, and other possessions allowed nomads to move deep into the open steppe with their herds of cattle and sheep. These wagons moved slowly, at walking pace, and may not have covered much distance each day, as the herd moved from one source of fodder to the next. Their cultural significance is apparent from the appearance of "wagon graves," which have a wheel buried in each corner, so that the grave itself forms a kind of wagon, carrying its occupant into the afterlife. Such graves first appear on the Black Sea plains around 3300 B.C.E. The distinctive tradition of wagon nomadism in this region persisted for thousands of years; it is mentioned by the Greek historian Herodotus in the fifth century B.C.E., was adopted by the Mongols in the thirteenth century C.E., and survived into the modern era.

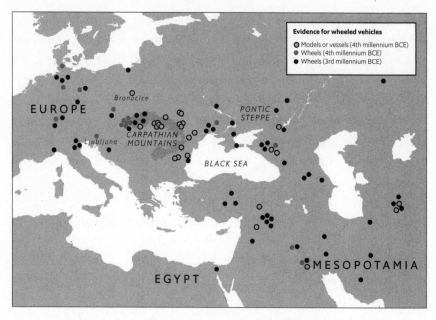

Map showing where the earliest known wheels (and depictions of wheels)
have been found, from Europe to Mesopotamia.

In Mesopotamia, meanwhile, the four-wheeled wagon was adopted for
military and ceremonial use. The Royal Standard of Ur, a Mesopotamian
artifact dated to around 2600 B.C.E., depicts four-wheeled battle vehicles
being pulled by onagers (similar to donkeys) as part of a ritual procession. Four of the wagons carry a driver, a warrior, and a supply of javelins, which suggests they were used as mobile battle platforms. Enemy
combatants are shown being crushed under their wheels. Yet these wagons
may not have proved terribly useful in combat: they offered little protection to the driver or warrior, would not been have able to move quickly,
and, lacking steering, would not have been very maneuverable. Their
main uses may have been to transport the king and his generals to the
battlefield (the king is depicted with his own battle wagon, without any
javelins), to provide observation posts, and to intimidate the enemy. They
may also have formed part of victory and funeral parades. As the historian
Stefan Burmeister puts it, wheeled vehicles "brilliantly combined locomotion with social elevation," raising Mesopotamian rulers above their

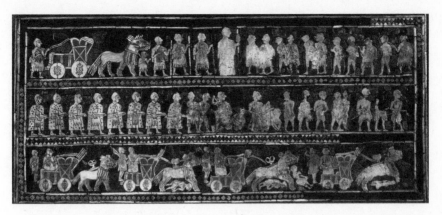

Depiction of wheeled vehicles in Mesopotamia, from the Royal Standard of Ur,
dated to around 2600 B.C.E.

subjects and granting them the superpower of being able to move while
standing still.

Wheeled vehicles were sufficiently unusual in this period in that they
had little or no impact on the layout of settlements or early cities. Some
of the earliest human settlements even seem to have lacked streets between
the buildings; instead, houses were constructed right next to each other,
and people moved between them by walking across their roofs, with
hatches providing access to the buildings below. Mesopotamian cities had
thoroughfares between their main gates and, in some cases, ceremonial
avenues, which would have been large enough to allow the use of wheeled
vehicles in parades. Their irregular mazes of narrow streets provided
protection against sun and windblown dust; wide, straight streets suitable for vehicles were unnecessary because goods were transported by
porters or pack animals. In Europe and Mesopotamia, the layout of
settlements—what we now call urban planning—was entirely driven by
the needs of people, not vehicles. For the nomads who lived in their
wagons, by contrast, their built environment was not merely influenced
by their vehicles—it consisted of them.

Wagons were clearly used in very different ways in these three regions.
The wheels depicted on the Royal Standard of Ur even look different
from European and Black Sea examples: they are made of three wooden
pieces that fit together, but the pieces are curved rather than straight

planks. This suggests that it was the idea of the wheel, rather than the specific knowledge of how to make it, that spread from its original birthplace. Once you've seen a wheel, after all, you can describe it to someone else or try to make your own—something that is not possible with, say, novel metallurgical or agricultural techniques based on specialist knowledge. Even so, wheels were only adopted in situations where the time and effort needed to make them could be justified. And that explains the surprising fact that, for thousands of years after their invention, wheels were not widely used.

THE RISE AND FALL OF THE CHARIOT

The Egyptians, for example, built the pyramids during the third millennium B.C.E. without the use of any wheels at all. They were surely familiar with the concept—their trade with neighboring Mesopotamia encompassed both goods (such as gold) and ideas (such as writing)—but when it came to the wheel, Egyptians were unimpressed. For moving things around, wheeled vehicles were not really needed; why bother with them when you have the Nile, the lifeline running through Egyptian civilization? In Egypt, as in Mesopotamia, heavy loads were most easily transported on water, using barges or rafts. On land, the Egyptians employed levers and rollers to move the large stone blocks used in construction. In any case no wheeled vehicle in existence could have borne their weight. Other cultures also chose to ignore the wheel. One common explanation for this is that wheeled vehicles require the availability of draft animals. But the Egyptians had oxen to pull their plows, yet still chose to ignore wheels, as did the cattle-herding societies of sub-Saharan Africa. And in the Americas, where wheels are found on small animal figurines, people could easily have built hand-drawn mine carts. But evidently they concluded that wheeled vehicles were not worth the bother.

Wagons with four solid wheels were heavy and slow and, lacking steering, could only make gentle turns, which limited their usefulness. Two-wheeled vehicles, or carts, which had emerged by 3000 B.C.E., were more maneuverable and could make much tighter turns, particularly if the wheels could turn independently, rather than being fixed at the ends of a single axle. Starting in around 2000 B.C.E., these two-wheelers began to evolve into a new and much faster vehicle: the chariot. Like a cart, it had two wheels, with the load balanced over a single axle. But chariots had spoked rather than solid wheels. These wheels could be much larger and lighter, which reduced rolling resistance and allowed chariots to achieve unprecedented speeds. Higher speeds were also possible because chariots were pulled not by oxen but by horses, which had been domesticated in the northern steppes starting around 3500 B.C.E. Two or four trotting horses could pull a chariot at 8 mph, more than twice the speed of an ox-drawn cart or wagon; galloping horses could pull a chariot faster still, at least on flat and relatively open ground.

Making a spoked wheel is far more complicated than making a solid one because it must be assembled from dozens of carefully shaped parts that have to fit together precisely. Making spoked wheels was the work of dedicated wheelwrights using specialist tools. The appeal of spoked wheels is not simply that they are lighter and allow vehicles to move faster. The maximum size of a solid, three-plank wheel is limited by the size of the planks available, which in turn is limited by the diameter of the largest available trees. Large spoked wheels, however, could be constructed even when large trees were not available, as was the case on the Black Sea plain, where they seem to have first emerged. The use of spoked wheels, in some cases as large as two meters in diameter, also allowed chariots to be driven at speed even over somewhat uneven terrain. Once the idea of the horse-drawn, two-wheeled chariot had emerged, it spread quickly, initially throughout the Middle East, and ultimately as far west as the British Isles and as far east as China. And no wonder, because chariots proved to be a transformational technology on the battlefield.

The pioneers of fast, lightweight military chariots were the Hittites, who used them to conquer most of Anatolia (modern-day Turkey) by 1700 B.C.E. This prompted neighboring peoples to adopt war chariots, including the Egyptians, who began using wheels for the first time. Capable of reaching the unprecedented and awesome speed of 25 mph, such chariots became closely associated with kingly prestige and military prowess. They were typically drawn by two horses and were used as mobile battle platforms that carried two or three people: a driver, an archer, and, in some cases, a shield bearer. The Egyptians further refined the chariot by paring down the design to make it even lighter and faster: one chariot found in the tomb of Tutankhamen weighed a mere thirty-five kilograms. (A wagon with four solid wheels, by contrast, might have weighed six hundred to seven hundred kilograms, and a cart with two solid wheels about half that.)

During battles, chariots would either face off directly in opposing rows (with archers firing at enemy chariots) or support infantry by harrying enemy troops with volleys of arrows. Chariots also carried spears, which could be thrown at closer range. The Battle of Kadesh, in 1274 B.C.E., is thought to have been the largest chariot battle in history, involving around five thousand chariots and more than fifty thousand soldiers. It pitted the Egyptians under the young king Rameses II, five years into his reign, against the Hittite king Muwatalli II. The Hittites lured the Egyptians into an ambush and scattered them with a surprise chariot attack. As his men began to retreat, Rameses leaped into his chariot and launched a counterattack. Leading several charges using the Egyptians' light, nimble chariots, Rameses inflicted heavy losses on the Hittite forces and their slower, heavier vehicles. The surviving Hittites ended up pinned against a river, where they abandoned their chariots and swam for their lives.

The battle is generally deemed by historians to have been a draw: the Egyptian forces ultimately failed to capture the city of Kadesh and returned home. But that did not stop Rameses from depicting himself as a heroic warrior, single-handedly turning the tide of the battle in his chariot, in a series of reliefs that were carved in temples across Egypt. These are perhaps the most famous examples of an entire genre of images from the era of chariot warfare, depicting warrior kings as they smite their enemies, parade in triumph, or hunt wild beasts in their vehicles. Rulers were buried with chariots as symbols of their military might; a total of six were found in Tutankhamen's tomb. Each would have taken about six hundred man-hours to build, according to a modern estimate. Access to these expensive, high-tech weapons signaled membership in the social and military elite. The Hittites and other peoples also depicted their gods riding in chariots, which implied that chariot-riding kings were their earthly representatives.

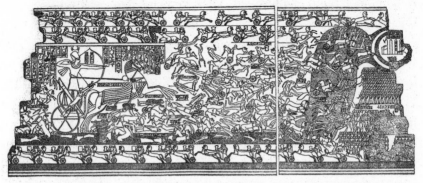

BATTLE SCENE FROM THE GREAT KADESH RELIEFS OF RAMSES II ON THE WALLS OF THE RAMESSEUM.

*Pharaoh Rameses II looking heroic in his chariot at the Battle of Kadesh,
as depicted in a relief on the walls of the Ramesseum in Thebes, Egypt.*

But the supremacy of the chariot on the battlefield did not last. Chariots could not be reliably used on uneven terrain, so their advantages were easily neutralized by placing obstacles across the battlefield to hinder their passage, or simply by avoiding battle on flat plains. Progress in horse breeding gradually produced larger, stronger animals that were capable of carrying a soldier in full armor. Cavalry units could move just as quickly as chariots, but were even more agile and could traverse uneven ground. That chariots were obsolete was vividly demonstrated at the Battle of Gaugamela in 331 B.C.E. The Persian king Darius III fielded chariots with scythes attached to their wheels and even had the battlefield cleared of bushes and vegetation that might impede their movement. But the Greek forces, led by Alexander the Great, opened their ranks to let the charging chariots pass, then surrounded and destroyed them. A mosaic found at the Roman town of Pompeii, based on an earlier Greek painting, depicts Alexander triumphant on his horse as a defeated Darius flees the battlefield in his chariot.

By the first century B.C.E, when Julius Caesar led the first Roman expedition to Britain, he was surprised to find that the British tribes were still using war chariots, which had fallen out of use in continental Europe. (Caesar noted that British warriors used the chariots to carry them into battle, where they would fight on foot while their chariots waited nearby, ready to pick them up if needed. They were, in effect, getaway vehicles.) Even as chariots began disappearing from the battlefield, however, they retained their association with kingly power and divine status. The gods were still assumed to ride chariots—the Greek sun god Helios was said to drive one across the sky every day, for example—and they were ridden in ceremonial processions by triumphant Roman generals, who would not have been seen dead in a chariot during an actual battle. Chariot racing was also an important part of the Olympic Games and a popular sport in Roman culture. With its thrilling speed and the potential for spectacular accidents, chariot racing was probably the world's first mass-spectator sport. Gaius Appuleius Diocles, a charioteer of the second century C.E., was both a celebrity and one of the best-paid athletes in history: his winnings are said to have exceeded 35 million sesterces, equivalent to more than $100 million today, ranking him among the Roman world's wealthiest men.

THE RULES OF THE ROMAN ROAD

The Romans may have shunned chariots on the battlefield, but they used less glamorous two-wheeled carts and four-wheeled wagons to carry military equipment and supplies, and to haul agricultural produce and other goods in and out of cities, taking advantage of the extensive and well-maintained Roman road network. Paving of roads began with the construction of the Via Appia, a military highway running southeast from Rome, starting in 312 B.C.E., and soon became widespread, both within towns and outside them. Laws governing the minimum width of Roman roads and streets date back to the fifth century B.C.E. And some of the first formal rules governing the use of wheeled vehicles, and the earliest examples of urban environments being reshaped to accommodate them, also date to the Roman period.

The use of vehicles within the city of Rome seems to have been entirely forbidden for centuries after its founding. Its streets were evidently too narrow and crowded for vehicular traffic; goods were instead moved through the city streets using mules or human porters. To facilitate deliveries and construction, Julius Caesar introduced a law in 45 B.C.E., the

Lex Julia Municipalis, allowing the use of wheeled vehicles in the city, but only from dusk until dawn, when the streets were the least busy. This rule had the obvious merit that anyone breaking it would have to do so in broad daylight and would be clearly visible. The only exceptions were for vehicles carrying certain priests and priestesses, and materials required for the construction or maintenance of temples. Juvenal, a Roman poet, grumbled about the noise made by vehicles at night, which suggests that the Lex Julia was still in force in the early second century C.E.

A different approach to traffic management was imposed in Pompeii, a town 150 miles south of Rome. Pompeii was founded in the sixth century B.C.E. by the Oscan people and became a Roman colony in the first century B.C.E. It had a fairly regular grid of streets, but they had not been planned with vehicles in mind and were unable to cope with growing volumes of traffic as the town prospered, becoming a popular resort for wealthy Romans. So the local authorities introduced a series of traffic-control measures, including detours to alleviate pressure on particularly busy streets or junctions, and an increasingly elaborate system of alternating one-way streets, much like that found in modern-day Manhattan, to prevent blockages on narrow streets that were unable to accommodate

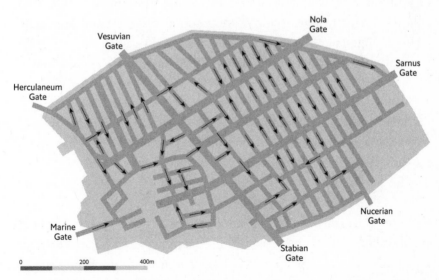

Map of Pompeii, showing its system of alternating one-way streets, much like that found in modern-day Manhattan (after Poehler, The Traffic Systems of Pompeii).

two-way traffic. The rules of Pompeii's traffic system, and the changing patterns of traffic flow, can be inferred from analysis of the shape of curbstones, particularly those at junctions, and the distinctive wear marks made on them by metal-rimmed wheels. Evidence from multiple Roman sites suggests that other towns introduced similar measures.

Timgad, a later Roman city founded around 100 C.E. in Algeria by Emperor Trajan, was planned from the start to accommodate vehicular traffic in a way that Pompeii had not been. One third of the city's area, more than twice the proportion in Pompeii, was given over to streets, which were on average more than fifteen feet across. They were all wide enough for two-lane traffic and were laid out on a regular grid. Many streets had colonnaded sidewalks to separate pedestrians and vehicles. An abundance of ramps, stable areas, and stone troughs to provide water for animals suggest that Timgad was built to support a higher density of traffic than Pompeii.

And when it came to two-way traffic, Romans clearly preferred to drive on the right, judging by evidence from wear marks on curbstones and the positioning of ramps in Pompeii, Timgad, and other Roman sites. As with many other aspects of Roman life, the evidence is most abundant in Pompeii, as a result of the city's preservation under a blanket of volcanic ash after the eruption of Vesuvius in 79 C.E. About three quarters of Pompeii's streets could accommodate only a single lane of traffic, but analysis of hundreds of wear marks on its larger, two-lane streets indicates that vehicles almost always traveled on the right. On the Via di Nola, for example, one of the city's main thoroughfares, 89 percent of the wear marks are associated with right-side driving. Visual depictions of Roman funeral processions and chariot races, on funerary urns and in mosaics, also indicate a preference for driving on the right.

This preference may have been practical in nature. Most people are right-handed, and when driving a cart or wagon being pulled by two or four horses, a right-handed person will prefer to sit on the left-hand side of the vehicle, or on the rearmost, left-hand horse, to be able to reach all the animals with a whip held in the right hand. And when sitting on the left, it is easier to drive on the right because it puts the driver close to the center of the road, providing better visibility of oncoming traffic and of vehicles passing on the other side of the road. For the Romans, right-side driving also had positive religious connotations. They likened life to a forked path where the virtuous choice was always on the right, and when entering temples and other buildings, they tried to ensure that their right foot was the first to cross the threshold. This is why *sinister* (the Latin word for "left") also came to mean "evil" or "unlucky."

The need for rules and infrastructure to accommodate vehicles was starting to shape the layout of cities and the texture of urban life. In Rome, vehicles and pedestrians were segregated across time: the narrow streets belonged to people during the day and to vehicles at night. In Timgad, they were segregated across space, with raised and colonnaded sidewalks for people, and wide roads to allow traffic to circulate—an early manifestation of the mistaken idea that providing more space for vehicles is the way to prevent traffic jams. But a countervailing trend was the Roman preference, starting in the first century C.E., for wide, ornamental boulevards that were closed to traffic and served as grand, pedestrianized public spaces flanked by civic buildings, fountains, and public amenities. Pompeii's system of traffic detours was necessary, in part, because of the closure of some of its main thoroughfares to vehicular traffic. The Romans were among the first to grapple with the challenges of traffic management, and the need to balance the provision of a pleasant environment for pedestrians versus the efficient flow of vehicles.

Do we still rely on Roman standards today? According to a popular internet meme, modern railway gauges in America are directly descended from the widths of the ruts in Roman roads, as found in Pompeii and other Roman sites. The American gauge was supposedly chosen to match the standard railway gauge in Britain, which in turn matched the standard gauge for horse-drawn carts and wagons—and that, so the story goes, was chosen to allow vehicles to run in the ruts in old Roman roads. American standard gauge (4 feet 8.5 inches, or 1.43 meters) does closely match the average Roman gauge (derived from wheel ruts) of 1.4 meters. But ever since the first wheeled vehicles emerged, their gauge has been consistent, falling in the range of 1.3 to 1.6 meters, with an average of 1.45 meters. Moreover, several gauges seem to have been in use in the Roman world, and the ruts in Pompeii (which were worn down by the passing traffic, rather than deliberately cut to act as tramways for vehicles) are wide enough to cope with a range of gauges from 1.3 to 1.6 meters. Also, multiple gauges were in use for farm wagons in Britain before the invention of railways, and both British and American railways used a variety of gauges before standardizing on 1.43 meters.

So there is no direct line of descent from Roman wagons to modern trains. Instead, it is more accurate to say that for thousands of years vehicles had their wheels, on average, about 1.43 meters apart. Another problem with this theory is that it assumes that rutted Roman roads remained in continuous use in Britain until the eighteenth century. In fact, most Roman roads fell into disrepair after the end of Roman rule. In much of North Africa, roads and wheeled vehicles were abandoned altogether in favor of camels. In Europe, meanwhile, horses emerged as the most prestigious means of transport. The adoption of the wheel had hit another bump in the historical road.

2

Your Carriage Awaits

Moreover, as Man *is the most noblest of all Creatures, and all foure-footed*
Beasts *are ordayned for his use and service; so a* Cart *is the Embleme of a*
Man, *and a* Coach *is the Figure of a* Beast; *For as* Man *hath two legges,
a* Cart *hath two wheeles . . . as much as* Men *are superior to* Beasts, *so
much are honest and needfull* Carts *more nobly to be regarded and esteemed,
above needlesse, upstart, fantasticall, and Time-troubling* Coaches.

—JOHN TAYLOR, "THE WORLD RUNNES ON WHEELES," 1623

WHY REAL MEN RODE HORSES

When a giant statue of the Roman emperor Marcus Aurelius was commissioned around 176 C.E., there was only one form it could possibly take if
it was to reflect the majesty of the world's most powerful man. Marcus
Aurelius presided over a period of relative political stability during the era
now known as the golden age of Rome. He was respected as a just ruler
and a skilled general who oversaw successful military campaigns against
the Parthian Empire, the kingdom of Armenia, and assorted Germanic
tribes. And thanks to his writings, he came to be revered as a philosopher
as well as an emperor. The statue, 4.25 meters (14 feet) tall, was made of

bronze covered in a layer of gold. It depicted the emperor wearing a toga, raising his right arm in triumph—and sitting on a horse.

Ever since cavalry had superseded war chariots on the battlefields, rulers had chosen to present themselves as heroic equestrians rather than charioteers, and horses had become the preferred means of transport for high-status men. In Rome, the emperor and his entourage would always take to the field on horseback, which both elevated them above ordinary soldiers and gave them a better view of the battle. (This was in an era before stirrups and rigid saddles, so they rode bareback, or sitting on layers of cloth—something modern swords-and-sandals movies often get wrong.) A relief on a triumphal arch erected at around the same time shows vanquished enemies submitting to Marcus Aurelius as he towers over them on his horse. The giant statue may originally have featured a defeated enemy chieftain cowering beneath the horse's raised front foot.

While men rode horses, wheeled vehicles had come to be associated with Rome's elite women. The prohibition on the use of passenger vehicles within Roman towns and cities was slowly relaxed from the first century C.E., starting at the top. Messalina and Agrippina, respectively the third and fourth wives of the emperor Claudius, were given special permission by the Senate to ride in a *carpentum*, an ornate two-wheeled cart with an arched covering, cushions, and silk curtains. This privilege was then extended to all emperors' wives, then senators' wives, and finally all well-to-do women. Carts and wagons were used to transport goods. But for Roman politicians and generals, the rules were clear: the only dignified way to travel was on horseback.

The disdain for wheels was not limited to the Roman world. Heroic depictions of Persian and Assyrian rulers had switched to showing them on horseback, rather than driving chariots, centuries earlier. And in the post-Roman period, camels replaced wheeled vehicles across North Africa, and as far east as modern Afghanistan; unlike carts or wagons, camels did not need roads and could easily cross deserts. After the fall of Rome wheels held on in Europe, at least, in the form of carts and wagons that carried agricultural loads. But in the centuries that followed, high-ranking European men aspired to the ideal of the valiant knight on horseback and came to see riding in a cart or wagon, rather than on a horse, as humiliating and shameful, and to be avoided at all costs. Einhard, a ninth-century scholar in the court of Charlemagne, mocked earlier Frankish kings for riding "in a cart, drawn by a yoke of oxen driven, peasant-fashion, by a plowman." Charlemagne, he implied, was a proper king because he rode a horse. Similarly, Jordanus Ruffus, knight farrier to Holy Roman Emperor Frederick II, observed around 1250 that "no animal is more noble than the horse, since it is by horses that princes, magnates and knights are separated from lesser people." A lord, he declared, "cannot fittingly be seen among private citizens except through the mediation of a horse."

The Knight of the Cart, a twelfth-century poem by Chrétien de Troyes, a French writer, illustrates the low regard in which wheeled vehicles had come to be held in the medieval period. It tells the story of Lancelot, a legendary Arthurian knight, on a quest to rescue Queen Guinevere. Having lost his horse, Lancelot encounters a cart-driving dwarf. At the time, Chrétien explains, carts were used as tools of punishment: any man convicted of a crime was placed on a cart and paraded through the streets, losing his honor and all his legal rights. So when the dwarf says he will only tell Lancelot what has become of the queen if he boards his cart, Lancelot hesitates. But such is his love for Guinevere that he overcomes his reluctance and climbs aboard. He then finds that people will not help him in his quest because by riding in a cart he is taken to be a lowly criminal, while knights mock him for having traveled in such a dishonorable manner. He is told, "Any knight is disgraced throughout the land after being in a cart."

The tale reflects the view of the time that a man is not truly a man unless he is riding on a horse. For women, however, the opposite was true: riding on horseback was considered indecent (not to mention impractical, given women's clothing at the time). Instead, continuing the Roman tradition, the appropriate manner for high-status women to travel over long distances was in an enclosed wagon, away from prying eyes. Four-wheeled wagons had by this time become much easier to maneuver with the addition of steerable front wheels, a Roman innovation. Such a wagon would be driven by a postilion, or by a male driver who was not a member of the elite; any men accompanying the wagon would be

on horseback. Particularly ornate vehicles were used as bridal conveyances at weddings—a stereotype that lives on in fairy tales in which knights
on horseback fall in love with princesses who travel in bejeweled carriages.
Consider, for example, the arrival of Beatrice of Naples in Hungary in
1476:

> The Princess, then bride-elect to Matthias Corvinus, King of
> Hungary, came to Buda in 1476 with a large suite. The bridegroom-
> King, accompanied by three thousand mounted noblemen, went to
> meet her at Fehérvár where she arrived in a gilded coach covered
> with gold-embroidered green velvet. The members of the Princess's
> suite travelled in seven richly gilded coaches, each of which was
> drawn by six horses; the coachmen wore velvet suits with gold
> buttons.

But this was hardly an everyday occurrence. By the year 1500 the
majority of wheeled vehicles, in the parts of the world where they were
still being used at all, were lowly two-wheeled agricultural carts. Five
thousand years after the invention of the wheel, it was still not in widespread use. In North Africa and much of the Middle East it had been
abandoned altogether; medieval Arabic and Persian do not even have
words for wheeled vehicles, and travelers' accounts as late as the eighteenth
century remark on their total absence in the Arab world. In Europe, meanwhile, wheeled vehicles had come to be seen as socially unacceptable by
elite men. But then, during the sixteenth century, European attitudes
toward wheeled vehicles underwent a sudden turnaround. You might call
it a revolution.

HOW COACHES BECAME COOL

The clue to the trigger for this change in attitudes, and its geographic
origin, lies in a single word: *kocsi*. Kocs (which is pronounced "coach")
was a Hungarian village on the road from Buda to Vienna. Somehow
this village gave its name to a kind of four-wheeled vehicle, the *kocsi*
(pronounced "coachee"), and as the adoption of this vehicle spread

westward to other European countries, the name traveled with it and was incorporated as a loanword into other languages: first into Czech and Serbian, and then into German, Dutch, Italian, French, Spanish, and English. Something new about the coach meant it was deemed an acceptable form of transport for high-status men, who put aside their disdain for wheeled conveyances. Yet there was nothing particularly new about its design: although coaches had steerable front wheels, and various forms of suspension, both of those innovations were hundreds of years old. Instead, some other factor prompted the coach's rapid adoption, by persuading men that riding in one was just as manly as riding a horse. So what was it?

Perhaps it was simply speed: coaches may have been particularly light and fast compared with previous forms of four-wheeled wagon. But it seems more likely that, like chariots before them, coaches came to be held in high regard because of their military connotations—and, in particular, a novel military use for wagons that emerged in the late fifteenth century. Facing the threat of the expanding Ottoman Empire, Hungarian commanders adopted a new tactic: arranging wagons on the battlefield in a ring and chaining them together to form a wagon fort, a mobile defensive fortification that could resist cavalry charges. The wagons, equipped with gunports, also acted as protected platforms from which men could fire a small cannon or an early form of gun called an arquebus. This cutting-edge combination of wagons and gunpowder weapons made armored knights on horseback look suddenly old-fashioned. And that may explain why men across Europe decided that riding in fancy wagons was not so embarrassing after all—provided they were referred to as coaches, a name borrowed from the country where this new idea had emerged.

By 1560, the thriving city of Antwerp, which had emerged as the financial center of Europe, had more than five hundred coaches. (There were said to be just two coaches in London at the time, and three in Paris.) Enthusiasm for coaches spread quickly, starting with European royalty. A chronicler in England recorded that in 1564 Walter Rippon—who had supposedly built "the first coche that ever was made in England," for the Earl of Rutland, in 1555—constructed "the first hollow turning coche for Her Majesty [Elizabeth I], being then her servant." This vehicle was covered (hollow) and had a pivoted front axle (turning). Fancy coaches were favored gifts between European monarchs: in 1582 Henri III of France gave Elizabeth an "exceeding marvellous princely coche" as a gift, after she had sent him some English hunting dogs. This was not merely an act of generosity: it was also a display of one-upmanship because the coach was the pinnacle of transport technology, and Henri wanted to demonstrate the skill of his French coachmakers.

Coaches rapidly became status symbols and "coaching" (driving for pleasure in a coach) emerged as a leisure activity, and a means of showing off, among people wealthy enough to own one or more coaches. This raised concerns in some quarters that noblemen might lose the ability to ride horses, which would make them less useful in a military conflict. In 1588 one German prince, Julius von Braunschweig, introduced rules to discourage coaching, on the grounds that "the manly virtues, dignity, courage, honor and loyalty of the German nation were impaired, as carriage-driving was equal to idling and indolence." But this did little to stem the popularity of coach driving, or the competition between coach owners to impress onlookers with the luxury and opulence of their vehicles.

For those unable to afford their own coaches, the new vehicles could be hired for short journeys within cities. In London, as the roads began to fill up with coach traffic, a bill was debated in Parliament in 1601 "to restrain the excessive use of coaches." By this time the Moroccan embassy in London had four coaches and the Russian embassy had eight; in 1603, at the accession of James I, the French delegation consisted of thirty coaches. Traffic jams, one Londoner observed, were so bad at times that coaches were "like mutton pies in a cook's oven, hardly can you thrust a pole between." Many parts of London were "villainously pestered" by the new vehicles. Watermen, who had traditionally ferried Londoners around in hired boats on the Thames River, saw a dramatic drop in their income as coaches ate into their business. John Taylor, a London waterman who rowed actors and playwrights across the river and subsequently became a poet, denounced the rise of coaches in his 1622 poem "An Arrant Thief." He observed that in 1558 "when Queen Elizabeth came to the crown, A coach in England then was scarcely known." But now, for him and his fellow watermen, "all our profit runs away on wheels" because of the rise of the "upstart Hell-cart-coaches." The following year he complained in another poem of "upstart four-wheeled tortoises," "damming up the streets and lanes"; this was, he declared, "the rattling, roaring, rumbling age, and The World runnes on Wheeles." A law passed in 1662 limited the number of such "hackney carriages" to four hundred, but this proved inadequate, and the limit was raised to seven hundred in 1694. And the number of private carriages was far higher.

The new willingness to ride in coaches, and to hire them when needed, also led to the establishment of long-distance coach services that ran on fixed routes, with regular stops every ten miles or so to allow for horses to be changed and passengers to refresh themselves. Breaking the journey into several stages in this way gave rise to the name *stagecoach*. An advertisement that appeared in 1667, for example, promoted a "Flying Machine" providing regular service from London to the city of Bath, a distance of 105 miles, in three days: "All those desirous to pass from London to Bath, or any other place on their Road, let them repair to the Bell Savage on Ludgate Hill in London and the White Lion at Bath, at both which places they may be received in a Stage Coach every Monday, Wednesday, and Friday, which performs the whole journey in Three Days (if God permit), and sets forth at five in the morning." Seats in this coach cost one pound and five shillings each, and each passenger was entitled to bring luggage weighing fourteen pounds. (A typical laborer's wage in London at the time was about £30 a year, so this was something only the wealthy could afford.)

Like hackney carriages, stagecoaches proved controversial. A novelty a century earlier, coaches had swiftly taken over the roads. A pamphlet published in London in 1673 denounced stagecoaches as a great evil, on the basis that "those who travel in these coaches contracted an idle habit of body; became weary and listless when they rode a few miles, and were then unable or unwilling to travel on horseback, and not able to endure frost, snow or rain." But the same year another writer declared, "There is of late such an admirable commodiousness, both for men and women, to travel from London to the principal towns in the country, that the like hath not been known in the world, and that is by stage-coaches, wherein any one may be transported to any place, sheltered from foul weather and foul ways . . . and this not only at a low price, but with such velocity and speed in one hour, as that the posts in some forraign countreys make in a day." In fact, early stagecoaches were no faster than walking, achieving an average speed of 3 mph along roads that were little more than muddy tracks, and exposing passengers to the dangers of both accidents and highwaymen. Such was the dire state of roads in this period that in 1703 a coach carrying Archduke Charles, the future Holy Roman emperor, overturned twelve times during a fifty-mile journey from London to Petworth. But coaches did at least make intercity travel slightly more comfortable by protecting passengers from the elements.

Being able to hire a hackney carriage, or buy a ticket for a stagecoach, was convenient for those unable to afford their own vehicles. But coaches were such an important emblem of wealth that *The Laws of Gallantry*, a French guide to manners published in 1640, noted that the first question that would be asked about a new entrant to society was "Does he own a carriage?" As a result some people, such as the English diarist and naval administrator Samuel Pepys, felt "almost ashamed to be seen in a hackney." When he eventually acquired a coach himself, Pepys wrote in his diary that it was "a mighty pleasure to go alone with my poor wife in a coach of our own to a play and make us appear mighty great, I think, in the world." After more than two millennia out of the limelight, wheeled vehicles had, once again, become powerful and desirable status symbols.

ARISTOCRATS ON THE LEFT, DEMOCRATS ON THE RIGHT

As the fashion for coaches spread across Europe, the design of buildings changed in response. Archways to allow coaches to enter and leave, along with internal courtyards to collect and deposit passengers, became standard features of large dwellings. But the influence of the newly popular vehicles went further: they started to influence the layout of cities. Streets were widened and straightened to ease the passage of coaches, and new cities were laid out with broad, straight avenues converging in the center. The need to accommodate coach traffic also provided a convenient excuse to do away with narrow, irregular streets that made it easy for insurrectionists to seal off part of a city behind barricades.

Another innovation was the creation of parks with large, tree-lined carriageways where the wealthy could parade around and show off to each other in their fancy vehicles. Marie de Médicis, the queen of Henri IV, introduced this idea to Paris in 1616. The Cours-la-Reine, next to the Seine River, was modeled on the roadway, known as the Corso, next to the Arno River in Florence. "Here it is that the Gallants, & the Ladys of the Court take the ayre & divert themselves," observed the English diarist John Evelyn, "the middle Circle being Capable to Containe an hundred coaches to turne commodiously." The Cours-la-Reine was thirty-eight meters wide and two kilometers long, which was enough room, Evelyn noted, for five or six lanes of carriages. The gates at each end were manned by Swiss guards with strict orders to admit only the cream of society. Similar spaces were established in Madrid (the Prado), in Rome (on the site of the old Roman Forum) and in London (Hyde Park).

Carriages at the Cours-la-Reine in Paris, early seventeenth century.
The ritual circulation of carriages was a high-status social event.

The word *cours* came to refer both to these spaces and to the ritual circulation of carriages at a particular time of day. A French visitor to London noted that the cours in Hyde Park differed in one important respect from that in Paris: rented carriages were allowed to take part. In Paris, anyone who showed up at the Cours-la-Reine in a rented vehicle would be whistled at by everyone else until the person departed in humiliation. Philippe Zoete de Laeke, a Dutch aristocrat who regularly took part in the Paris cours in the 1650s, described it as a "confusion of carriages" and a "great jam" and once claimed to have counted more than two thousand coaches, which must have made it difficult for any of them to move at all. On another occasion he saw a noblewoman's carriage overturn, throwing her and three other occupants on the ground, after her driver tried to cut into a line of traffic and collided with another coach. The competition between carriages and their occupants intensified whenever the king took part in the cours. All other carriages were obliged to give way, just as modern traffic parts to allow the passage of emergency vehicles. But everyone also wanted to get close to the king. The resulting altercations between coachmen would sometimes turn violent.

The free-for-all of the cours highlighted the need for formal rules to regulate the flow of traffic, and in particular the basic question of which side of the road vehicles should drive on. Why some countries ended up driving on the right, and others on the left, is the subject of much speculation. But it seems that for much of the medieval period there was no hard-and-fast rule: vehicles generally tried to stay in the middle of the road, and their main concern was avoiding hazards such as ditches and potholes. The rules for passing other vehicles, whether traveling in the same direction or in the opposite direction, varied widely. German rules in this period, for example, specified that the less loaded vehicle had to make way for the more heavily laden one, which suggests that most roads were single-track and the sidedness of driving was not something people paid much attention to. But traffic would only flow smoothly along the new, wide avenues being built in cities across Europe if everyone agreed which side of the road to drive on, which began to be formalized in the eighteenth century.

Whether a particular country or region chose to drive on the right or left seems to have been largely a matter of chance, because both have their merits. On roads that are wide enough for two lanes of traffic, and with vehicles pulled by two or more horses, driving on the right would have been the natural choice (as in the Roman period, and for the same reasons). However, mounting and leading horses is, for right-handed people, most easily done from the horse's left side (whether or not the rider is wearing a sword). So those riding horses, who mount them from the roadside, might have been more inclined to ride on the left. This may be the origin of the French custom that aristocrats on horseback traveled on the left of the road, and everyone else on the right. During the French Revolution, however, aristocrats would understandably have preferred to keep a low profile by switching to the right-hand side, and a rule making driving on the right compulsory was introduced in 1794. In the years that followed, as Napoléon Bonaparte swept through Europe, he enforced right-hand driving in the countries he conquered. But European countries outside his dominion that drove on the left, including Britain, Portugal, and Sweden, continued to do so. (Portugal and Sweden switched to right-hand driving in the twentieth century.) In Britain and its colonies, the established custom of driving on the left was only formalized in law in 1835. Some former British colonies, including India and Australia, still drive on the left. In colonial America, however, right-hand driving seems to have been preferred from the start, though it was not until 1804 that New York became the first state to make this mandatory on public roads. All other states had followed suit by the 1860s. That some countries ended up driving on the left, and others on the right, is an example of path dependency—the way decisions made in the past can constrain behaviors and choices in the future, making change difficult. The history of transport is, appropriately enough, full of path dependencies.

People riding in carriages didn't just want roads to be wider and better regulated. They also wanted them to be smoother, which spurred the development of new techniques to improve the quality of roads, both within towns and between them. The most important change was the inversion of the usual approach, dating back to Roman times, of laying large stone slabs on top of a bed of smaller stones. Given the damage that iron-rimmed wheels can do to such slabs—clearly visible in the rutted roads of Pompeii—road builders switched to laying down large slabs first, with a layer of smaller stones on top. After conducting a series of experiments starting in the 1780s, John McAdam, a Scottish engineer, refined this approach with his proposal that roads be surfaced using small, sharp-edged stones made from crushed rock, rather than rounded pebbles. The straight edges of these small stones caused them to pack together more tightly as vehicles passed over them, rather than being scattered. McAdam's approach, which became known as a macadam surface, was formally adopted in Britain in the 1820s and spread to other countries. (The treatment of macadam surfaces with tar, patented in 1902, led to the word *tarmac*.)

Better roads, together with improvements to coach design, such as steel-spring suspension and brakes, made possible higher average speeds of 8–12 mph. In 1750 it took two days for a stagecoach to travel between London and Cambridge, a distance of about sixty-five miles, with an overnight stop halfway (which works out to an average speed of about 3 mph). But by 1820 the journey could be completed within seven hours, equivalent to an average speed of more than 9 mph. People marveled as faster stagecoaches shrank the distances between towns and allowed long journeys that had previously taken weeks to be completed in days. But wheeled transport was still unaffordable for most people—until a new kind of vehicle took to the roads in the 1820s.

DEMOCRACY ON WHEELS

The idea of a shared carriage, like a stagecoach, but with a larger passenger capacity and operating within a city, had first been tried in Paris in the seventeenth century. The entrepreneur behind the service, rather unexpectedly, was the French mathematician and philosopher Blaise Pascal. Today he is remembered for his pioneering work in probability theory and the physics of fluids (the unit for pressure is named after him). And as a philosopher, he is most famous for an argument known as Pascal's wager: the idea that, lacking proof of God's existence, people should believe in him anyway, because if he does exist, he will send nonbelievers to hell. But Pascal was a practical inventor as well as a great thinker. In the 1640s he built some of the earliest mechanical calculating machines, precursors of the digital computer. And in the 1660s he came up with a plan for a shared transport system, based on carriages that ran on fixed routes and could seat eight passengers. Granted a monopoly from Louis XIV and funded by aristocratic backers, the *carrosses à cinq sols*, or five-penny coaches, began operating in March 1662. They were extremely popular to begin with, but concerns about the mixing of social classes meant their use was swiftly restricted to "bourgeoisie and people of merit"— just the sort of people, in short, who would worry that traveling in a shared coach showed that they could not afford one of their own. As a result the service struggled to make money and was shut down in 1675.

The idea was revived in the 1820s by Stanislaus Baudry, another Frenchman. The proprietor of a flour mill in the city of Nantes, Baudry had set up a public bath next door, taking advantage of the excess heat produced by the steam engine that powered his mill. To encourage people in Nantes to visit his baths on the outskirts of the city, he began running a free carriage to and from the city center in 1826, hoping to recoup the operating cost from greater admissions to his baths. But he soon noticed that people were taking his free carriage without actually visiting the baths. This suggested there was demand for a regular service in and out of the city. So Baudry quickly pivoted to becoming a transport operator, with two specially built carriages, each capable of carrying sixteen paying passengers, operating on different routes with fixed stops. The service was immediately profitable, and the distinctive, larger vehicle on which it relied was dubbed the *omnibus*, which means "for all" in Latin. In 1828 Baudry was granted permission to operate a hundred omnibuses along ten routes in Paris, which were an instant success. Rival operators sprang up, and within two years ten omnibus firms were operating a total of 264 coaches in the city.

The idea was copied in other countries. An omnibus service was launched in London in 1829, with vehicles capable of carrying twenty passengers, though they were initially banned from the city center, where hackney coaches had a monopoly. But this monopoly was withdrawn in

1832, resulting in the rapid growth of omnibus services, with 620 vehicles running by 1838. Omnibuses also spread to New York City, where a newspaper heralded "the age of the omnibus" in 1833, and to other European and American cities in the 1830s and 1840s.

As its name indicates, the omnibus was open to all. It became a symbol of democracy, with good reason. Though omnibuses were mostly used by middle-class riders, some cities introduced subsidies to extend access to the poorest workers. Those who took advantage of these cut-price or "commuted" fares became known as commuters. A French commentator in the nineteenth century hailed the omnibus as a "sanctuary of equality" that was used by everyone. An observer in New York City extolled the way that people from different social classes used the same omnibus, albeit at different times, from junior clerks heading to work early in the morning to wealthy women going shopping later in the day. In Britain, omnibus riders came to be seen as representative of the population at large, thanks to Walter Bagehot, a British political writer who wrote in 1863 that "public opinion . . . is the opinion of the bald-headed man at the back of the omnibus." This observation may explain the subsequent adoption by English courts of the hypothetical "man on the Clapham omnibus" as the standard for an ordinary, reasonable person.

Compared with previous vehicles, from war chariots to fancy coaches, the omnibus was far more egalitarian. Its popularity signaled the democratization, at long last, of wheeled transport. It had taken more than five thousand years since the invention of the first wheel. In 1623 the poet John Taylor had declared that "The World runnes on Wheeles." That was a bit premature. But in the first half of the nineteenth century wheeled vehicles, pulled by animals, finally became a common means of transport for ordinary people in many parts of the world.

3

Under One's Own Steam

Soon shall thy force, gigantic steam afar
Drag the slow barge or urge the rapid car.

—Erasmus Darwin, 1791

DO THE LOCOMOTION

In the year 1800 wooden vehicles pulled by animals were the most advanced form of land-based transport on the planet and had been for more than five millennia. Admittedly, nineteenth-century coaches had features that the earliest wagons had lacked, such as metal-rimmed and spoked wheels, steering, steel-spring suspension, and glass windows. But the basic idea had been the same for thousands of years: wooden wheels supporting a rectangular wooden structure, with a pole and yoke to allow one or more animals to pull the whole thing along. During the nineteenth century, however, new materials and propulsion technologies made possible entirely new kinds of vehicle, and the technology of human transport changed more in one hundred years than it had in the previous five thousand. Attitudes toward high-speed travel, and personal freedom, were redefined by two entirely new types of vehicle, one bursting into prominence in the first half of the century, the other in the second: the steam train and the bicycle.

The idea of steam power was known to the ancient Greeks, but practical devices that exploited steam power to do useful work first emerged in the eighteenth century. The stationary steam engine constructed by the English inventor Thomas Newcomen in 1712, building on the work of previous experimenters, was used to pump water out of flooded coal mines. Early steam engines were large (Newcomen engines were typically housed in buildings three stories tall) and inefficient, but this did not matter much because they were powered by coal, and being next to a coal mine meant the fuel was available in abundance.

Over the following decades Newcomen's design was improved by successive inventors, notably by James Watt, a Scottish engineer who was asked to repair a Newcomen engine in 1763 and quickly saw how its wasteful design could be improved upon. His addition of a separate condensing chamber reduced the amount of heat lost during operation, greatly improving efficiency: Watt's steam engine used half as much coal as a comparable Newcomen engine. Just as important, Watt modified his engine to produce rotary motion, rather than the back-and-forth pumping action of a Newcomen engine, which allowed Watt's engine to be used to drive machinery of various kinds in the emerging factories and mills of the industrial revolution. Such machinery had previously been driven by waterwheels, and Watt's steam engine meant factories no longer had to be located next to rivers, as long as coal was available. His improved design also accelerated efforts to develop steam engines that were small enough to drive a wheeled vehicle.

The first attempt to build a steam-powered vehicle seems to have been made by Nicolas-Joseph Cugnot, a French inventor, who built a steam wagon to pull artillery for the French army in 1769. It was apparently capable of hauling a load weighing four or five tons at a walking speed of around 3 mph. The scaled-down (but still large) steam engine was mounted above the vehicle's single front wheel, which it drove directly and which could be pivoted by the driver using a steering tiller; two wheels were at the back. But swiveling the front wheel required turning the entire steam engine, so it required great strength, which made the vehicle difficult

The steam-powered artillery carriage built by Nicolas-Joseph Cugnot, a French inventor, in 1769. Swiveling the front wheel involved moving the entire mechanism of the steam engine, making the vehicle difficult to control.

to control—and may explain why it crashed into a wall during testing and was severely damaged. The French government then withdrew its funding.

Richard Trevithick, a British inventor, took a different approach with the vehicle he built in 1801. It was a steam engine mounted on four wheels, the rear ones being driven by the reciprocating motion of a piston, with smaller front wheels controlled by a tiller for steering. This machine made its maiden run up Camborne Hill in Cornwall on December 24, 1801, with Trevithick operating the steam engine, his associate Andrew Vivian handling the steering, and five or six other men hanging on to small platforms at the back and front of the vehicle. Though they only went a mile or so, this seems to have been the first time passengers had traveled under mechanical power. On the machine's next outing, on Christmas Day, a woman described it as a "walking, puffing devil," and the name stuck. But a few days later, during a test run on a rutted road, *Puffing Devil* overturned. Trevithick and his men righted the machine with the help of some passersby and left it in the outhouse of an inn. But while they were enjoying a meal of "roast goose and proper drinks," the engine caught fire and was destroyed.

Having proved that a steam-powered vehicle was technically feasible, Trevithick decided not to rebuild it, but instead moved on to a new, three-wheeled design explicitly intended to carry passengers. The *London Steam Carriage* consisted of a passenger compartment mounted on large rear wheels, eight feet in diameter, driven by a steam engine. The driver, sitting in front of the passenger compartment, steered the vehicle using a tiller to direct its single front wheel. This contraption was tested over several months in London, usually in the early hours of the morning when the roads were clear. It was capable of speeds as high as 12 mph. But it proved jarringly uncomfortable to ride, caused damage to the roads due to its great weight, and was difficult to steer, crashing into a railing. Critics pointed out that horse-drawn carriages were quieter and cheaper to operate, dashing Trevithick's hopes of selling his invention to operators of stagecoach services. Steam power, it seemed, was an impractical way to power road vehicles.

But Trevithick refused to give up. Given the difficulty of steering, particularly on uneven roads, he realized that steam-powered vehicles would be better suited to running on rails, of the kind used in mines. Exactly where and when the idea of using fixed tracks to guide mine

The London Steam Carriage *built by Richard Trevithick in 1803.*

carts first arose is unclear, but wooden tracks were in use across Europe by the sixteenth century, and by the early nineteenth century mine carts running on iron rails, known as tramways, were coming into use in British mines and ironworks to move coal and ore. The carts were pushed by hand underground and hauled by horses over longer distances outdoors. Applying steam power to hauling mine carts made sense because no steering mechanism was needed, coal for fuel would be readily available, and a steam engine could easily haul a train of several linked carts.

In 1804 Samuel Homfray, an English industrialist who operated an ironworks in South Wales, made a wager with a rival industrialist, Richard Crawshay. Homfray was a member of a consortium that had built a ten-mile tramway from the mining center of Merthyr Tydfil to a nearby canal, and he employed Trevithick to build a steam locomotive that could run on the rails. He bet Crawshay five hundred guineas that the locomotive would be able to haul ten tons of iron to the canal and then haul the empty wagons back to Homfray's ironworks. After a few test runs over shorter distances, the demonstration took place on February 21, 1804, in the presence of Homfray, Crawshay, and a government engineer who had come to observe. Trevithick wrote to a friend the next day, "We carried ten tons of iron in five wagons, and seventy men riding on them the whole of the journey . . . The gentleman that bet 500 guineas against it rode the whole of the journey with us, and is satisfied that he has lost the bet." This was the first steam railway journey in history.

The weight of the locomotive was too much for the tramway, however, so Homfray subsequently reverted to using horse-drawn wagons. It's unclear whether Homfray ever received his winnings because the referee overseeing the wager thought that the damage done to the rails, and the fact that the locomotive's boiler had leaked on the return journey, meant the demonstration had not been totally successful. But the important thing for Trevithick was that he had proved the feasibility of steam railways and the ability of locomotives to take the place of horse-drawn traction. "The public until now called me a scheming fellow, but now their tone is much altered," he proudly wrote to his friend.

To publicize his ideas, and his prowess at designing steam locomotives, Trevithick established a "steam circus" at Bloomsbury, in London, in the summer of 1808. For the price of one shilling, visitors could be pulled around a circular track by his latest locomotive, the *Catch Me Who Can*, at speeds of 12 mph, making it the first locomotive to haul fare-paying passengers. Trevithick's aim was to show that railways were faster than traveling by horse. But the weight of the locomotive (around eight tons) proved too much for the rails, causing it to come off the track. Trevithick was forced to close the circus, and the resulting financial losses contributed to his bankruptcy the following year. He gave up on the idea of steam-powered vehicles and focused instead on applying fixed steam engines to pumping and other industrial uses, for which there was strong demand.

Other engineers continued to experiment with the use of steam locomotives, however, in particular to haul coal, and over the following years the power and reliability of steam locomotives steadily improved. The Stockton and Darlington railway in northeast England, which opened in September 1825, was the first public railway to make use of steam traction. Coal was hauled along the twenty-five-mile route using steam locomotives built by George Stephenson, a British engineer, though horse-drawn trains were also used in the early years. Passenger coaches were initially hauled entirely by horses (the owners of the line did not operate passenger services themselves, but charged others for use of the rails). But mixing horse-drawn and locomotive-hauled trains on the line was dangerous and inefficient, and in 1828 the owners of the line decided to switch entirely to steam. The decision was controversial: the notion that steam traction was fast, cheap, and reliable enough to replace horses was considered unproven.

To resolve this question once and for all, a contest called the Rainhill Trials was held in October 1829. A railway was under construction to link the English industrial cities of Liverpool and Manchester; a joke at the time was that it took less time to ship goods thirty-three hundred miles from America to Liverpool than it did to move them thirty-five miles from Liverpool to Manchester by canal. A twin-track railway would solve the problem, and Stephenson, who had been appointed its engineer, was determined that it would use steam locomotives to haul both goods and people. But not everyone was convinced this was a good idea. So a weeklong competition was held on a straight, two-mile section of the track, by the village of Rainhill, to find a locomotive that weighed no more than 4.5 tons, cost less than £550, and could haul three times its own weight over thirty-five miles, at a speed of at least 10 mph. Ten locomotives were entered into the competition, but only five took part.

The winner was *Rocket*, designed by George Stephenson and his son Robert. It averaged 12 mph during its test run but was capable of 30 mph and was the only locomotive to complete the trials, after various technical failures caused all the rival locomotives (including one powered by a horse walking on a treadmill) to drop out. The Stephensons duly won the contract to supply locomotives for the new railway, which opened on September 15, 1830. But the inaugural run, with a procession of eight trains and attended by the prime minister, was marred by tragedy when a popular local politician, William Huskisson, was hit by *Rocket* and died. After this inauspicious start, however, the railway proved an instant financial success. Though built to transport goods, it unexpectedly became immensely profitable as a passenger railway. It was the first intercity service, the first to offer discounted tickets for day-trippers, and the first railway used for rapid delivery of mail and newspapers.

The dramatic success of the Liverpool and Manchester railway triggered a mania for railway investment in Britain, where more than fifty new lines, covering sixteen hundred miles, were soon been approved by Parliament. Other countries followed Britain's example in the 1830s and 1840s, building intercity rail links and extending commuter lines around major cities. By making it quicker and easier to get in and out of city centers, rail lines stimulated rapid urban expansion. For the first time, people no longer needed to live close to where they worked, but could travel back and forth each day, without the need to own a horse. Railway lines also made it easier to distribute manufactured goods and agricultural products. This led to the emergence of railroad cities, whose economies boomed as a result of their rail connections, notably in America, which had thirty thousand miles of track by 1860—more than the rest of the world combined. These industrial hubs offered new economic opportunities, making them magnets for European migrants.

Railways transformed urban life, changing the face of existing cities and giving birth to new ones. Cities linked by rail were suddenly closer together, in effect, redefining national geography, too. The connection of New York to Philadelphia by rail in 1834, for example, reduced the journey time between America's two largest cities from two days to five hours. The need to regulate train timetables prompted the introduction of standardized national timekeeping systems. All this happened within a few years in the mid-nineteenth century. But what most struck people at the time was that railways let them travel at unprecedented speed. "What can be more palpably absurd and ridiculous than the prospect held out of locomotives travelling twice as fast as stagecoaches!" asked the *Quarterly Review*, a British periodical, in 1825. Nobody knew what effect, if any, high-speed travel would have on the human body. Would it prevent people from breathing properly, or thinking straight? When the steam locomotive *Tom Thumb* hauled thirty-six passengers on a test run in 1830 on the Baltimore & Ohio Railroad, an eyewitness observed that "some excited gentlemen of the party pulled out memorandum books, and when at the highest speed, which was eighteen miles an hour, wrote their names and some connected sentences, to prove that even at that great velocity it was possible to do so."

Railways swiftly displaced stagecoaches on intercity routes. But as previously noted, faster and more efficient transport between cities increased demand for rapid transport of people and goods within them, which required a greater number of horse-drawn vehicles. Railway companies in British cities bought large numbers of horses to provide local delivery, with major stations devoting as much space to stabling as they did to locomotive sheds. As a London stable keeper recalled in 1873, "We thought when the railways first came in that we should have nothing to do, but it has not turned out so . . . For every new railway you want fresh horses . . . Because there is the work to be done to and fro." The price of large, powerful cart horses increased by 25–30 percent between 1850 and 1873. Railway travel also increased demand for horse-drawn passenger services within cities, to move people to and from stations, or to ferry them from one station to another in horse-drawn omnibuses. The number of horse-drawn cabs in London increased tenfold between 1830, the dawn of the railway age, and 1900. Railways had made possible the transport of people and goods at unprecedented speeds. But rather than liberating cities from their dependence on horses, they increased it. As the historian F. M. L. Thompson put it, "The railway age was in fact the greatest age of the horse."

ICE-SKATING ON A MECHANICAL HORSE

Using steam power to propel a vehicle was one way to make a horseless carriage. But some inventors were exploring another approach, by building human-powered vehicles instead. The idea of a four-wheeled wagon that was propelled by its own rider had been around for several centuries: Giovanni Fontana, a Venetian engineer, had sketched a design for one in the early 1400s. The rider pulled on a rope wrapped around a cylinder, whose rotation drove the wheels via a series of gears. This was not a practical design for a vehicle. There was no steering, for a start. Other inventors came up with improved versions of this design, many of which involved a rider who sat in the front and steered the vehicle using reins, and a footman in the back of the vehicle who drove the wheels by pressing down wooden planks arranged as pedals.

Horseless carriages of this form were demonstrated by inventors in London in 1774 and Paris in 1779. And in 1813 Karl von Drais, a German physicist and inventor, built a horseless carriage that could carry four people, with one of them steering using a tiller, and another providing the motive power by pedaling. The problem with all these vehicles was that their size and weight made it difficult for humans to propel them at any speed. It was quicker to get out and walk.

But then Drais made a conceptual leap. He realized that instead of building a human-powered vehicle that imitated a carriage, it made more sense to imitate a horse. He may have been inspired by the volcanic eruption of Mount Tambora in April 1815, which spread a vast plume of dust and ash around the world, causing months of crop failures and food shortages in what became known as the "year without a summer." A mechanical, human-powered horse, Drais may have reasoned, would eliminate the expense of feeding a living one. In any event, he began work on an entirely new form of self-propelled transport, a two-wheeled wooden vehicle that looks to modern eyes like a bicycle without pedals. He called

The Laufmaschine or draisine, the forerunner of the modern bicycle, invented by Karl von Drais in 1817.

it the Laufmaschine (literally, "running machine"), and by June 1817 it was ready for its maiden voyage. Drais headed off from Mannheim, where he lived, along the well-maintained road to Schwetzingen. Sitting on the saddle of his contraption, he propelled it by planting his feet on the ground and pushing every few meters, while steering with handlebars attached to a tiller. After going four miles along the road, Drais turned round and headed home, traveling a total of eight miles in about an hour. His new invention was as fast as a trotting horse, but powered by its rider without much effort. The tricky part was keeping it balanced while gliding along, and maintaining that balance when pushing with the feet, which took some practice. Drais drew a comparison with the skills needed for ice-skating.

To publicize his invention, he announced the following month that he would ride forty miles, between Karlsruhe and Kehl, in four hours. He duly did so, with the local police chief confirming that Drais had completed the journey, which started at noon, by four P.M. Published accounts began to refer to his invention as the "draisine," and Drais issued an illustrated pamphlet describing the design, which prompted other people to try building their own. (In his drawings, Drais artfully concealed the cord-operated brake mechanism behind one of the rider's legs, to throw builders of unauthorized copies off the scent.) He obtained patents on the design in several countries, registering it in France in 1818 under the new name *vélocipède*, derived from the Latin words for "swift" and "foot." In England, knockoffs of his invention were known as hobby-horses or dandy chargers. The first example in America appeared in February 1819, when a maker of musical instruments, James Stewart, built one based on a drawing received from Europe. He advertised it as "a new mode of travelling, combining the advantages of carriage, horse and foot." People flocked to see it demonstrated at the concert hall in Baltimore, and soon copies were proliferating. That summer there was a craze for velocipedes in several cities: they could be rented in public parks in Boston, New York, Washington, and elsewhere, with tuition offered to new riders. "A few lessons are sufficient to overcome the difficulties necessarily attendant on its novelty," observed a New York newspaper.

But enthusiasm for this new mode of transport died out as quickly as it had arisen. After the "year without a summer" of 1816, the weather returned to normal just as Drais and his invention were first taking to the roads. Good harvests in the northern hemisphere in 1817 caused the prices of food and fodder to drop. Even though the velocipede did not require feeding, it was expensive to buy, which meant it was still only affordable to the wealthy, who preferred riding horses. Velocipede enthusiasts, meanwhile, were starting to get a bad reputation. With its rigid wooden or metal wheels, the velocipede was painful to ride on uneven or rutted roads, so riders preferred to whiz around on paved sidewalks. But this was dangerous and had been banned in several cities by the end of 1817, including the velocipede's own hometown of Mannheim. It was a similar story in America, where a New York newspaper printed a letter in July 1819 from a man who had seen a four-year-old boy knocked down and injured by two men riding velocipedes on the sidewalk. The man complained that "our peaceable citizens, our wives and our children, cannot enjoy a walk in the evening, without the danger of being run over by some of these new-created animals." By the end of the year velocipedes had also been barred from the sidewalks of many American cities.

A few European enthusiasts kept the flame alive, setting new speed records on velocipedes and taking part in clandestine races. But by the 1830s railways had become the most exciting and talked-about transport technology for people who wanted to get around quickly without using a horse. Trains might not have granted people quite the same sense of giddy personal freedom that the velocipede did, but nor did they require riders to learn any tricky new skills.

Still, inventors continued to tinker with variants of the velocipede, some of which had three or four wheels. Finally, in the 1860s, came the breakthrough: the addition of pedals, initially fixed to the front wheel, that allowed riders to drive the wheel directly with their feet, rather than repeatedly pushing against the ground. Exactly where (and with whom) this idea originated is unclear and is fiercely debated by historians of the bicycle. But it had certainly happened by 1865: the entry for *vélocipède* in a French dictionary published that year defines it as

> a sort of wooden horse, placed on two wheels, on which one balances, while giving oneself a forward impulse by the feet. On the modern velocipede the feet are put onto stirrups formed as cranks that make the big wheel turn and provide a high speed.

This "modern velocipede" may well have been a three-wheeler, the kind of vehicle on which pedals possibly first appeared. Initially, people were understandably afraid of putting their feet on pedals while riding; they would have been less apprehensive when riding a three-wheeler, which was in no danger of tipping over. But in April 1866 a French news-paper, *Le Journal de l'Ain*, unambiguously described a *vélocipède* bicycle (i.e., a two-wheeled velocipede) with pedals on its front wheel. Various people claimed to have pioneered this arrangement, chief among them two Frenchmen, Pierre Lallement and Pierre Michaux, and the fight over patent rights went on for decades. But whoever invented them, pedals led to renewed interest in the *vélocipède* bicycle. The new machines were greeted with astonishment because, unlike old-style velocipedes, which could be kept upright by the rider's legs, those with pedals seemed to stay upright as if by magic—and the faster they moved, the more stable they became. That a two-wheeler "should maintain an upright position is, to the superficial observer, one of the most surprising feats of practical mechanics," noted a letter published in *Scientific American* in 1868.

Numerous variations on this new design began to appear on both sides of the Atlantic. There was a craze for "high wheeler" designs with large front wheels, which enabled skilled riders to achieve higher speeds but were difficult to mount and dismount. These machines (also known as penny-farthings) were favored in competitive racing and other public displays, but were too expensive and impractical for general use. Meanwhile a steady accumulation of other innovations became part of the standard design of what came to be known, in English, as the bicycle. These included the use of ball bearings to keep the wheels turning smoothly; tubular steel frames to reduce weight; improved brakes; lightweight metal wheels with wire spokes; freewheel mechanisms that let the rider glide without pedaling; rubber rims around the wheel, which evolved into pneumatic tires; and chain drive of the rear wheel, which solved the problem that direct pedaling of the front wheel interfered with steering. By the late 1880s all these elements had been combined into a recognizably modern design with two equal-sized wheels, known as the safety bicycle. This name was intended to emphasize that bicycles, which had previously been regarded as expensive and dangerous toys for wealthy young men, were now suitable for use by everyone.

The new design ushered in a golden age, during which cycling flourished as a leisure activity and a means of truly personal locomotion. It let people travel as quickly as they could on horseback, but without the expense of buying, feeding, and maintaining a horse. And unlike trains, which offered high-speed travel subject to a strict timetable and between fixed points, bicycles could go anywhere. Granting riders unprecedented autonomy and freedom, bicycles came to be seen as agents of wider social change. This was not simply because women cyclists challenged the impracticality of Victorian clothing and took to wearing trousers or bloomers instead. Beloved of suffragettes and socialists, bicycles became

Advertisement for an early "safety" bicycle.

more broadly associated with personal emancipation and social progress. American civil rights campaigner Susan B. Anthony declared that the bicycle had "done more to emancipate women than anything else in the world. I stand and rejoice every time I see a woman ride by on a wheel. It gives woman a feeling of freedom and self-reliance." The *Century* magazine called the bicycle "the great leveller," suggesting that "it puts the poor man on a level with the rich, enabling him to 'sing the song of the open road' as freely as the millionaire."

That was overdoing it. But bicycles did have immediate social impact in one area in particular: romance. They broadened people's social circles, letting cyclists travel beyond their own communities and greatly increasing the number of potential marriage partners. Cycling became a popular social activity that allowed young men and women to escape the oversight of chaperones. As one newspaper explained in 1899, "The chief merit of the bicycle in the eyes of the young is that it dispenses with the chaperon . . . It imparts open air freedom and freshness to a life heretofore cribbed, crabbed, cabined and confined by convention." Another account, from 1896, explains, "Cycling parties are often got up, and the ride is still young when the cyclists tend to sort themselves into couples, each couple usually consisting of a lad and a lass . . . rushing through wooded tracts and sunlit meadows is extremely conductive to a fatal form of sentimentality." Tandem bicycles, allowing couples to ride together, were immortalized in the 1892 song "Daisy Bell" ("a bicycle built for two"). Even flat tires provided romantic opportunities. Women were not expected to be able to repair their own bicycles, but to rely on male gallantry: "There are many punctures done on purpose, which necessitates a tete-a-tete walk home—for surely no gentleman would allow a lady to walk home by herself."

Admittedly, there were concerns that frequent cycling would lead to the development of "bicycle face," a deformation of the features, or "cyclemania," an unhealthy obsession with cycling at speed. Scandalized Victorians also worried that cycling made women infertile, loosened their morals, led them to develop overly masculine musculature, and generally threatened the natural order of things. But such lurid fears proved unfounded, and as bikes became cheaper and more commonplace, cycling came to be seen primarily as a form of transport rather than a social activity.

THE ROAD TO THE AUTOMOBILE

Steam trains had shown that horseless transport could be fast. Bicycles had shown that it could be personal. Could it be both? Was it possible to build a vehicle that was as fast as a train, as convenient and personal as a bicycle, and could travel on existing roads like a horse? One way to do it, which inventors had never quite given up on, was to add a steam engine to a carriage, as Cugnot and Trevithick had done. The success of steam railways prompted renewed interest in such "steam wagons" in the 1830s, on both sides of the Atlantic. There were even a few short-lived efforts to operate steam-powered omnibus services in English cities. But steam wagons failed to catch on for a combination of reasons.

The first was that they worked best on smooth roads, which were noticeably lacking at the time. (Steam-powered transport fared much better on rails, and on water in the form of paddle steamers.) Second, steam vehicles were frowned on by city authorities because of the noise and smoke they produced, and because of concerns about boiler explosions. Steam vehicles were explicitly banned from the streets of London in 1840 for just this reason, and many other cities followed suit. Finally, steam vehicles had to contend with opposition from railway and stagecoach companies, which were concerned that steam wagons, running on ordinary roads, might threaten their business, and they lobbied for, and won, legislation to prevent steam vehicles from posing a threat. (The most famous restriction was the so-called Red Flag law in Britain, passed in 1865, which required any "locomotive on the highway" to have a crew of three, one of whom had to walk at least sixty yards in front of the vehicle holding a red flag or lantern to give other road users sufficient warning of its approach.) Such rules ensured that steam vehicles were unable to compete with trains, stagecoaches, or horse-drawn omnibuses—and discouraged innovation in powered road transport by inventors trying to build self-propelled carriages.

Instead it was the idea of rails, rather than steam power, that ended up being borrowed from steam trains and applied to urban transport, in the form of horse-drawn buses, known as horsecars or trams, that ran on rails laid on city streets. Running buses on rails, rather than on uneven roads, reduced friction and enabled horses to pull greater loads. That in turn meant that fewer horses were needed per vehicle, which reduced running costs, increased speeds, and made possible much lower fares, typically less than half that of a traditional omnibus, which broadened access. Horsecars took hold in cities across Europe and America starting in the 1850s, often displacing omnibus services, which came to be seen as "tardy and annoying" by comparison, according to one contemporary observer.

In New York City, horsecar ridership increased from 23 million in 1857 to 161 million in 1880, by which time the city had nearly twelve thousand horses pulling fifteen hundred cars over more than 136 miles of track. Once again, railways had had the paradoxical effect of making cities even more dependent on horses. Horsecars also started to affect the layout and expansion of cities, particularly in America. By providing fast, frequent, and cheap connections, horsecars hastened the trend to divide cities into distinct business and residential districts.

Even as horsecars proliferated and steam wagons failed to gain traction, the idea of combining the speed of a train with the personal freedom and flexibility of a bicycle refused to die. Rather than adding a steam engine to a carriage, some inventors decided to take a different approach: Could an engine be added to a bicycle? Adding a huge, heavy steam engine was clearly impractical. But in Germany, a number of engineers were experimenting with a different kind of engine, which had been developed in the 1850s by a Belgian inventor, Étienne Lenoir. Unlike a steam engine, which applies heat from burning fuel to the outside of a water-filled cylinder, Lenoir's engine burned a gaseous mixture of fuel and air inside a cylinder—ignited with an electrical spark—which pushed a piston. This design is accordingly known as an internal combustion engine. Lenoir sold several engines to drive machinery in factories, one of which was seen by Nikolaus Otto, a German engineer.

Otto added several refinements to make Lenoir's design more efficient and set up a company to sell his new engine for use in factories. In the years that followed Otto further improved the design, in particular by having the piston compress the fuel-air mixture before ignition (the engine ran on a type of petroleum spirit known as ligroin), and by controlling the combustion to make the engine run more smoothly. By the late 1870s Otto's company was selling hundreds of engines every year to drive factory machinery. But Otto was not interested in trying to apply his invention to transport, to the frustration of Gottlieb Daimler, his factory manager. So in 1882 Daimler and his friend Wilhelm Maybach, another of Otto's employees, resigned in order to set up their own company to build engine-powered vehicles. They set about making the internal combustion engine smaller and lighter, and increasing its operating speed from around 150 revolutions per minute (rpm) to several hundred, boosting its power output. In 1885 they attached their new, smaller engine to a bicycle. Daimler's son Paul, aged seventeen, took this vehicle out for a six-mile spin on November 18, 1885. It was the first motorcycle, and the first vehicle powered by an internal combustion engine.

Just as it was taking to the road, another German engineer, Carl Benz, was putting the finishing touches on a vehicle of his own. Benz, like Daimler and Maybach, had applied his experience in building stationary engines for factory use to develop a small internal combustion engine for use in road vehicles. He was a keen cyclist, but rather than attach his engine to a bicycle, he built a large tricycle around his engine. He called the resulting vehicle, patented in January 1886, the Motorwagen. Despite having only three wheels and being based in large part on bicycle parts (including drive chains and wire-spoked wheels), it is considered to be the first modern automobile because it was the first road vehicle to be designed from scratch around an internal combustion engine, as opposed to an existing vehicle to which an engine had been added. The Motorwagen could seat a driver and a passenger and had a maximum speed of about 10 mph. It was first shown in public in July 1886. By this time Daimler and Maybach had installed one of their engines in a

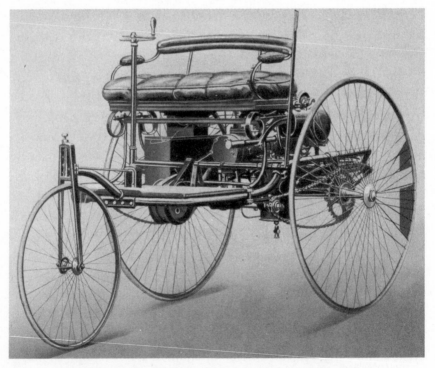

The Benz Patent Motorwagen, the first true automobile, from 1886.

four-seater carriage, creating the first four-wheeled motor vehicle. Like Benz's Motorwagen, it was capable of about 10 mph. Rather than building their own vehicles, however, Daimler and Maybach decided to establish a company to make engines and sell them for use in vehicles of all kinds.

Thus it was the bicycle, rather than the steam engine, that paved the way for the automobile. And the bicycle paved the way in a more literal sense, too. Starting in the 1880s, cyclists began to lobby for better roads. In Britain, the Roads Improvement Association was founded by cyclists in 1886, inspiring a similar Good Roads movement in America. Cyclists also fought for the removal of restrictions on where they could ride: bicycles were banned on some bridges, for example, and in Central Park in New York City, where the roads were reserved for fancy carriages—a Gilded Age version of the seventeenth-century Paris cours. Smoother surfaces, and legal precedents establishing the right to use new kinds of vehicles on public highways, removed obstructions that might have hampered the subsequent progress of the automobile. As the mayor of Brooklyn put it in 1896, "The bicycle has done more for good roads, and will do more for good roads in future, than any other form of vehicle." Bicycles also "directed men's minds to the possibilities of independent, long-distance travel over the ordinary highway," noted Hiram Percy Maxim, an American engineer, when recalling his experience of the 1890s. The bicycle "created a new demand which was beyond the ability of the railroads to supply. Then it came about that the bicycle could not satisfy the demand which it had created. A mechanically propelled vehicle was wanted instead of a foot-propelled one, and we now know that the automobile was the answer."

HORSE MANURE, REVISITED

The bicycle craze of the 1890s coincided with growing concern about the environmental impact of horses in cities, where they pulled private carriages, omnibuses and horsecars, goods wagons and taxicabs. But the limits of the horse-powered city were becoming apparent. In New York City, the horsecars were at capacity by the 1880s, with services running every minute in the rush hour on the busiest routes. To move more people and goods around, horse-drawn vehicles were getting bigger, which meant they needed larger teams of larger horses, which took up more space on the road and generated more manure. Stables were getting bigger, too; the one that opened in 1888 belonging to the Seventh Avenue Street Railway housed twenty-five hundred horses on four floors and was said to be the largest in the world. And then there were the manure dumps. New York City had fourteen of them by 1870, where manure was stored, often for months at a time, before being sold as fertilizer. In the 1880s, as the volume of manure increased, the price collapsed due to oversupply, which made it even more difficult to get rid of. "He does earn his living, yet he is a very costly animal," the *New York Times* said of the horse in 1881. An alternative, it observed, could not come soon enough:

> In crowded cities the practical objections to the animal increase as his services do . . . Not the least serious objection is the droppings from the animals, which make street-filth especially disgusting. The streets, especially the many that are occupied by surface railroads, are incessantly manured . . . In the fact that cities have been made by building around the horse there is no necessity for keeping him permanently as their center . . . let him be considered indispensable, as an instrument, until some better instrument enables us to dispense with him.

The newspaper was still complaining in 1894: "A horse within a city is a nuisance—a nuisance with palliations, to be sure." But something had changed. The sense that reliance on horses was unsustainable had given way to a feeling that change was not just inevitable, but imminent. "Every civilized being with a particle of imagination must gladly foresee," the paper declared, that "the days of vehicles propelled by horses are drawing somewhat rapidly to a close." The automobile, it seemed, had arrived in the nick of time to liberate cities from the tyranny of the horse. But how would people react to the coming of this new machine?

4

The Rubber Hits the Road

It began by being a scientific experiment, went on to become the instrument of the adventurous, then became the toy of the rich, then the ambition of the poor, and finally the servant of everyone.

—Filson Young, *The Living Age*, 1911

BERTHA BENZ'S ROAD TRIP

The first person in history to use an automobile in a recognizably modern way—simply to get from A to B—was Bertha Benz, the wife of Carl Benz. Early on an August morning in 1888, and without telling her husband, she and her two teenaged sons, Eugen and Richard, climbed aboard a three-wheeled prototype Motorwagen and set off on a road trip from Mannheim to visit Bertha's mother in Pforzheim, sixty-five miles away. Her aim was to demonstrate to her husband that his invention, which had previously been tested only in the courtyard of his workshop, was reliable enough to be used for long-distance travel. Bertha Benz's journey has been much mythologized over the years, but the story goes that to avoid waking her husband, she and her sons wheeled the vehicle out of his workshop onto the road outside before starting the engine—and that she left a deliberately vague note on the kitchen table saying she had gone to visit her mother, but without saying how.

Bertha Benz had been instrumental in the development of the first automobile, and not just because her dowry had helped to fund its construction. She had also ridden alongside her husband on several test drives and took a keen interest in its technical details, which proved to be useful during her journey. She knew that with its single-cylinder engine and two gears, the Motorwagen would struggle to climb anything more than the gentlest hill. Accordingly, one reason she took her sons along was so they could get out and push if necessary. Keeping the vehicle going meant regularly refilling the carburetor with fuel (there was no separate fuel tank, just a small reservoir on top of the engine) and topping up the radiator with water. Ligroin, the type of petroleum spirit the engine was designed to run on, was sold by pharmacists for use as a household solvent. So Mrs. Benz chose a route that passed through several towns with chemists' shops. She made her first refueling stop at the town pharmacy in Wiesloch, a town along the route. Water could be had along the way from taverns, streams, or troughs used by horses.

As expected, going up hills required some manual assistance. Two astonished farmers were asked to lend a hand to get the automobile up one particularly steep hill. Not everyone approved of this strange new contraption: some onlookers are said to have found it so terrifying that they fell to their knees in prayer. But Mrs. Benz had other things to worry about. She supposedly had to unblock a fuel line by poking it with a hatpin; she also used her garters to plug a leaky valve and replace the worn-through insulation on a short-circuiting ignition wire. There was no danger of flats, however, because the vehicle had steel rims on its rear wheels, and a solid-rubber tire on its front wheel. She informed her husband of her progress by telegram, and she and her sons eventually arrived at her mother's house at dusk. A few days later they drove home, this time via a less hilly route, once again stopping for ligroin and water as they went. They also stopped to ask a cobbler to add a layer of leather to the vehicle's brake shoes, to make the brakes more effective.

The world's first-ever family road trip by car led to several improvements in the Motorwagen. At his wife's suggestion, Carl Benz added an extra, lower gear to enable the vehicle to climb hills without having to be pushed. He also improved the brakes, which had had trouble slowing the vehicle when it was going downhill, and he retained Bertha's innovation of leather-covered brake shoes. But most important, his wife's journey, and the amazement it caused, gave Benz the confidence to press ahead with promoting his invention as salable. The Motorwagen was rapturously received at an exhibition in Munich the following month, at which Benz won a gold medal and attracted much attention from the press. He began commercial sales of his vehicles shortly afterward. Today Bertha Benz's route is marked with memorial signs, and the pharmacy in Wiesloch where she bought ligroin proudly claims to be the world's first gas station. Her daring journey introduced the automobile to the world and showed that it was suitable for everyday use, give or take the odd hatpin. Provoking a mixture of bewilderment, admiration, and fear, her journey provided a foretaste of public reactions to the automobile. But it was just one vehicle puttering along a country road. In the years that followed, as automobiles began to proliferate, attitudes toward them underwent rapid change.

GETTING TO THE STARTING LINE

The modern automotive era can be said to have begun with an unusual race. It was organized by *Le Petit Journal*, a hugely popular French newspaper with a reputation for circulation-boosting publicity stunts, whose owners hoped to capitalize on the growing interest in the new technology of horseless carriages. But how practical were such vehicles, what were their limitations, and which kind had the most promise? "At the end of the 19th century, human inventiveness, which in less than 100 years has created steam power, gas, electricity, and other types of propulsion, has still not found the means to get rid of horses and replace them with a mechanical form of propulsion for vehicles," the paper declared in December 1893. "It is this problem, the interesting question of the replacement of horse-drawn vehicles, that the *Petit Journal* wishes to address in 1894, in the hope of taking a big step forward."

The paper announced that it would hold a contest the following summer to assess the viability of horseless carriages as a practical means of transport, and to determine which of the various forms of propulsion—steam, electricity, or petrol engine—was most suitable for general use. Entrants would be required to drive their vehicles from Paris to the city of Rouen, in Normandy, a distance of seventy-nine miles. Each vehicle could be powered by any form of propulsion, and the contest was open to competitors from any country. The vehicles would be judged not by their speed, however, but by whether they were safe, easy to use, and economical to run—a stipulation that ruled out vehicles that required a stoker or a mechanic in addition to the driver. The first prize, for the entrant that most closely met these criteria, would be five thousand francs.

In the following weeks 102 entrants paid the ten-franc fee to register for the competition. But when the competitors gathered in Paris for the preliminary heats on July 18, 1894, only twenty-six vehicles showed up, all of which were powered either by steam or petrol engines. No entrants based on electricity, or more exotic propulsion technologies such as compressed air, hydraulics, and "gravity," made it to the starting line. The twenty-six entrants took part in a public procession through the streets of Paris—in effect, a moving exhibition of the state of the art in automotive technology—which attracted large and enthusiastic crowds.

Over the next three days, the contestants, divided into five groups, took part in a qualifying round, with each group required to complete a fifty-kilometer (thirty-one-mile) route within a different suburb of Paris. Each group consisted of a mixture of steam and petrol vehicles from a variety of manufacturers, so that spectators along each route would get a sense of the variety of horseless-carriage types and designs and could see how they compared with one another in performance. All of this provided entertainment for the onlookers, exposure for the vehicle manufacturers, and publicity for *Le Petit Journal*.

The competitors and their vehicles offered a who's who of the emerging motor industry. They included Count Jules-Albert de Dion, a French noble whose twin passions were dueling and fiddling with steam engines. He had entered the competition driving a steam tractor built by his own company, which towed an ordinary carriage behind it, the steam tractor thus being used as a direct substitute for a horse. Other steam-powered entrants included several vehicles powered by Serpollet steam engines, including one belonging to a forward-thinking Paris department store, and a rather delicate-looking steam tricycle.

The petrol-powered entrants included an improved version of the Motorwagen, the Benz Velo, which had gone on sale earlier that year. Among other improvements, it had four wheels rather than three. But Carl Benz himself was not present that day in Paris; instead his company was represented by Émile Roger, a French entrepreneur and bicycle manufacturer. He had been Benz's second customer for the Motorwagen, after it had gone on sale in 1888, and had subsequently acquired the exclusive right to build and sell Benz vehicles in France.

There were also five petrol-driven machines made by Peugeot, a French manufacturer, and four built by Panhard et Levassor, another French firm—one of them driven by Émile Levassor, one of the company's founders, and another by Hippolyte Panhard, the son of Levassor's cofounder. Their company, which had sold about hundred vehicles to customers in and around Paris since 1890, had pioneered putting a petrol engine at the front of a vehicle (rather than at the back, under the seats) and having it drive the rear wheels—an arrangement known as the Système Panhard which was gradually being adopted by other manufacturers. All these vehicles were steered using tillers, with the exception of one Panhard vehicle, which had been modified by its owner, Alfred Vacheron. He had replaced the tiller with an experimental device: a steering wheel. Spectators watching the various vehicles rumble past were unwittingly catching glimpses of the future of motoring.

Among those watching the proceedings was Gottlieb Daimler, who (along with his colleague Wilhem Maybach) had designed the engines being used to power several of the petrol-driven vehicles taking part in the race. In France, their engine design had been licensed to Panhard et Levassor, which used it to power their own vehicles and also supplied engines to Peugeot. By the time of the Paris–Rouen race, however, Daimler and Maybach had fallen out with their investors, who had forced them to sell all their shares and patents and resign from their own company. So as Daimler watched the vehicles preparing for the race, he must have had mixed feelings. As a firm believer in the superiority of the internal combustion engine, he wanted the petrol-powered vehicles to

Alfred Vacheron, one of the participants in the Paris–Rouen race of 1894.

outperform the steam-driven ones, and he was no doubt rooting in particular for those built by Peugeot and by Panhard et Levassor. But he had lost control of the company he had created to commercialize the technology.

AND THEY'RE OFF!

After three days of trials, twenty-one vehicles had qualified for the main event, which took place on Sunday, July 22. The *New York Herald*'s correspondent in Paris reported that crowds "several thousand strong" gathered to watch the race begin, with the cars departing at thirty-second intervals. It was a clear, sunny day and spectators lined the route, with some following the vehicles on bicycles, horses, or on foot:

> The start was made shortly before eight o'clock, twenty-one vehicles taking part. They were of all sizes and descriptions, some holding a round dozen of persons and some only two. Some were of elegant appearance and others were cumbrous. The start went off well, with

the crowd applauding those carriages which took their fancy and making game of those that seemed behind the age. There were several of the latter, for it is a recognised fact that there is yet a lot of room for perfecting these horseless carriages.

Throwing up clouds of dust, the twenty-one competing vehicles made their way westward out of Paris toward the town of Mantes, roughly halfway along the route. One of the steam-driven wagons soon dropped out after breaking an axle. The Count de Dion's steam tractor was the first to reach Mantes, at around eleven A.M. The eminent passengers in his vehicle, the Prince de Sagan and Captain La Place, were "white with dust," an eyewitness noted, but expressed themselves "delighted" by their journey. Next to arrive, about ten minutes later, were Albert Lemaître, driving a Peugeot, and Émile Levassor, in one of his own vehicles. By noon the rest of the vehicles had appeared, the arrival time for each being noted, and the competitors stopped for a ninety-minute lunch break. At one thirty P.M. a bugle was sounded, and the competitors started on the second leg of the journey toward Rouen.

Most of the vehicles moved at a sedate speed of about 10 mph, so the resulting procession, with its attendant train of spectators on bicycles and horses, took several minutes to pass the spectators gathered in towns and villages along the route. Some spectators waved flags, while others offered flowers or fruit to the passing drivers. There were a few mishaps on the crowded road: seven dogs were run over during the day, and one cyclist was injured. During the afternoon a boiler tube on one of the steam vehicles burst, injuring one of its operators and causing another dropout. Several vehicles sustained damage to their thin rubber tires. The Count de Dion, who continued to lead the pack, took a wrong turn up a steep hill, ended up in a potato field, and needed help to get back onto the road again.

The New York Herald's correspondent reported that he had set out on his bicycle from Mantes at twelve thirty P.M., during the lunch break, in the hope of reaching Rouen before any of the competitors, but was over-taken along the way by the Count de Dion, "going on the level at the rate of twenty-eight kilometers, or seventeen and a half miles an hour.

The carriage charged hills like an express train." Having led the field all day, the Count de Dion was the first to reach Rouen, arriving early in the evening, closely followed by two Peugeot vehicles and two Panhard et Levassors. The final vehicle arrived in Rouen shortly before nine P.M. Of the twenty-one vehicles that had set out from Paris that morning, seventeen completed the journey, all but three of them petrol powered. Three steam vehicles and one petrol-driven one had dropped out en route.

At the prize ceremony the following day, the Count de Dion, whose steam tractor had traveled the fastest and finished first, was nonetheless awarded the second prize of two thousand francs. The aim of the contest was, after all, to determine whether self-propelled vehicles could be safe, easy to use, and economical to run. The judges ruled that his steam-powered vehicle could not be the overall winner because it required a skilled mechanic to keep the engine going and was expensive to operate. Instead, the first prize of five thousand francs was awarded jointly to Peugeot and Panhard et Levassor, whose vehicles "came closest to the ideal" by "employing the petrol motor invented by Herr Daimler." Third prize went to a Serpollet steam carriage, and fourth prize was split between two entrants who had made innovative modifications to their vehicles—one of them being Alfred Vacheron, for championing the use of a steering wheel. The fifth prize went to Émile Roger, the driver of the Benz vehicle, who had finished fourteenth. In short, the organizers ensured that all the major manufacturers who had taken part ended up with a prize of some kind.

It was a curious race, given that the fastest vehicle did not win first prize, the first-prize winners finished second, and the real winner only became apparent in hindsight. The true victor that day was arguably the petrol-driven internal combustion engine, and in particular the one designed by Daimler. He had not entered the competition directly, but his engine had powered nine of the twelve petrol-powered vehicles that completed the course, including the four that shared first prize. Daimler was singled out for special praise by the judges, who said his efforts had "turned petroleum or gasoline fuel into a practical solution" for self-propelled vehicles. It seemed likely that there would be a surge in demand for Daimler engines. But Daimler and Maybach were no longer

The steam tractor built by Count Jules-Albert de Dion pulled a type of two-wheeled carriage known as a calèche. Although he finished first in the Paris–Rouen race of 1894, the Count de Dion did not win first prize because his vehicle was deemed too complicated and expensive to operate.

involved with the company that owned the rights to the winning design. By this time they had, however, devised an even better version, called the Phoenix, which their old company's licensees wanted to get their hands on. To resolve the mess a friend of Daimler's, a British investor named Frederick Simms, agreed to inject funds into the company on the condition that Daimler and Maybach rejoined it, bringing their new design with them, and were reinstated as executives. In 1895 the two men duly returned to the company they had cofounded.

Daimler's son Paul, the pioneering motorcyclist, who also attended the race, recalled the striking contrast between the operators of steam- and petrol-powered vehicles: "It was a curious spectacle seeing these disparate vehicle types racing against each other: the stokers on the heavy steamers, dripping with perspiration and covered with soot, working hard to put on fuel; the drivers of the small steam-powered three-wheelers keeping a watchful eye on the pressure and water level in the small, skillfully fitted tubular boiler and regulating the oil firing; and then in contrast to all that the drivers of the petrol- and paraffin-powered cars sitting calmly in the driver's seat, operating a lever now and again, as if they were simply out for a pleasure trip—an utterly peculiar image of contrasts that has remained with me ever since."

The race was reported on by newspapers around the world. The *New York Herald* described the event in a special edition on July 23. In London the *Pall Mall Gazette* carried a summary on July 24, noting that "the race for automatic vehicles which took place on Sunday from Paris to Rouen appears to have been a decided success." The *New York Times*, quoting the *London Telegraph*, listed the results in a report in early August, under the headline "Winners in the Road-Wagon Race." And in November the *New York Herald* reported, "Paris is becoming enthusiastic on the subject of horseless carriages. Another competitive race, similar to the one from Paris to Rouen in July last, has been arranged to take place in June next, the route being from Paris to Bordeaux and return."

"THE UTTER DISCARDING OF HORSEFLESH"

This second event, which took place on June 11, 1895, was bigger in every way. For one thing, it was much longer: the distance from Paris to Bordeaux and back was 730 miles, nearly ten times the distance from Paris to Rouen. (France was, at the time, blessed with some of the best roads in Europe, thanks in part to investments a century earlier by Napoléon, who recognized that well-maintained roads would allow him to move troops around quickly.) The first prize, of 31,500 francs, was much bigger, too. This time twenty-two vehicles assembled on the starting line, most of them petrol powered, but with a handful of steam vehicles, and two electric ones, whose drivers had prearranged stops to replace their batteries at regular intervals along the route. Unlike the previous year's event, this was a true race: the prize would be awarded to the vehicle that completed the course in the shortest time. But some things about the race seemed familiar: as in 1894, it pitted the Count de Dion, in his steam tractor, against Émile Levassor, driving one of his firm's petrol vehicles, now powered by the new Daimler Phoenix engine.

And once again, the Count de Dion took an early lead. But when he stopped to take on fuel and water, Levassor overtook him and remained in front for the rest of the race. After driving almost continuously for two days and nights, with only brief stops for refreshments, he arrived back in Paris on June 13, having achieved an average speed of 15 mph. In total, nine of the twenty-one entrants completed the race, the first eight places being taken by petrol vehicles, and a steam vehicle coming in last. Neither electric vehicle completed the course. But when the prizes were announced, Levassor was not named the winner, on a technicality: the race was supposed to be for vehicles with four seats, and his only had two, as did the vehicle that had finished second. So the grand prize went to Paul Koechlin, the driver of a Peugeot, who had finished third, eleven hours behind Levassor. This caused an outcry, and the organizers agreed that in future races the prize should go to the fastest vehicle.

But the main thing that was bigger about the 1895 event was the amount of publicity it attracted. "Judging from the great interest taken recently in experiments having for their aim the substitution of mechanical appliances in the place of horses for the propulsion of carriages and other road vehicles, it looks as if we will before long see a revolution in this direction," observed the *Pall Mall Gazette* in September 1895. And, it observed, the race had cemented the place of the internal combustion engine as the technology that would displace the horse. "France has demonstrated to the satisfaction of all unbiased observers that conveyances worked by the aid of petroleum motors are less than half as costly to maintain as horses for the same service, and that they have other obvious advantages which are sure to lead eventually to the utter discarding of horseflesh," the paper declared. "To be sure, these *voitures mécaniques avec moteur à petrole* look odd, but that is because we have been accustomed to see a nag instead of a box of machinery in the front of our vehicle." Even the Count de Dion had soon switched his company from making steam-powered vehicles to petrol-powered ones.

The 1895 race was the spur for many other competitions and city-to-city races in the years that followed, not just in France, but also in other countries, which worried that they might be falling behind in this important new field. In England, the *Engineer* magazine immediately offered a thousand-guinea prize in a contest to determine the best road vehicle produced in the country. The 1895 race also inspired a similar event in America. Staged in Chicago on Thanksgiving Day, November 28, 1895, it was sponsored by the *Chicago Times-Herald* and offered a $5,000 prize. All these competitions prompted engineers and drivers to try to outdo one another, advancing the state of the automotive art and providing publicity for manufacturers, in a motor-racing tradition that has continued ever since. An editorial in the inaugural edition of the *Horseless Age*, published in New York in November 1895, captured the sudden sense of excitement around the technology in America:

> The change in public sentiment from indifference to enthusiasm was to occur in an incredibly short period of time. The first race for motor vehicles from Paris to Rouen, which occurred in [July] 1894, set more of our inventive minds at work upon the motor problem, but it brought forth no general response from the American people. But the race from Paris to Bordeaux and return last June was such a phenomenal performance that all Christendom paused for a moment to fasten its eyes upon the flying automobiles. 750 miles in 48 hours and 53 minutes! The self-propelled vehicle was then an accomplished fact. The mechanical world immediately began to discuss it. The newspapers printed the story of the achievement and sent it into every hamlet . . . Then the American people seem to awaken with a start to the importance of the motor vehicle.

As this excerpt shows, coverage of the French races had introduced the French word *automobile* into the English language—a much less unwieldy term than *horseless carriage*. But not everyone wanted to use it. The *Horseless Age* preferred *motor vehicle*, a choice it defended on the basis that *motor* could be combined with other existing words to describe motor bicycles, motor wagons, motor carriages, and so on. "At present the people seem to be wedded to the name 'horseless carriage,' but . . . it seems quite certain that this awkward expression will gradually be discarded in favor of the briefer, more terse and expressive terms mentioned above," the magazine declared in an editorial in December 1895. In Britain the terms *autocar* and *automotor* had some support, as shown by the title of the *Automotor and Horseless Vehicle Journal*, but these were denounced by the *Horseless Age* as "heathenish abominations" because they implied that "the vehicle runs without human aid." In January 1899 the *New York Times* weighed in: "There is something uncanny about these new-fangled vehicles. They are all unutterably ugly and never a one of them has been provided with a good, or even an endurable, name." The *Times* rejected *automobile* on the etymological grounds that it combined *auto* (from Greek) with *mobile* (from Latin). It also complained that "speakers of English have been fatally attracted by the irrelevant word 'horseless.'" But the *Times* was soon regularly using *automobile*, and the word *car*, which had previously referred to wheeled vehicles of all kinds, including train carriages and streetcars running on rails, came to refer more specifically to motor vehicles in the early years of the twentieth century. Meanwhile *motor car*, often abbreviated to *car*, became the preferred term in Britain, where *automobile* or *auto* never caught on.

FROM NOVELTY TO NUISANCE

Bertha Benz's road trip in 1888 had been witnessed by bemused onlookers numbering a few dozen at most. Huge crowds turned out to see the grand car races of the 1890s. By the turn of the century, dozens of manufacturers in Europe and America were selling thousands of cars to wealthy enthusiasts, who were starting to make regular use of them on public roads. In 1900 around six thousand vehicles were produced in Europe (mostly in France) and four thousand in the United States, bringing the number of vehicles on the roads to around eight thousand on each side of the Atlantic. Public attitudes shifted as the automobile went from being an occasional novelty to an everyday nuisance because of the reckless behavior of many early motorists.

Louis Baudry de Saunier, a French journalist, noted in 1900 that "the automobile makes even the calmest man burn with an inextinguishable thirst for speed." In 1902 a writer for the *Overland Monthly*, a California magazine, expressed the hope that "in time the intoxication of the rapid motion of the automobile will wear off, and the pleasure of using such machines will be found in the opportunity that it gives to enjoy fresh air, change of scene and the beauties of nature, with the sense of freedom and independence that cannot be enjoyed in railroad trains." But this hope was misplaced. "I know kind, well-bred, and considerate people who, as soon as they feel the steering wheel in their hands and the gas pedal under their foot, are seized by an automotive frenzy," wrote Adolf Schmal, an Austrian writer, in his handbook for motorists, published in 1913. "It seems as if everything we normally call good breeding is suddenly extinguished in them."

Schmal assumed that motorists would be well-bred because the expense of buying a car meant that early drivers were, by necessity, wealthy members of the social elite. The appearance of cars on the road represented more than just the intrusion of a new kind of vehicle: it was an intrusion by the rich in particular. Early automobiles were loud because silencers (or mufflers) had yet to be made compulsory, and drivers made liberal use of their horns to warn people of their approach.

On country roads, people bemoaned the clouds of dust stirred up by cars, which were far worse than anything horses or wagons could produce. "Motor-car dust is a perennial pest which renders living in suburban and country houses situated on important roads most unhealthy and uncomfortable," observed an American diplomat stationed in Geneva, in 1905. The French Riviera, one of the first places in the world where motoring for pleasure became fashionable, was particularly badly affected. "I am informed that it has been found impossible of late to either lease or sell certain villas in the French Riviera, and that the paradise of the motorist has become the inferno of the inhabitant," the diplomat wrote. But he noted that in Geneva, and elsewhere in Switzerland, the local authorities had responded by applying "antidust preparations"—hot coal tar or asphalt—to the roads. Surfacing roads in this way turned out to be effective in reducing the dust kicked up by cars. Some people even paid for the surfacing of the roads in front of their houses. But applying such treatments to all existing roads seemed impractical because it would cost so much. So instead people called for tighter speed limits or for vehicles to be restricted to particular routes.

Noise and dust were not the only problems from the proliferation of automobiles. People and animals were also at risk. Chickens were often caught under the wheels, and some drivers were accused of taking pleasure in running them down deliberately. Attitudes toward chickens highlighted the gulf between poor farmers and wealthy drivers. *Le Figaro*, a French newspaper, even told the tale in 1913 of the "automotive chicken," which had supposedly been specially bred by farmers to rush in front of cars, so its owner could then claim five francs in compensation. Horses were another source of conflict. Motorists disliked being held back by slow-moving horse-drawn vehicles and felt that sentimental, old-fashioned attitudes toward horses were hampering the progress of the automobile in a more general sense, too. It was unfair to blame reckless drivers for endangering other road users, proponents of the automobile argued, when horses caused far more accidents. The danger posed by motoring was overstated, they complained, while accidents involving horses were overlooked as being just part of the natural order of things. "The noble horse, despite all its virtues still stupider than a motorist, remains untouchable, although it has been proven a hundred times that horses and horse-drawn wagons cause more accidents than automobiles," lamented a German motoring journal in 1904. An Italian magazine took a similar position in 1912: "Horses, trams, trains can collide, smash, kill half the world, and nobody cares," yet there was an outcry "if an automobile leaves a scratch on an urchin who dances in front of it, or on a drunken carter who is driving without a light."

The character of Mr. Toad, in Kenneth Grahame's novel *The Wind in the Willows*, is the embodiment of the reckless and inconsiderate upper-class motorist, a stereotype that would have been widely recognized at the time of the book's publication in 1908. In the story, Mr. Toad is a crazed follower of the latest fads and has become an obsessive motorist after having his horse-drawn vehicle forced off the road by a passing automobile. "What dust clouds shall spring up before me as I speed on my reckless way!" he declares, on his conversion from horse-drawn to motor vehicles. Before long he has crashed seven cars, been in the hospital three times, and paid a fortune in fines for motoring offenses. His friends try to prevent him from pursuing his dangerous hobby by placing him under house arrest, but he escapes, steals a car, and ends up in prison. He then escapes, steals the same car again, and drives it into a river.

The real-life inspiration for Mr. Toad may well have been William K. Vanderbilt II, an American millionaire and car enthusiast. He caught the motoring bug in 1888, aged ten, when he rode a steam-powered tricycle in the south of France. Ten years later he ordered a motor tricycle—built by the Count de Dion's company, no less, and powered by an internal combustion engine—and had it shipped to New York. (Around fifteen thousand of these de Dion tricycles were sold between 1897 and 1901, making it one of the first motor vehicles to be widely distributed.) Vanderbilt acquired a large collection of vehicles, and his Toad-like motoring escapades are said to have led to the imposition of the first speed limits near his home in Newport, Rhode Island, in 1900, and on Long Island, in 1902. He also antagonized people farther afield during a series of European motor tours. In 1899, during a visit to France, he killed two dogs that were attacking the tires on his vehicle and had to flee from an angry mob. On another occasion he had to fire warning shots to disperse a crowd threatening him with whips and rocks—tellingly, he always carried a revolver with him for protection. His gun was taken from him by an angry mob after he hit a child with his car in Italy in 1906, and the police had to intervene to rescue him. In 1909, Swiss farmers attacked him and threatened to set fire to his vehicle.

Little wonder with people such as Vanderbilt at large on the roads that hostility toward motorists in this period was widespread. A pioneering German female motorist recorded in her diary in 1905, "A journey by automobile through Holland is dangerous, since most of the rural population hates motorists fanatically. We even encountered older men, their faces contorted with anger, who, without any provocation, threw fist-sized stones at us." Other tactics to discourage motorists in this era included sprinkling nails or broken glass on roads, tying ropes and wires across the lanes, and throwing volleys of fresh dung. Between 1904 and 1906, farmers around Rochester, Minnesota, plowed up the roads to prevent the passage of automobiles; others, near Sacramento, California, dug ditches across roads in 1909 and captured thirteen cars. Handbooks for German motorists from this period recommend carrying a weapon for protection. Some motorists considered it advisable to leave the scene of an accident as soon as possible, for fear of retribution from angry farmers. A law passed in Germany in 1909 even allowed motorists to do this, provided they reported the accident promptly to the police. A German parliamentarian, conversely, advised wagon drivers in 1910 to buy guns to defend themselves from motorists.

In a speech in 1906, Woodrow Wilson, then president of Princeton University, worried that loutish motorists were fanning the flames of resentment toward the rich: "Nothing has spread socialistic feeling in this country more than the use of automobiles. To the countryman they are a picture of arrogance of wealth with all its independence and carelessness." Car fans, for their part, denounced critics as enemies of progress. "Who are these people who cry for government help against the motorists? They are the same ones who didn't want gas lighting half a century ago and who petitioned the King of Prussia to stop the railroad being built from Berlin to Potsdam," noted a German writer in 1906. In 1908 Octave Mirbeau, a French writer, satirized such complaints from motorists: "How frustrating, how thoroughly disheartening it is that these pigheaded, obstructive villagers, whose hens, dogs and sometimes children I mow down, fail to appreciate that I represent Progress and universal happiness. I intend to bring them these benefits in spite of themselves, even if they don't live to enjoy them!"

There were some attempts to ban cars altogether in the 1890s and early 1900s, though most such efforts were either short-lived or never actually enforced. Parts of Germany and Switzerland banned cars on Sundays to preserve the sanctity of the Sunday stroll. For the most part, however, the advent of the car was met with a growing body of rules regulating its use: speed limits, the registration of vehicles, licensing of drivers, requiring the use of lights at night, and so on. In Britain, for example, the infamous Red Flag law was withdrawn in 1896. In its place came new rules allowing road vehicles weighing less than three tons to drive no faster than 14 mph, with a reminder that they should keep to the left. The Motor Car Act of 1903 updated these rules, introducing vehicle registration and the licensing of drivers (though no test was required), increasing the speed limit from 14 mph to 20 mph, and making reckless driving an offense for which drivers could be imprisoned for up to three months. The threat of imprisonment was deemed necessary because fines were failing to deter wealthy "road hogs" or "motor scorchers," as dangerous motorists were starting to become known, from bad behavior.

But ultimately it was not laws that would change attitudes toward the automobile, but familiarity. Hostility toward cars and drivers began to diminish as vehicles became more affordable. As car ownership came within reach of more people, in cities and countryside alike, some of the initial objections to the automobile, such as the noise and dust, came to be seen as a price worth paying for the greater freedom, convenience, and affordability it offered compared with horse-drawn vehicles. Perhaps surprisingly, given that Europe had been the birthplace of the technology, this happened in America first, thanks to one car in particular: the Ford Model T.

You Are What You Drive

A family's motor indicated its social rank as precisely as the grades of the peerage determined the rank of an English family.

—SINCLAIR LEWIS, *BABBITT*, 1922

THE CAR THAT CHANGED EVERYTHING

Anyone who wanted to buy a car in America in 1908 had no shortage of options. Car advertisements from that year offered prospective buyers a bewildering choice of vehicles from dozens of different carmakers, the majority of them now long forgotten. What most of these advertisements had in common was an emphasis on the social cachet associated with car ownership. And no wonder, because cars were expensive: the average price of an American-built petrol car that year was $2,834 (equivalent to about $80,000 today), while an imported European model cost, on average, $6,730 (equivalent to about $200,000). As the text and images of the advertisements clearly signal, cars were playthings for the rich. Advertisements for Pierce-Arrow cars, which ranged in price from $3,950 to $7,200, depict men and women in formal dress, attended by chauffeurs, valets, and butlers, as they glide between high-society engagements.

In some cases the setting is less formal, the top hats and dinner jackets replaced by boaters and blazers, or men in tennis gear leaning languidly on their expensive vehicles. Pierce-Arrow broughams (a style of car modeled on a carriage, where the driver sits outside an enclosed passenger cabin) are said to have "the smartness of a well-appointed carriage." Other brands made similar claims. Advertisements for the 1908 Oldsmobile Model Z, which cost $4,200, promise "an aristocratic, dignified car," while the Model M (a mere $2,750) is described as "a strictly high-class car embodying style, comfort and roadability." In its advertisements, the Peerless Motor Car Company (slogan: "All that the name implies") features two high-society women being chauffeured around New York. Many of these advertisements also refer to the cars' performance and reliability, as indicated by their prowess in speed trials, hill climbs, and long-distance endurance races. This was a way to reassure potential buyers that as well as making them look good, the cars in question would not cause them embarrassment. What use, after all, is a car that indicates your wealth and status if it breaks down outside the opera?

So the approach taken by the Ford Motor Company for its new Model T, which was launched in October 1908, was (like the car itself) something of a departure from the norm. Most of the advertisement is text, not imagery, and rather than being aspirational, its tone is practical and no-nonsense: "high priced quality in a low priced car . . . the Ford car will run more miles for less money than any other touring car manufactured." Instead of showing the car in a high-society setting, surrounded by well-dressed people, it is shown on its own, on a plain background. And instead of being buried in the small print at the bottom, or not mentioned at all, the price is prominent in the headline. And no wonder, because the Model T was being offered for sale at "the hitherto unheard of price of $850." Here was a car intended to expand and democratize car ownership. Who was it aimed at? The advertisement did not depict a target customer or context of use, implying it was for anyone, anywhere: a "universal car," as the company soon began to call it.

In the years before the Model T's introduction the American car market was, roughly speaking, divided into two categories. On the one hand were horseless carriages: lightweight vehicles that were, as their

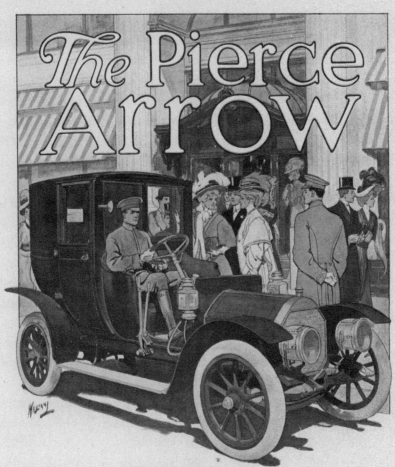

PIERCE ARROW ENCLOSED CARS

We offer for the coming season four types of enclosed cars of the following horse-power and prices:

	24 H.P. 4 cylinder	36 H.P. 6 cylinder	40 H.P. 4 cylinder	48 H.P. 6 cylinder	60 H.P. 6 cylinder
Landaulet	$3950	$4600	......	......	......
Brougham	3900	4550	......	......	......
Landau	......	......	$5500	$6200	$7200
Suburban	......	......	5400	6100	7100

These are built on the same chassis as the Pierce Arrow Cars which made perfect scores and won the Trophies in both the Glidden and the Hower Tours.

THE GEORGE N. PIERCE COMPANY, BUFFALO, N. Y.

Members Association Licensed Automobile Manufacturers

Advertisement for Pierce-Arrow, 1908. The company's advertisements invariably showed the cars in high-society settings.

name and shape implied, clearly descended from horse-drawn carriages, but powered by a rear-mounted petrol engine, and steered using a tiller. A classic example was the Oldsmobile Curved Dash, introduced in 1901. Such cars, commonly known as runabouts, were open topped, with no windshield, and only a single row of seats. Their lack of power meant they were only suitable for short trips on good roads. The other style of vehicle was the so-called touring car, also known as the French-style design because of its front-mounted engine, an idea that had been pioneered by the French manufacturer Panhard in 1891. The design of touring cars owed nothing to carriages or tricycles; they were instead seen as "highway locomotives" capable of high speeds over long distances, like trains. These heavier, more powerful vehicles also offered greater comfort and reliability, with more rugged axles and better suspension, giving them the ability to cope with almost any road conditions. All this made them far more expensive than runabouts, but their greater versatility meant they started to dominate the market, displacing what one 1908 newspaper report called the "spindly, fragile 'horseless carriages'" that had come before. This pushed up average selling prices. In 1903, two thirds of new cars sold in America cost less than $1,375; but by 1907, two thirds cost more than that.

Henry Ford was one of several carmakers who saw an opportunity to build a vehicle that combined the power and ruggedness of a touring car with the low cost of a runabout (i.e., coming in at less than $1,000). His company had launched a successful two-passenger runabout, the Model N, in 1906 for $500, and followed it up with the essentially similar Model R and Model S. "The greatest need to-day is a light, low-priced car with an up-to-date engine of ample horsepower, and built of the very best material," Ford wrote in *Automobile* magazine in 1906. "One that will go anywhere a car of double the horsepower will; that is in every way an automobile and not a toy; and, most important of all, one that will not be a wrecker of tires and a spoiler of the owner's disposition. It must be powerful enough for American roads and capable of carrying its passengers anywhere that a horse-drawn vehicle will go without the driver being afraid of ruining his car." The problem was that the larger engine a touring car needed to negotiate hills and bad roads meant that the rest of the car had to be bigger, stronger, and heavier, too—making it more expensive.

The challenge was to find a way to build an engine that was light yet powerful. Ford's answer was to use vanadium steel, a strong but light-weight alloy that was coming into use in Europe, but had yet to become available commercially in America. Ford put together a team to figure out how to make and use this new material, then designed and built an entirely new car based on it. The result was the Model T, which had the power of a touring car without being as large, heavy, or expensive. As the advertisement introducing it noted, "Vanadium steel, the finest and costliest steel manufactured, is used throughout the entire car . . . the axles, shafts, connecting rods, springs, gears, brackets etc are all of vanadium steel." Ford claimed that it was at least 50 percent stronger than other forms of steel. But could the diminutive Model T really deliver the touring-car performance? Proof came in the summer of 1909, when two Model Ts competed with heavier and more expensive vehicles in a forty-one-hundred-mile race from New York to Seattle. Press coverage of the race contrasted the appearance of the Model Ts with that of their larger rivals, deriding them as "pygmies" and "midgets." But when a Model T was the first to cross the finish line, critics changed their tune. "One thing—and a very important one—that was not taken into consideration by those who prophesied defeat for the Fords, was the fact that the little cars had more horse power to comparative weight than the larger and racier looking machines," noted the *New York Times*, putting its finger on the source of the Model Ts' advantage.

The Model T was not the cheapest car on the market when it went on sale—runabouts could be had for less—but it offered an unprecedented degree of power and durability for the price. It cost little more than a runabout, but it could handle hills and rutted country roads. Available as a runabout, a five-seater touring car, or a delivery van, all built on the same chassis, it appealed to a range of customers. Ford emphasized this versatility in its advertising, promoting the Model T as "the farmer's car" and "the merchant's car" and "the family car," before calling it simply "the universal car." The Model T captured 11 percent of the American car market in its first year on sale, and in the years that followed

Advertisement for the original Ford Model T, 1908. The text, like the car itself, is practical and no-nonsense.

its market share steadily ticked upwards, from 27 percent in 1911 to 46 percent in 1914 to 55 percent in 1923, while the price ticked steadily downward, from $850 in 1908 to $298 in 1923. By extending car ownership down the income scale, the Model T brought motoring to the masses. Its runaway success stemmed not just from its use of vanadium steel, but also from its low production cost, which in turn depended on the radical new way in which it was built: on a moving assembly line. The Model T did more than just redefine how cars were built. It set the twentieth-century template for mass production of consumer goods of all kinds.

ANY COLOR, AS LONG AS IT'S BLACK

The idea of what we now call mass production using interchangeable parts had originated in the nineteenth century and was originally known as "the American system of manufactures." It could be used to manufacture large quantities of a specific product through the assembly of standardized, interchangeable parts, made to sufficiently precise tolerances, by low-skilled (and hence low-wage) workers. This approach was originally used to make shoes, guns, and clocks, and in the early twentieth century it was extended to cars, starting with the Oldsmobile Curved Dash in 1901, production of which had reached an unprecedented fifty-five hundred units a year by 1904. The slotting together of predesigned parts meant that the manufacture of some components could also be farmed out: the Curved Dash's engine was built by one supplier, and its transmission by another. This encouraged parts suppliers to cluster around large manufacturers, resulting in the emergence of car-making hubs, notably in Detroit.

The earliest Model T Fords were built using this established style of mass production, with workers adding components to a stationary, incomplete vehicle. But in the summer of 1913 Ford began to experiment with moving, electrically driven assembly lines, an idea the company borrowed from meatpacking plants in Chicago, where multiple workers collaborated to disassemble animal carcasses being carried along by an overhead "trolley" system. To begin with, a moving assembly line was used to assemble the Model T's magneto (part of the ignition system), and over the following year the process was gradually expanded to cover the whole vehicle. A moving assembly line meant workers stayed still and repeatedly performed the same task on an incomplete vehicle as it went past them. This limited how long they could take and forced them to become skilled at performing a particular operation quickly. "The man who puts in a bolt does not put on the nut; the man who puts on a nut does not tighten it," Ford later explained.

In all, the Model T's construction was decomposed into 7,882 separate tasks. This degree of specialization, combined with the regimented coordination of a moving assembly line, took mass production to new level of efficiency. Production time for a single vehicle fell from twelve hours to ninety-three minutes, with a new car rolling off the line every three minutes. It was noisy and tedious for workers, but it was also surprisingly well paid: from 1914 Ford paid $5 for an eight-hour day, about double the industry's going rate. Strange as it may seem, paying higher wages was yet another way of cutting costs and improving efficiency. In 1913, the year before the $5 wage was introduced, 71 percent of Ford's new hires had left within five days. Paying higher wages reduced employee turnover, and hence the amount of time needed for training. Ford claimed that "the payment of five dollars a day for an eight-hour day was one of the finest cost-cutting moves we ever made." Average earnings in the United States in 1914 were $335, whereas a Ford employee working five-day weeks for fifty weeks would make $1,250. This also meant that many Ford workers could actually afford the machines they were building, particularly as the price fell.

Production of the Model T was also famously streamlined by Ford's decision to offer it in one color only: black. When it first went on sale, the Model T had been offered in a range of colors. But the fewer the variations in the final product, the more efficient mass production becomes, and the easier it is to manage the resulting inventory. So when Ford adopted the moving assembly line in 1914, it standardized all Model T production on a single color. It is sometimes claimed that black was chosen because it dried faster than any other color, allowing the assembly line to run more quickly. But there is no basis for this claim in Ford engineering documents or contemporary accounts written by employees. The particular fast-drying, high-gloss, fade-resistant, and dampproof paint process used in the Model T would have worked just as well with other dark pigments. Black was simply the cheapest option. So black it was.

Ford's new mass-production process was hailed as a machine every bit as revolutionary as the vehicles it produced. It cranked out millions of units of the same car, but at a steadily decreasing price: every doubling of cumulative Ford Model T output led to a fall of about 16 percent in cost per unit, by one calculation. The more cars Ford made, the more affordable they became, expanding car ownership still further. Ford's apparently miraculous factory was opened to visitors and was promoted in books, postcards, films, advertisements, and exhibitions. A working assembly line was even built at the San Francisco Panama-Pacific International Exposition in 1915, producing a Model T every ten minutes for three hours each day, in front of awed spectators. Ford replicated its assembly lines at home and abroad, starting in Canada, then expanding

is abandoned, and that GM should set itself the goal of producing
of cars in each price area" so that "the price steps should not be
to leave wide gaps in the line." The old GM range of seven brands,
of them overlapping, with models ranging in price from $795 to
would be replaced by six models in six price bands, from $450
00, with no gaps between them. The key idea, as Sloan put it, was
producing a full line of cars graded upward in quality and price."
s at different prices could then appeal to different customers, and
became wealthier and more demanding, they could move up GM's
of brands.

ll looked good on paper. But Sloan's plan initially went nowhere.
t had been ousted in another boardroom coup in 1920, and his
sor, Pierre S. du Pont, became distracted by a disastrous project to
a Chevrolet with a new kind of air-cooled engine, which ended
vehicles sold being recalled and destroyed. Not until after this
e, when Sloan was made president and chief executive of GM in
was he able to put his plan into action, slimming down the port-
of brands and adjusting the pricing and product lines of those
ning to minimize overlap. With this more coherent ladder of car
s in place, GM's advertising could boast that the company offered
for every purse and purpose," explicitly listing the brands in order
iving the price range for each. The company also created a new
, Pontiac, to fill the price gap between Chevrolet, at the bottom of
dder, and Oakland, on the next rung up. Pontiac represented a
er deviation from Ford's approach, in which carmakers focused on
ng a single model. The Pontiac would be developed by Chevrolet
ould be built by Oakland, which would also continue to make cars
r its own name. The aim was, as Sloan put it, to "demonstrate that
production of automobiles could be reconciled with variety in
uct. This was again the opposite of the old Ford concept, which we
stently met and opposed at every turn."

M's emphasis on choice and variety, as opposed to Ford's one-size-
ll approach, was not the only way in which the two firms were oppo-
GM had embraced the idea of allowing customers to pay for cars
stallments, a practice that emerged around 1910 and accounted for

into Europe, Latin America, and Japan. By 1921 the Model T accounted
for 57 percent of world automobile production; by 1923 Ford's assembly
lines were cranking out 2 million vehicles a year, up from eleven thousand in 1909.

The growth of car ownership in America was particularly astonishing.
In 1900 around 8,000 motor vehicles were on the road in Europe, with
a similar number in the United States; by 1910 those numbers had jumped
to about 300,000 in Europe and 458,000 in America; but by 1920 the
figures were 1 million and 8 million. The number of automobiles on
American roads had increased a thousandfold in twenty years—a rate of
growth that is more commonly associated with computer technology.
America had taken the automobile to heart earlier and more quickly than
any other country for a number of reasons. Incomes were higher than in
Europe, cars were cheaper, and fuel was less heavily taxed because it did
not have to be imported (America was the world's leading oil producer).
By 1910, Los Angeles had the highest rate of car ownership on earth,
thanks to its wealthy inhabitants, good roads, and warm climate, which
allowed year-round driving (most vehicles were not enclosed). The
number of horses on American roads went into rapid decline, falling by
60 percent in the biggest cities between 1910 and 1920. By the mid-1920s
only 3–6 percent of vehicles were still being drawn by horses.

Ford's distinctive manufacturing approach came to be known as
Fordism and was copied both by other carmakers and in other industries. As the New York Times put it in 1931, "Fordism became a fetish for
industrialists everywhere . . . the promise of mass production, the resultant economy in costs, the reduction in overhead, the ability to produce
a good article at an unbelievably low price, became the basis of new
industrial cult." While Charlie Chaplin satirized the relentless, dehumanizing experience of working on a production line in his film Modern
Times, other observers hailed the Fordist approach as a great boon to social
justice and equality. By democratizing ownership, mass production would
erase social distinctions based on status goods such as cars, suggested Lewis
Mumford, an American historian and philosopher: "the machine has
achieved potentially a new collective economy, in which the possession
of goods is a meaningless distinction, since the machine can produce all

our essential goods in unparalleled quantities, falling on the just and unjust, the foolish and wise, like the rain itself."

But the efficiency and uniformity of the Model T's production was to be its undoing. Henry Ford genuinely believed that it was the only car people would ever need and took pride in how little it changed over the years. Indeed, in its advertising the company did not even mention tweaks to the design, such as addition of curved fenders in 1915 or electric lights in 1925. Ford's advertisements were as spartan as the Model T itself, emphasizing the car's low purchase price and running cost, and its manufacturer's dedication to producing one vehicle as cheaply and efficiently as possible. But the company's refusal to update the design had become a liability. The Model T looked old-fashioned (even if some of its innards has been updated, for example with the addition of an electric starter). Its 20-horsepower engine, powerful by comparison with other cars in 1908, had been overtaken by the 1920s. Meanwhile, and other carmakers also offered better performance, comfort and styling. The Model T's unchanging features and basic design became a joke, but that was fine with Ford, which revelled in its no-nonsense reputation for cheapness and reliability. Even the Model T's name was utilitarian compared with those of other cars, which took their names from famous racing drivers (Chevrolet, Rickenbacker), weapons (Arrow, Rocket) or prestigious terms associated with royalty (Sovereign, Sultan) or classical mythology (Phoenix, Vulcan). The more Ford optimized the production of a single vehicle, the less able it was to move with the times. The first mass-market car, the Model T introduced millions of people to car ownership around the world. By the mid-1920s Model Ts accounted for half the cars on American roads, but that was the problem: American customers began to want something a bit different. The Model T was cheap and reliable, but buyers wanted more.

THE OPPOSITE OF FORD

General Motors was founded in 1908, the same year the Model T was launched. Its founder, William C. Durant, had made a fortune in carriage-making and decided to move into cars. He established GM as a holding

company and immediately acquired Buick, controlled, followed by a string of other carma Oldsmobile, and Cadillac, in the months that fo companies that made car components, accesso Manufacturers of all kinds of products, from car branching out into carmaking (Buick had ori Durant's plan was to assemble a collection of carm under separate brands, or marques, but would b ciency and lower costs by pooling some activities he overextended himself in his acquisition spree a by other shareholders in 1910. Durant respon carmaker with the race-car driver Louis Chevro neered a return to GM in 1916, and a merger w him in charge of the combined firm, in 1918.

GM's sprawling portfolio of car brands was the approach, with its obsessive focus on a single mod starting to shift. With cars becoming far more affo one no longer had the same social cachet—what started to matter a lot more instead. GM's struct separate carmakers offered buyers plenty of choic ranged from Chevrolet at the low end through Oakl Booth and Sheridan, to Buick and Cadillac at the t lineup, having been assembled through acquisition, was lots of overlap between brands in the middle the lowest-price car was too expensive (the ch $795, cost far more than a Model T, which cost abc Manufacturing quality varied hugely between and Sheridan and Scripps-Booth had poor sales and were and Oakland cars relied on outdated designs. Wit North America of 393,000 cars across all its brands distant second to Ford, with sales of 1.1 million. And Ford's dominance at the low end of the market, "we tion," Alfred P. Sloan, then GM's operating vice presi

Sloan was given the job of devising a plan to rev line. He proposed that duplication should be elimi

65 percent of new car sales by 1925. The company saw this as a rising trend it could capitalize on and established its own finance arm, the General Motors Acceptance Corporation, in 1919, to provide credit to its customers, becoming the first carmaker to do so. Ford, by contrast, was fiercely opposed to the idea and demanded payment in full up front. GM also welcomed used-car trade-ins against new models, to encourage prospective customers to move up its brand ladder. "Middle-income buyers, assisted by the trade-in and instalment financing, created the demand, not for basic transportation, but for progress in new cars, for comfort, convenience, power, and style," noted Sloan. When it came to styling, GM's cars reflected the growing enthusiasm for fully enclosed, "closed body," designs that could be used in any weather, with solid roofs and side windows. Closed bodies were unusual before the First World War, but the proportion of American cars with closed-body designs rose from 10 percent in 1919 to 85 percent in 1927. Having predated this trend, the Model T was an open-car design, with a fold-down roof and no side windows, and its chassis had not been designed to support a heavier closed body. Ford's manufacturing prowess might have been second to none, but its product had failed to move with the times.

And encouraging car buyers to move with the times was to be the final piece of Sloan's new strategy. As the market became increasingly saturated, the challenge of selling cars in volume was to get existing car owners to upgrade, rather than making cars cheap enough to entice first-time buyers. So with his ladder of car brands in place, Sloan added a further twist: "annual model renewal." This meant changing the appearance of each model every year, while leaving things mostly unchanged under the hood. In many cases the engine and chassis were shared across several different models, dressed up with different body stylings and sold under different GM brands. But in the styling of the exterior, Sloan decreed that there would be "continuous, eternal change," with annual design changes to make old models seem outdated and new ones more stylish and fashionable. He referred to this approach as "dynamic obsolescence."

This would only work if the cars were styled in a way that people found alluring, changing enough to make each year's new model look distinctive, while also maintaining continuity with previous models and avoiding radical changes that might deter buyers. So GM placed a lot of emphasis on color and design. It collaborated with DuPont, a chemicals giant that owned a large stake in GM, to develop DuCo, a fast-drying and durable lacquer resin that could be made in a range of colors including blues, greens, brown, and orange. In 1923 GM experimented with these new colors on its Oakland brand. With seven new Oakland models due to launch in 1924, GM painted a prototype of each one in bright DuCo blue, with accents in red or orange, and sent the cars on a nationwide tour of dealers. This provided a road test for the durability of the paint, which performed well, and the cars were the stars of the New York Automobile Show, where they ended their tour in December. Orders poured in from customers drawn to this exciting new color. "DuCo has become so popular," reported one executive, "that customers are now demanding it." GM duly applied DuCo colors across its entire product

GM marketed its cars as fashion items, placing great emphasis on design, styling, and color, with a hierarchy of brands at different prices to segment the market.

into Europe, Latin America, and Japan. By 1921 the Model T accounted for 57 percent of world automobile production; by 1923 Ford's assembly lines were cranking out 2 million vehicles a year, up from eleven thousand in 1909.

The growth of car ownership in America was particularly astonishing. In 1900 around 8,000 motor vehicles were on the road in Europe, with a similar number in the United States; by 1910 those numbers had jumped to about 300,000 in Europe and 458,000 in America; but by 1920 the figures were 1 million and 8 million. The number of automobiles on American roads had increased a thousandfold in twenty years—a rate of growth that is more commonly associated with computer technology. America had taken the automobile to heart earlier and more quickly than any other country for a number of reasons. Incomes were higher than in Europe, cars were cheaper, and fuel was less heavily taxed because it did not have to be imported (America was the world's leading oil producer). By 1910, Los Angeles had the highest rate of car ownership on earth, thanks to its wealthy inhabitants, good roads, and warm climate, which allowed year-round driving (most vehicles were not enclosed). The number of horses on American roads went into rapid decline, falling by 60 percent in the biggest cities between 1910 and 1920. By the mid-1920s only 3–6 percent of vehicles were still being drawn by horses.

Ford's distinctive manufacturing approach came to be known as Fordism and was copied both by other carmakers and in other industries. As the *New York Times* put it in 1931, "Fordism became a fetish for industrialists everywhere . . . the promise of mass production, the resultant economy in costs, the reduction in overhead, the ability to produce a good article at an unbelievably low price, became the basis of new industrial cult." While Charlie Chaplin satirized the relentless, dehumanizing experience of working on a production line in his film *Modern Times*, other observers hailed the Fordist approach as a great boon to social justice and equality. By democratizing ownership, mass production would erase social distinctions based on status goods such as cars, suggested Lewis Mumford, an American historian and philosopher: "the machine has achieved potentially a new collective economy, in which the possession of goods is a meaningless distinction, since the machine can produce all our essential goods in unparalleled quantities, falling on the just and unjust, the foolish and wise, like the rain itself."

But the efficiency and uniformity of the Model T's production was to be its undoing. Henry Ford genuinely believed that it was the only car people would ever need and took pride in how little it changed over the years. Indeed, in its advertising the company did not even mention tweaks to the design, such as addition of curved fenders in 1915 or electric lights in 1925. Ford's advertisements were as spartan as the Model T itself, emphasizing the car's low purchase price and running cost, and its manufacturer's dedication to producing one vehicle as cheaply and efficiently as possible. But the company's refusal to update the design had become a liability. The Model T looked old-fashioned (even if some of its innards has been updated, for example with the addition of an electric starter). Its 20-horsepower engine, powerful by comparison with other cars in 1908, had been overtaken by the 1920s. Meanwhile, and other carmakers also offered better performance, comfort and styling. The Model T's unchanging features and basic design became a joke, but that was fine with Ford, which revelled in its no-nonsense reputation for cheapness and reliability. Even the Model T's name was utilitarian compared with those of other cars, which took their names from famous racing drivers (Chevrolet, Rickenbacker), weapons (Arrow, Rocket) or prestigious terms associated with royalty (Sovereign, Sultan) or classical mythology (Phoenix, Vulcan). The more Ford optimized the production of a single vehicle, the less able it was to move with the times. The first mass-market car, the Model T introduced millions of people to car ownership around the world. By the mid-1920s Model Ts accounted for half the cars on American roads, but that was the problem: American customers began to want something a bit different. The Model T was cheap and reliable, but buyers wanted more.

THE OPPOSITE OF FORD

General Motors was founded in 1908, the same year the Model T was launched. Its founder, William C. Durant, had made a fortune in carriage-making and decided to move into cars. He established GM as a holding company and immediately acquired Buick, a carmaker he already controlled, followed by a string of other carmakers, including Oakland, Oldsmobile, and Cadillac, in the months that followed. GM also bought companies that made car components, accessories, varnish, and paint. Manufacturers of all kinds of products, from carriages to birdcages, were branching out into carmaking (Buick had originally made bathtubs). Durant's plan was to assemble a collection of carmakers that would operate under separate brands, or marques, but would benefit from greater efficiency and lower costs by pooling some activities behind the scenes. But he overextended himself in his acquisition spree and was ousted from GM by other shareholders in 1910. Durant responded by starting a rival carmaker with the race-car driver Louis Chevrolet. Durant then engineered a return to GM in 1916, and a merger with Chevrolet, putting him in charge of the combined firm, in 1918.

GM's sprawling portfolio of car brands was the direct opposite of Ford's approach, with its obsessive focus on a single model. But the market was starting to shift. With cars becoming far more affordable, merely owning one no longer had the same social cachet—what sort of car you owned started to matter a lot more instead. GM's structure as a collection of separate carmakers offered buyers plenty of choice. By 1920 its lineup ranged from Chevrolet at the low end through Oakland and Olds, Scripps-Booth and Sheridan, to Buick and Cadillac at the top. But GM's product lineup, having been assembled through acquisition, was a shambles. There was lots of overlap between brands in the middle of the range, while the lowest-price car was too expensive (the cheapest Chevrolet, at $795, cost far more than a Model T, which cost about $500 at the time). Manufacturing quality varied hugely between and even within brands. Sheridan and Scripps-Booth had poor sales and were losing money; Olds and Oakland cars relied on outdated designs. With collective sales in North America of 393,000 cars across all its brands in 1920, GM was a distant second to Ford, with sales of 1.1 million. And with no response to Ford's dominance at the low end of the market, "we were in a bad situation," Alfred P. Sloan, then GM's operating vice president, later recalled.

Sloan was given the job of devising a plan to revamp GM's product line. He proposed that duplication should be eliminated, loss-making divisions abandoned, and that GM should set itself the goal of producing "a line of cars in each price area" so that "the price steps should not be such as to leave wide gaps in the line." The old GM range of seven brands, many of them overlapping, with models ranging in price from $795 to $5,690, would be replaced by six models in six price bands, from $450 to $3,500, with no gaps between them. The key idea, as Sloan put it, was "mass-producing a full line of cars graded upward in quality and price." Models at different prices could then appeal to different customers, and as they became wealthier and more demanding, they could move up GM's ladder of brands.

It all looked good on paper. But Sloan's plan initially went nowhere. Durant had been ousted in another boardroom coup in 1920, and his successor, Pierre S. du Pont, became distracted by a disastrous project to build a Chevrolet with a new kind of air-cooled engine, which ended in all vehicles sold being recalled and destroyed. Not until after this debacle, when Sloan was made president and chief executive of GM in 1923, was he able to put his plan into action, slimming down the portfolio of brands and adjusting the pricing and product lines of those remaining to minimize overlap. With this more coherent ladder of car brands in place, GM's advertising could boast that the company offered "a car for every purse and purpose," explicitly listing the brands in order and giving the price range for each. The company also created a new brand, Pontiac, to fill the price gap between Chevrolet, at the bottom of the ladder, and Oakland, on the next rung up. Pontiac represented a further deviation from Ford's approach, in which carmakers focused on making a single model. The Pontiac would be developed by Chevrolet but would be built by Oakland, which would also continue to make cars under its own name. The aim was, as Sloan put it, to "demonstrate that mass production of automobiles could be reconciled with variety in product. This was again the opposite of the old Ford concept, which we persistently met and opposed at every turn."

GM's emphasis on choice and variety, as opposed to Ford's one-size-fits-all approach, was not the only way in which the two firms were opposites. GM had embraced the idea of allowing customers to pay for cars in installments, a practice that emerged around 1910 and accounted for

65 percent of new car sales by 1925. The company saw this as a rising trend it could capitalize on and established its own finance arm, the General Motors Acceptance Corporation, in 1919, to provide credit to its customers, becoming the first carmaker to do so. Ford, by contrast, was fiercely opposed to the idea and demanded payment in full up front. GM also welcomed used-car trade-ins against new models, to encourage prospective customers to move up its brand ladder. "Middle-income buyers, assisted by the trade-in and instalment financing, created the demand, not for basic transportation, but for progress in new cars, for comfort, convenience, power, and style," noted Sloan. When it came to styling, GM's cars reflected the growing enthusiasm for fully enclosed, "closed body," designs that could be used in any weather, with solid roofs and side windows. Closed bodies were unusual before the First World War, but the proportion of American cars with closed-body designs rose from 10 percent in 1919 to 85 percent in 1927. Having predated this trend, the Model T was an open-car design, with a fold-down roof and no side windows, and its chassis had not been designed to support a heavier closed body. Ford's manufacturing prowess might have been second to none, but its product had failed to move with the times.

And encouraging car buyers to move with the times was to be the final piece of Sloan's new strategy. As the market became increasingly saturated, the challenge of selling cars in volume was to get existing car owners to upgrade, rather than making cars cheap enough to entice first-time buyers. So with his ladder of car brands in place, Sloan added a further twist: "annual model renewal." This meant changing the appearance of each model every year, while leaving things mostly unchanged under the hood. In many cases the engine and chassis were shared across several different models, dressed up with different body stylings and sold under different GM brands. But in the styling of the exterior, Sloan decreed that there would be "continuous, eternal change," with annual design changes to make old models seem outdated and new ones more stylish and fashionable. He referred to this approach as "dynamic obsolescence."

This would only work if the cars were styled in a way that people found alluring, changing enough to make each year's new model look distinctive, while also maintaining continuity with previous models and avoiding radical changes that might deter buyers. So GM placed a lot of emphasis on color and design. It collaborated with DuPont, a chemicals giant that owned a large stake in GM, to develop DuCo, a fast-drying and durable lacquer resin that could be made in a range of colors including blues, greens, brown, and orange. In 1923 GM experimented with these new colors on its Oakland brand. With seven new Oakland models due to launch in 1924, GM painted a prototype of each one in bright DuCo blue, with accents in red or orange, and sent the cars on a nationwide tour of dealers. This provided a road test for the durability of the paint, which performed well, and the cars were the stars of the New York Automobile Show, where they ended their tour in December. Orders poured in from customers drawn to this exciting new color. "DuCo has become so popular," reported one executive, "that customers are now demanding it." GM duly applied DuCo colors across its entire product

GM marketed its cars as fashion items, placing great emphasis on design, styling, and color, with a hierarchy of brands at different prices to segment the market.

range. By 1925 DuPont was selling DuCo to all of GM's divisions and fourteen other carmakers. It was the opposite of Ford's all-black approach.

As color became a key selling point, DuPont established an advisory service to monitor, develop, and recommend color choices to carmakers. It was headed by H. Ledyard Towle, a man ideally suited to the role: having trained as a painter, he worked as a camouflage artist in the First World War, designing dazzle patterns used to hide ships, then went into advertising, working both for DuPont and several GM divisions. Like a fashion designer, Towle understood how color, materials, and body shape could work together, but the bodies he was dressing happened to be those of cars. Towle went to Europe every year to attend car shows and fashion shows alike, to ensure that car styling aligned with wider fashion trends. The impresario of automotive color, his prognostications were widely printed in American newspapers. In one article, published in January 1927, he declared, "The beauty of color in the American automobile now being presented to the public surpasses anything ever seen in its line in any exhibition of motor cars. Black has almost entirely disappeared. In its place has come a wealth of warm, appealing, beautiful harmonies, which indicate that the motor car industry has now entered fully into the new and significant American desire for color . . . the beauty of color can be had in the most inexpensive as well as the most costly car."

Manufacturers of other products also began offering their products in a range of colors that could change to follow fashion. *Fortune* magazine in 1930 described a "suddenly kaleidoscopic world" in which color was employed as "a master salesman"; it called this development "the color revolution." As a DuCo advertisement put it, "To be Modern is to be Colorful." It was a far cry from selling cars only in black.

In 1928 Towle left DuPont to work for GM, where his pioneering work in color came together with the trailblazing car designs of Harley J. Earl. Earl had learned his trade from his father, a former carriage-builder who switched to customizing car bodies. Their family firm, based in Hollywood, did work for film stars who wanted their cars to look a bit different and was acquired by a local Cadillac dealer, who retained Earl as the head of its custom body shop. This brought Earl to the attention of Cadillac's top brass, who asked him to design a new model, the LaSalle, which was intended to offer the styling of an expensive, hand-built European car but could be mass-produced.

Earl drew heavily on the design of the Hispano-Suiza H6B, an elegant luxury car favored by wealthy Europeans, and the LaSalle was marketed as the car "of those who lead"; one advertisement claimed, "Wherever the admired and the notable are gathering, observe the frequency with which a LaSalle rolls to the entrance. The famous, the beautiful, the social arbiters—the roster of LaSalle ownership is studded with their sparkling names." Fortunately, the advertisement assured would-be buyers whose sophistication outran their finances, "You may possess a LaSalle on the liberal term-payment plan of the General Motors Acceptance Corporation." Launched in 1927, the LaSalle was an immediate success, prompting GM to establish its Art and Color Section, the industry's first dedicated design department, and to put Earl in charge of it. Under his leadership GM vehicles pioneered many elements of automotive design over the next thirty years—most famously the addition of tail fins, which made their debut on a 1948 Cadillac and went on to be adopted across the industry during the 1950s and 1960s. Earl also introduced the use of clay modeling in automotive design and invented the idea of the concept car, a one-off prototype built to generate publicity and assess market reaction to new design ideas.

With their emphasis on constantly updated styling, GM's new cars appealed to buyers looking for something more exciting than a Model T. They no longer wanted cars to be cheap: with GM's encouragement, they wanted style and prestige instead. Choice of car became a form of self-expression and a signifier of social status, not just for the wealthy but for a wider public. Keeping current with the latest model, or moving up the ladder to a more expensive brand, let people advertise their wealth and success (even if they were paying for the car "on time," as installment plans were known). By contrast, Ford had fallen behind the times with its aging product and its refusal to offer financing.

As GM gained ground, even reductions in the Model T's price were insufficient to revive Ford's sales. By 1926 the Model T's market share had fallen to 30 percent of cars sold in America, from its peak of 55 percent three years earlier. Ford ceased production in May 1927, shortly after the

15-millionth Model T had rolled off the line, then spent a year retooling its factories to build a new, more modern replacement, the Model A, which was launched in 1928. Tellingly, it could be purchased on an installment plan, had a closed-body design—and was offered in four colors. But it was too little, too late, and by the end of the 1920s GM had overtaken Ford to become the world's leading carmaker.

GM's ensuing dominance came as a surprise even to Sloan, who had assumed that his firm's approach, and what he called Ford's "static-model utility car" model, would coexist and compete. "I had no idea in 1927 that the old Ford policy was washed out and that the General Motors policy of upgraded cars had won," he later wrote. But the proof was the emergence of Chrysler as the number three player in the American market. It had, Sloan noted, "come up from nowhere with tremendous vitality and with a market policy similar to General Motors'," namely, a portfolio of brands at different prices, including Chrysler, Plymouth, DeSoto, and Dodge. Even Ford eventually adopted this approach. It had purchased Lincoln, a luxury carmaker, in 1922, though it was initially operated as a separate company, and in 1938 Ford established a new midrange brand, Mercury, to sit between Ford and Lincoln. Today, with few exceptions, carmakers consist of collections of brands aimed at different market segments, following GM's example.

Sloan turned GM into more than just a model for the car industry. His reorganization of the company ensured that day-to-day decisions were devolved to the managers of each division, but financial oversight was centralized, with each division reporting its results, and being allocated resources, in a standardized way. Just as Henry Ford had defined the template for efficient mass production, Alfred Sloan created the template for the twentieth-century multidivisional corporation and in turn became the most famous businessman on the planet. Not merely the world's largest carmaker, GM became the world's largest company altogether. At its height it accounted for more than half of America's automobile market, and more than 10 percent of its national economy—making it far bigger, in comparative terms, than any technology giant today.

The GM model took the vehicle-as-status-symbol, an idea as old as wheeled vehicles themselves, to a new level. "You are what you drive," the importance of design, annual model updates, buying on credit, and upgrading often—these ideas have all persisted into the modern era. They all began with GM in the 1920s. Ford reinvented how cars were made, but GM reinvented the way cars were sold.

THE TREADMILL OF OWNERSHIP

And not just cars. GM's approach to market segmentation and advertising provided the template for American consumerism more broadly. Many of the things GM pioneered seem obvious in hindsight. But that is only because GM's approach was so successful that it has become the standard model not just for the car industry, but for other industries, too, from domestic appliances to clothes retailing to electronics. It is now standard practice for companies to offer a range of products at different price points, often under different brands—and to make annual changes in color and design, which make last year's products look dated. Consumers find themselves on an treadmill of acquisition, feeling a constant need to upgrade. In some ways it is understandable that this model first took hold in the car industry. Cars are, after housing, the most expensive things most people buy, which means that the kind of car you choose to buy can be a reliable indicator of wealth. Cars are also, by their nature, visible in public with their owners in a way that washing machines or widescreen televisions, say, are not.

In recent years, however, the idea that "you are what you drive" has come under pressure from various attempts to provide the benefits of cars without having to own them. Today a ride can be summoned when needed from a ride-hailing service such as Uber or Lyft. Car-sharing clubs make renting a car for a few hours, or a couple of days, quick and easy using a smartphone app. Some start-ups are experimenting with services that let drivers subscribe to a car, paying a monthly fee for use of a specific vehicle or a pool of shared cars. Lynk & Co., a Chinese firm that describes itself as "Netflix for cars," says it will let users subscribe for as little as one month at a time. Ride-hailing companies are also experimenting with offering their services via a monthly subscription, just as mobile phones went from per-minute billing to monthly bundles. John Zimmer, the cofounder of Lyft, told the *Wall Street Journal* in 2018, "Where I see this going is instead of getting keys for a sixteenth birthday—which used to be that symbol of freedom in America—you get a Lyft subscription." Even Ford, GM, and other carmakers talk of pivoting from selling vehicles to selling "mobility services," though so far their investments in car-sharing and ride-hailing firms have not come to much. It would involve a wrenching change in their century-old business model, and the undoing of a hundred years of car-industry marketing about the social cachet of car ownership.

One sign that this might be possible is that consumers seem to be transferring their allegiance to another product—the very product that underpins many of these alternatives to car ownership. That product is, of course, the smartphone. Just as in the car industry, smartphone manufacturers unveil new models each year, with new features and subtle changes in style. Consumers know that other people will read a lot into their choice of brand, model, and color scheme. And just like cars, handsets can be customized and personalized with aftermarket accessories. Writing in 1971, Henri Lefebvre, a French philosopher, called the automobile "the epitome of possessions" because of its unique ability to signal social status. But today the smartphone is fast taking its place. And compared with cars, smartphones are arguably more democratic. Even though the most expensive models cost more than $1,000, the range in price from the cheapest to the most expensive is much smaller than for cars. Billionaires generally drive fancier cars than the rest of the population, but they carry the same smartphones. Yet even in these most quintessentially modern products, the far-reaching influence of the car industry of the 1920s can still be seen. Smartphones are built on assembly lines that Henry Ford would recognize—and their marketing follows the rules laid down by Alfred Sloan.

6

Who Owns the Streets?

The obvious solution . . . lies only in a radical revision of our conception of what a city street is for.

—*Engineering News-Record*, 1922

"THE AUTOMOBILE HAS TASTED BLOOD"

On the evening of September 13, 1899, Henry H. Bliss, a New York real estate broker, stepped off a streetcar as it came to a halt at the junction of Central Park West and Seventy-fourth Street. Bliss, a well-known figure in the business community, had been on a date, and as he turned to help his companion down from the vehicle, he was hit by a passing automobile and caught beneath its wheels. He was taken to a nearby hospital but died of his injuries a few hours later. He was the first pedestrian to be killed by an automobile in the United States.

The driver of the car, Arthur Smith, was arrested and charged with homicide. He insisted that the collision was unavoidable. He had been swerving to avoid a heavy truck, and Bliss had stepped directly into his path. "The Automobile has Tasted Blood," declared one newspaper headline. But most papers referred to Bliss's death as an accident, rather than blaming automobiles in general or Smith in particular (the charges against him were dropped, on the basis that Bliss's death was unintentional). Under the headline "Fatally Hurt by Automobile," the *New York Times* noted that incident had occurred on a road known as Dangerous Stretch because of the many accidents that had taken place there over the summer. But a pedestrian being killed by an automobile was something new.

Bliss was not, in fact, the first such victim. In 1896 an Englishwoman, Bridget Driscoll, had been knocked down and fatally injured by a petrol-powered car in London. Its driver, like Arthur Smith, was arrested but released without charge; the coroner who examined Driscoll's body said he hoped "such a thing would never happen again." But happen again it did, and the death toll rose steadily in the early years of the twentieth century as cars proliferated.

One reason was that automobiles were faster and less predictable when compared with horse-drawn vehicles, which could not change direction quickly, or with horsecars and streetcars, whose courses were predetermined by the rails they ran on. It did not help that most drivers in this period were, by necessity, inexperienced. There were no restrictions on who could drive motor vehicles, drivers were unfamiliar with the behavior of vehicles traveling at speed, and there were no laws against driving while intoxicated with alcohol. A more fundamental change was that the pattern of street use was also in flux. Having long been shared by pedestrians and horse-drawn vehicles, and used as public spaces where children played and pushcart vendors plied their trade, streets were now having to make room for increasing numbers of streetcars, cyclists, and, most of all, automobiles.

The result was a much more chaotic environment, particularly in America, which was home to the vast majority of the world's cars in the early twentieth century. As their numbers shot up, so did the number of fatalities on American roads, from thirty-six in 1900 to eleven thousand in 1920. The questions raised by Bliss's death in 1899 were a taste of things to come. Who was to blame for accidents, and were they really unavoidable? How could the roads be regulated to square the needs of drivers with the safety of other road users? The debate over road safety that played out in America during the 1920s led to rules and conventions that were subsequently adopted around the world and are still in force a century later. Everyone alive today has grown up with these rules, and it is difficult to imagine things working any other way. Street furniture, including traffic lights and signs, was also introduced to regulate the flow of both cars and pedestrians. The events of the 1920s reshaped the relationship between people and vehicles, and the nature of city streets, in ways that have persisted ever since.

CHILDREN VERSUS CARS

Most of those killed on America's roads in the early twentieth century were pedestrians, and most of those pedestrians were children. Although drivers involved in fatal accidents faced heavy fines and were often charged with manslaughter, such sanctions seemed to have little effect. As the death toll rose, public outrage found expression in hostile newspaper coverage of dangerous drivers. Reports of accidents frequently contrasted the innocence of victims (whether children, young women, or the elderly) with the guilt of drivers (often drunk, speeding, or criminals fleeing the scene of a crime). "In the view of some of the press, the automobile is today a juggernaut, a motoring speed-monster, intent on killing and maiming all who stand in its way," one chronicler of the industry noted with despair in 1916. Drivers were depicted as deliberate "killers" or "murderers." Cartoons showed the grim reaper behind the wheel. Pedestrians complained that cars had invaded the streets and deprived them of their former rights and freedoms. Because people had previously been free to step into the streets whenever they liked, the onus was on motorists, as newcomers, to avoid collisions—so drivers were widely assumed to be at fault in any accident.

Safety campaigners organized marches in many American cities, calling on motorists to exercise more caution. The National Safety Council (NSC), an existing body that oversaw workplace safety, expanded its remit to address road safety as well. Many women joined its affiliated local councils to campaign for safer roads and greater protection for children, transforming a business-oriented organization into something more like

Illustration depicting cars as killing machines, New York Times,
November 23, 1924.

a social movement. Cities began to observe "Safety First" weeks, in which local chambers of commerce, the police, Boy Scouts, schools, churches, and newspapers worked together with safety councils and local auto clubs to promote road safety. Auto clubs took part because they were keen to be seen as part of the solution, not part of the problem; they blamed accidents on a small number of inconsiderate drivers. The expansion of road-safety campaigns in America was overseen by Charles Price, a former salesman who was put in charge of reducing accidents at an agricultural-machinery company. Price swiftly reinvented himself as a safety expert and had become head of the NSC in 1919. Regular safety campaigns were taking place in fifty American cities by 1923.

As well as demonizing dangerous drivers, safety campaigns also memorialized children, like soldiers who had fallen in war. Detroit adopted the custom of ringing church bells after each road death, and announcing the victim's name in schools. In Memphis, the safety council put up a black flag wherever a child was killed on the roads. Baltimore's innovation, in 1922, was a giant monument in wood and plaster, twenty-five feet tall, painted to resemble a stone war memorial and bearing the names of 130 children killed by cars in the previous year. That same year New York held a safety procession of 10,000 children, including a "memorial division" of 1,054 children, each of whom represented an accident victim killed during 1921. A delegation of Boy Scouts carried a papier-mâché tombstone, and open-top cars conveyed children who had been maimed in road accidents. The safety parade in Washington, D.C., included a group dressed up as shroud-wearing corpses; that in Louisville had models of coffins and skeletons. In St. Louis, an airship dropped flowers around a newly unveiled safety monument as a band played a dirge. "Drivers of automobiles must be taught to adhere to the doctrines of the St. Louis Safety Council," said the mayor in his speech.

Yet although everyone supported the idea of safety, there was no consensus about exactly what that meant in practice. To keep the unlikely coalition of campaigners, industry interests, and car clubs together, safety campaigns were rather vague, emphasizing the importance of caution and adherence to local safety rules. But these rules varied widely, as different cities took different approaches. In many places, the police imposed speed limits, typically of 10 mph or less, though these were difficult to enforce, and in some cases were so low that they could not be obeyed without causing cars' engines to stall. Some cities experimented with one-way streets to regulate the flow of traffic; in others, horse-drawn vehicles were given right of way over motor vehicles. Whether motorists had to defer to pedestrians, or vice versa, also varied from place to place or was left unspecified beyond general appeals to common sense and "safety first." Little wonder the result was deadly chaos.

SILENT POLICEMEN AND MILWAUKEE MUSHROOMS

Efforts to formalize the rules of the road had first begun in 1900 in New York, which led the way because it had the most vehicles of any American city—and because it was the home town of an eccentric billionaire with an unusual obsession for traffic regulation. William Phelps Eno inherited a fortune in 1899 from his father, and rather than going into the family real estate business, he devoted himself instead to the cause of road safety, publishing a manifesto on the topic in January 1900. Though few motor vehicles were on the streets in New York, he could see that automobiles were likely to grow in number and wanted to preempt any problems that might arise. He was confident that "properly understood and regulated, several times the present traffic in our streets could go on with less delay, more safety and more comfort than what there is now." Eno established himself as an expert in "scientific" traffic management, despite having dropped out of college and having no formal qualifications.

In 1903 he had one hundred thousand copies printed of his four-page pamphlet, "Rules of Driving," after officials in New York City agreed to distribute it and adopt its rules. Eno's motto was *ex chao ordo* (order from chaos), and his rules chiefly consisted of a formalization of existing customs. Motorists were directed to drive on the right and pass on the left; to use hand signals when turning; to yield to emergency vehicles; and not to exceed a "safe and proper" speed (though no actual figure was given). But Eno also threw in a few ideas of his own. His most important innovation was the notion of the "wide" or "outside" turn—that when turning left, drivers should not simply swerve across the road and cut off the corner, but turn as late as possible, as though driving around an imaginary post in the center of the road. Indeed, at Eno's suggestion, posts were installed at some junctions in New York in 1904 as a reminder of "the necessity of passing around the central point."

As other cities began to adopt traffic regulations of their own, they borrowed some of Eno's rules from New York, and in particular that of the outside left turn, which became standard practice. In 1915, as part of the mobilization for the First World War, national traffic rules were drawn up for the first time, and Eno got the outside left turn included. This prompted many cities to install posts or signs in the center of intersections, often marked with the words KEEP TO THE RIGHT. This was the first example of street furniture that told drivers what to do, instead of assuming they were familiar with the local traffic rules. By specifying the path a vehicle should take as it rounded a corner, and forcing it to slow down, these signs, which came to be known as silent policemen, improved safety for pedestrians. They were also much cheaper than stationing a police officer to act as a "cornerman" to regulate traffic at a busy junction, something that many cities were starting to find increasingly costly.

But although there was general agreement about the outside left turn, the devices used to enforce it varied from one city to another, confusing motorists who ventured away from their hometown. "If we were to collect specimens of traffic control devices from those cities where traffic regulation is active, we could fill a museum with signs and signals, no two of which would be alike in color, shape, size or marking," noted a report on traffic control written in 1923. Some cities made their own silent policemen; others bought them from a thriving community of entrepreneurs who saw a lucrative market opening up and hoped their devices would become the national standard. They touted their wares to city officials at trade fairs such as the Good Roads Show, held in Chicago in 1922, where many variations on the silent policemen were on display, in a range of shapes and sizes, some illuminated, some not. There was plenty of scope for improvement because wooden posts were all too easily knocked down by careless (or malicious) drivers.

The City of Milwaukee found itself having to replace four hundred silent policemen every year and had given up on the idea by 1923 in favor of a local innovation: the Milwaukee mushroom. This perforated cast-iron dome, rather like an inverted colander, was fixed to the center of an intersection and illuminated from below. Motorists would drive around it, as they did with silent policemen, but advocates of the mushroom pointed out that if struck by a passing vehicle it would stay put, providing a warning jolt to the driver but doing no damage to the vehicle. Some judges had ruled that cities were liable for damage caused to vehicles that struck silent policemen, so this was an attractive feature. The mushroom seems to have been pioneered in Detroit a few years earlier, but without illumination; the illuminated "Milwaukee-type" mushroom proved popular for a few years in the 1920s, with several firms manufacturing competing versions. One model was even spring mounted, allowing it to retract into the road if a vehicle passed over it. Of the various competing forms of street furniture, however, mushrooms did not prove to be long-term survivors. Another device ended up ruling the streets: the traffic light.

GREEN LIGHT, GO!

The first traffic light was installed on Westminster Bridge in London in 1868, to improve the safety of pedestrians. John Peake Knight, a railway engineer, invented a set of semaphore arms, mounted on a tall post on the bridge, that could be raised and lowered manually by a policeman. Raised arms meant vehicles and horses had to stop "to allow the passage of Persons on Foot"; lowered arms meant vehicles and horses should exercise caution and "pass over the Crossing with care, and due regard to the safety of Foot Passengers." Crucially, the arms were accompanied by colored gaslights for visibility at night: red for "stop," and green for "caution"—the standard colors that had been adopted for signaling on railways in the 1840s (along with white for "all clear"). This pioneering traffic light did not last long, however. Less than a month after its installation, a gas leak caused it to explode, injuring the policeman operating it, and it was removed soon afterward.

The idea of traffic signals was revived in America in the early twentieth century, as car ownership exploded and twice-daily traffic jams became a regular occurrence in many cities. Contrary to suggestions that cars would reduce congestion because they would take up less space and move faster than horse-drawn vehicles, jams got worse, both because there were more vehicles, and because motorists had started storing their cars in the road. Manufacturers added ignition keys and door locks to cars around 1912, letting owners leave them unattended on the street during the working day or overnight, something that had not been possible with horse-drawn vehicles. Parked cars, a rarity in photos of American streets before 1910, are commonplace after 1915. This reduced the amount of street space for moving vehicles by 30–50 percent. With traffic gridlocked, police officers stationed at corners could do little to regulate its flow. And officers at one intersection had no way to coordinate with those at adjacent ones. Cities tried borrowing ideas from railways, with semaphore signals and tall towers that allowed police officers to see their counterparts at nearby junctions. But semaphore arms were hard to see (and invisible at night), and towers in the middle of intersections obstructed the flow of traffic.

The first electric traffic light was installed in Cleveland, Ohio, in 1914. Like its predecessor from 1868, it used two colors—red and green. But by this time the railway industry had switched the meanings of green and white, so that green meant "go" and white meant "caution." This was because the increasing use of gas and electric lighting meant that a white light (in a house, for example) could be mistaken for a "go" light when it was not in fact a railway signal. Given that green lights were not used except on signals, it was therefore safer for railway signals to use green for "go" and white for "caution." Another danger associated with the use of white for "go" was that if the colored lens on a red or green light was damaged and fell off, the signal would wrongly indicate "go," which could (and did) lead to railway accidents. Using green for "go" ensured that a damaged signal would indicate "caution" instead. So although the 1868 and 1914 traffic lights for road vehicles used the same colors, the meaning of the green light, borrowed in both cases from the railway industry, was "caution" in 1868, and "go" in 1914.

Cleveland's new electric traffic light was controlled by a police officer from a nearby booth. After all, the traffic lights would surely be ignored unless a policeman was nearby to enforce the rules. But the light's instantaneous switching from red to green and vice versa proved problematic for both motorists and pedestrians, so in 1917 William Potts, a Detroit police officer, added an amber light to indicate that the signal was about to change. Manually controlled traffic lights were adopted across America and spread to Europe in the 1920s, though it took a while for their colors to become standardized. On Fifth Avenue in New York City, for example, an amber light meant vehicles on the avenue should move and those on the cross streets should not, while a green one meant the opposite. On Broadway, meanwhile, lights followed the usual rule that red meant "stop" and green meant "go." That rule, and the idea that the red light should go above the green one, became an international standard in the 1920s with the help of the League of Nations, which held conferences on road signs and traffic rules starting in 1926. The United States did not participate, but as the world's leading automotive nation, it acted as a de facto standards-setter. France, Germany, Spain, and Japan also sent traffic engineers to America to find out about traffic management, with the result that other American traffic-control innovations (such as the octagonal Stop sign, invented by a Detroit policeman, Harry Jackson, in 1914) spread around the world.

In some cases, neighborhoods held celebrations when traffic lights were installed because they ensured that pedestrians had the right of way, at least some of the time, to cross the road. And it turned out that both drivers and pedestrians would obey traffic lights even if they were auto-matically controlled by a timer, rather than manually by a policeman. Automatic control ensured fairness and regularity and moved traffic faster by allowing precise control of timing at different junctions. "Staggered" lighting was set up so that lights would always be green for a motorist moving at a particular speed (usually 25 mph). The first such system, installed on Sixteenth Street in Washington, D.C., was said to have doubled the speed of commuter traffic.

As well as controlling the flow of vehicles, provided a formal frame-work for when pedestrians should cross the road: at a junction, and only when the light was red for traffic crossing their path. The introduction of traffic lights, combined with safety campaigns, the demonization of dangerous drivers, and attempts to codify traffic rules might have been expected to reduce road deaths. But the casualties continued to mount. The number of deaths on American roads jumped from 14,859 in 1922 to 17,870 in 1923, the biggest percentage increase for five years. The fragile alliance of safety campaigners, officials, commercial interests, and motoring clubs that had formed under the nebulous slogan of "safety first" began to splinter, and agreement on the importance of safety gave way to open disagreement about how best to achieve it.

THE INVENTION OF JAYWALKING

The car industry began to steer the debate in a totally new direction in 1923, not because of a sudden concern for pedestrian welfare, but out of concern for its own survival. After years of rapid growth, sales of cars had fallen for the first time, and many in the industry felt that the constant portrayal of their products as child-killing death machines was partly to blame. "Every automobile accident, whether serious or minor, causes a sales resistance," noted one car dealer in 1922. A former police commissioner in Detroit told an industry convention that carnage on the roads "is causing prejudice against the car owner that can only be mitigated by a reduction in the number of accidents." Industry bodies and car clubs, which had previously stood shoulder to shoulder with safety campaigners despite their constant vilification of drivers, decided a new approach was needed.

They were offered advice from an unexpected quarter: Charles Price, who had by this time left the National Safety Council. He had become disenchanted with its lurid and judgmental road-safety campaigns, with their emphasis on vilifying drivers. Having previously worked in industrial safety, which emphasized workers' role in keeping themselves safe around potentially dangerous machinery, Price felt the same approach should be applied to cars, by insisting on the responsibility of pedestrians to stay out of danger. "The machine itself is safe enough," he declared in an article published in *Automotive Industries*, a trade journal. He urged the industry to take the lead in promoting a different approach to road safety, to revive sales. "There is a great danger of large numbers of people beginning to look on the automobile as more of a menace than a blessing," he wrote. But if the industry could foster "the right attitude toward the motor vehicle . . . an even greater number of cars, tires, parts and equipment could be sold each year."

As well as slowing sales and rising road deaths, the industry faced another challenge: growing support for the idea of fitting mechanical devices, called governors, to cars to limit their maximum speed. This proposal had been floating around for a couple of years as a potential safety measure, but in 1923 it became a far more concrete prospect when forty-two thousand people in Cincinnati, or more than 10 percent of the population, signed a petition in favor of it. As a result, an ordinance mandating the use of speed governors was put to a public vote in the city. The industry was terrified that limiting the maximum speed of cars would depress sales even further and open the door to a regulatory free-for-all in which different cities would impose different safety requirements on carmakers. The industry mobilized to oppose the ordinance, forming a General Citizens' Committee, which was just a front for local car dealers, and taking out newspaper advertisements warning that mandating the use of governors would make the city inaccessible to motorists from elsewhere who did not have them, harming local businesses. The committee also wrote to every car owner in the city to warn that their freedoms were under attack and rallied the local automobile club to oppose the ordinance, which was decisively defeated.

Industry groups and car clubs realized that they could steer public opinion when they acted in concert. The day after the Cincinnati vote, the National Automobile Chamber of Commerce (NACC), an industry body, formed a safety committee. Together with the American Automobile Association (AAA), the leading motorists' club, it began planning a new and different kind of safety campaign: one that focused on "educating pedestrians" rather than drivers. Accidents, in this view, were primarily caused not by dangerous drivers, but by careless pedestrians, who needed to have new rules drummed into them to keep them safe. And the industry soon hit upon a way to do this, by weaponizing a particular word. Just as reckless motorists had been labeled joyriders and speed maniacs, so pedestrians were given an epithet that could be used to blame and shame them: jaywalker.

Jay was a slang term for a clueless country bumpkin who was unsure how to behave in the city, and a *jaywalker* was originally someone who got in the way, either on the sidewalk or on the road. Around 1915 police officers who oversaw busy intersections began to describe pedestrians who would not follow instructions as jaywalkers. The word then came to mean something more specific, namely someone who crossed the road in the middle of a block, rather than at a corner. This was of course how people had been crossing roads for centuries: wherever they felt like it. In footage of American streets from the early twentieth century, horse-drawn vehicles, streetcars, bicycles, and automobiles can be seen moving at roughly walking pace, with pedestrians weaving in between them. By the 1920s, cars accounted for most of the vehicles on the roads, and motorists were becoming increasingly frustrated by the limits this approach imposed on their speed.

The carmakers, dealers, auto clubs, and other pro-car interests, collectively known as motordom, duly launched a campaign to talk up the dangers of jaywalking. Outwardly this approach seemed to champion the safety of pedestrians, but by arguing that people should only cross at junctions and at right angles to the traffic, it promoted and reinforced the industry's position that the streets were now primarily for the use of motor vehicles. "Pedestrians must be educated to know that automobiles have rights," declared the NACC's leader, George Graham. He objected to newspaper coverage that depicted pedestrians as innocent victims of evil motorists when, in his view, "it is a fair question if the driver is actually responsible for more than half the cases." Graham established an "accident prevention department" to gather and analyze statistics from local coroners and supply them to reporters as evidence that most accidents were caused by reckless pedestrians. The effect was almost instant. "It is now the fashion to ascribe 70–90% of all accidents to jaywalking," noted Bruce Cobb, a New York magistrate, in November 1924. He suspected that "much of the blame heaped upon so-called 'jaywalkers' is but a smoke screen, to hide motordom's own shortcomings as well as to abridge the now existing legal rights of the foot travelers on our streets."

But motordom's most effective tactic was to get the government on its side. In December 1924, Herbert Hoover, then secretary of commerce, convened the first National Conference on Street and Highway Safety, with the aim of drawing up a set of safety rules that could be used across the country. The industry got Hoover to water down his initial hostility toward cars and installed its own representatives on the key committees, including the statistics committee, which began to report accident statistics to the press that blamed most accidents on pedestrians. These figures now had the imprimatur of a supposedly impartial government body. As the national safety rules were drawn up, the industry got its preferred approach—based on the vilification of jaywalking pedestrians, and road tested in one particular car-crazed city—baked into it.

In retrospect it seems oddly appropriate that it was Los Angeles that ended up setting the model for the rest of the country. By 1923 the city already had one car for every three inhabitants, more than twice the national average. The Los Angeles Traffic Commission, set up with the backing of the local automobile club and chaired by the head of a local car dealership, funded studies of traffic and made a series of recommendations that were adopted by the city in January 1925. "The old common law rule that every person, whether on foot or driving, has equal rights in all parts of the roadway must give way before the requirements of modern transportation," declared the code's author. The code excluded horse-drawn vehicles from the central business district in the evening rush hour, to speed the flow of traffic. It also imposed rules on pedestrians, confining them to crosswalks and imposing fines on jaywalkers. These driver-friendly rules were welcomed by local motorists.

But pedestrians were less keen, prompting E. B. Lefferts, head of the local automobile club, to arrange a publicity campaign to "educate" them about the new rules. The club distributed printed materials with the help of the police, and the new medium of radio was pressed into service, too, with nightly broadcasts about the anti-jaywalking rules. Lefferts persuaded the police not to impose fines on jaywalkers to begin with, on the basis that "the ridicule of their fellow citizens is far more effective than any other means which might be adopted." Instead, police officers were to blow their whistles at jaywalkers and order them out of the road. Some pedestrians objected to this and were arrested, but most, Lefferts observed, "grinned sheepishly and scuttled back to the curb," where they found themselves "facing a large gallery of amused people." Lefferts encouraged the use of social pressure rather than legal sanctions to avoid antagonizing pedestrians, but also because he did not want the legality of the new rules to be tested. The police stepped up enforcement in April 1925 by adding plainclothes officers to enforce the anti-jaywalking ordinance. All this had the desired effect: by the end of the year, a local reporter noted, pedestrians had meekly learned to follow the rules.

The Los Angeles rules became the model for pedestrian regulation in other cities across America, enshrined in the Model Municipal Transport Ordinance, issued in 1928 by Hoover's national safety body. With government backing, behavior had shifted entirely by 1930, and the default was that streets were for cars, and pedestrians should limit themselves to crosswalks. The industry had successfully changed attitudes from always blaming the driver to assuming any collision was an unavoidable accident and probably the fault of a reckless pedestrian—and that cars, not people, had the first claim on the roads. As the chairman of Dodge put it in 1926, "The pedestrian cannot selfishly claim that he alone has all the rights and the motorist none." In fact, the opposite was true, and this has been the prevailing model ever since. Under the banner of road safety and pedestrian education, cars had taken over the streets. Walking in the street had gone from being a right to being wrong.

DRIVING ACROSS THE ATLANTIC

It was a similar story in Britain, Europe's leading automotive nation by this time. Like its counterpart in America, the leading safety organization, the National Safety First Association, grew out of an industrial-safety mind-set that favored the education of workers rather than regulation of machines and then transferred this approach to road safety. Free copies of its journal, *Safety First*, were distributed to police chiefs and local officials. Most people regarded the NSFA as either neutral or opposed to the motoring lobby. But it was in fact heavily funded and influenced by industry bodies and the Automobile Association, a club founded in 1905 to champion the rights of motorists.

Following the lead of the NACC in America, the NSFA's position was always to advocate education (particularly of pedestrians) rather than legislation. Through the use of statistics and scientific language it promoted the idea that the danger posed by motor vehicles was inevitable, and that a "science of road safety," developed by professional traffic engineers, police officers, and carmakers working together, was the best way to minimize it. The NSFA's publication of aggregated road-accident data took the focus off individual cases and made it easier to blame pedestrians for the growing number of fatalities. In 1929, Liverpool's chief constable declared that the city's pedestrians were the worst in the world and blamed them for 75 percent of traffic accidents. Amazingly for a safety organization, the NSFA campaigned against the introduction of driving tests and even opposed the reimposition of speed limits after their abolition, itself a triumph of industry lobbying, in 1930.

When London's introduction of rules to fine jaywalkers had no effect on the number of road deaths, it was taken as evidence that education, rather than legislation, was the most effective approach. An opinion poll showed that this view had become widely held by 1939. When asked how to reduce road accidents, the largest fraction of respondents (28 percent) said caution and common sense were the answer; only 5 percent suggested reducing the number of cars, or increasing penalties on offending motorists. As in America, albeit with a delay of a few years, campaigns against dangerous, Mr. Toad–like drivers had given way to enthusiasm for educating pedestrians, and ensuring that they kept off the roads, except at designated crossings. A law in 1934 codified the rules for pedestrian crossings, requiring cars to give way—and also formalizing the idea that, otherwise, cars had priority on the roads.

All this worked because British politicians of the era preferred to take a laissez-faire approach rather than to impose new regulations, and the police appreciated having safety materials handed to them on a plate. Little wonder that a pedestrian's rights group complained that this added up to "delegation to motorists of the task of saying what constitutes safety." It is notable that in Europe, laws to codify the legal responsibilities of motorists (for example, by making insurance compulsory) appeared first in Scandinavian countries that lacked a powerful motor industry to lobby against them. In Britain, the industry's coziness with politicians enabled it to prevent or delay the imposition of regulation. It also helped that, as in America, politicians, policemen, and journalists were all increasingly likely to own cars themselves and be wary of having their motoring freedoms curtailed.

Supporting the use of cars, and the car industry more widely, had also come to be seen as crucial to national progress. In 1916 the United States had overtaken Britain and its empire as the world's largest economy, and its dynamism was exemplified in its leadership in the manufacturing and adoption of automobiles. European nations did not want to be left behind and considered it important not to hamper the expansion of this vital new industry. As a British parliamentary report on road safety put it in 1937, "Propaganda should be employed for the purpose of making those who do not own motor-cars realize how much they owe to motor transport for the supply of their food, for passenger services and so on. There still remains in the public mind a prejudice against motor-cars, born no doubt in the old days when few people owned them, and when they were considered as luxuries rather than part of the essential national service, as they are today."

In Germany, similarly, Adolf Hitler was an outspoken advocate of mass car ownership along American lines, despite never learning to drive himself. Germany, the birthplace of the automobile, had fallen behind America, he believed, because previous governments had failed to promote the automobile's production and adoption. Instead, politicians and police officers, through taxes and traffic laws, had "co-operated to choke off and stamp out the development of German road traffic and with it the transportation industry as thoroughly as possible." In his first major speech after becoming chancellor of Germany in 1933, at the Berlin Motor Show, Hitler announced plans to abolish the registration tax on new cars, relax traffic laws, make driving licenses easier to obtain, build a network of motorways, and develop an affordable small car for the masses: the people's car, or Volkswagen.

Even though Germany had a bit more than half the population of the United States, Hitler observed, it had only five hundred thousand to six hundred thousand cars, compared with around 24 million on American roads. By emulating the popularity of the low-cost Ford Model T, his planned Volkswagen would, he hoped, enable Germany to reach at least 3 million cars on the roads and become a true automotive society, "as we can see has successfully been accomplished in the brilliant example of America." Although Hitler's regime imposed strict controls in many areas of life, the roads were not one of them. A new law in 1934 abolished all speed limits, both in cities and on the new highways, a network of roads built for the exclusive use of automobiles (hence the name *autobahn*). The result was an upsurge in road deaths: around eight thousand people died on Germany's roads between 1933 and 1939, making them the deadliest in Europe. But thanks to Hitler's support for motorization, the German car industry grew rapidly in the 1930s, employing 1.5 million workers and accounting for one job in twelve by 1938. It was carmaking, not rearmament, that powered Germany's recovery from the Great Depression.

THE ROAD NOT TAKEN

In Britain and Germany, as in America, the supremacy of the car had come to be seen as a vital ingredient of a modern economy—a key technology, like semiconductors or artificial intelligence today, capable of shaping the fate of nations. In a speech to a medical conference in 1937, a leading German surgeon, Martin Kirschner, argued against the reimposition of speed limits. Even though he admitted such measures would save many lives, he maintained that impeding the progress of the automobile would threaten "our societal relations, our wealth, our industry, our agriculture, the ability to defend ourselves, our international standing, in short, of our whole civilization and culture." Instead, he argued, he and his colleagues should focus on developing new approaches to trauma surgery as a way to reduce the death toll. This indicates the extent to which the adoption of the car, and the resulting danger posed to life and limb, had already come to be seen as an unfortunate but inevitable fact of life—an attitude that still prevails today.

But what of the road not taken? There was nothing inevitable about the way cars were adopted, first in America, and then by imitation in Europe and elsewhere. Are there other rules, and other ways of arranging urban spaces, that would have allowed cars to fit more smoothly into cities, rather than simply taking over the streets? Experiments in recent decades suggest that there are. A century on from the pivotal arguments of the 1920s, many cities are now returning some areas, at least, to something closer to the pre-car era. Two cities in particular show that pedestrian deaths are not inevitable and that mobility and safety need not be incompatible. Those cities are Oslo, the capital of Norway, and Helsinki, the capital of Finland, both of which reported zero pedestrian deaths in 2019. (Indeed, across the whole of Norway, no children died in traffic accidents that year; its roads are the world's safest.) Both Norway and Finland had previously signed up to Vision Zero, a safety initiative that began in Sweden that aims to eliminate all deaths and injuries on the roads.

Oslo and Helsinki, which each have populations of around seven hundred thousand, or about the same as Washington, D.C., used similar tactics to redesign their streets to improve safety. They imposed lower speed limits, gradually replaced on-street parking with cycle lanes and wider sidewalks for pedestrians, and excluded cars from some areas altogether. Helsinki has established a 745-mile network of bike paths, which are even cleared of snow in winter; Oslo raised parking charges and tolls to enter the city, established car-free zones around schools, and shifted some city-center deliveries from vans to electric cargo bikes. Together with high levels of investment in public transport, all this has reduced the volume and speed of traffic on city streets, with a resulting fall in deaths and injuries. In 2020 cities around the world, from Paris to Milan to Kampala, took advantage of coronavirus lockdowns to move in the same direction, creating new bike lanes and broadening sidewalks to reclaim street space from cars. Some cities have since made those changes permanent. Collectively, these moves signal an end to the assumption that streets belong chiefly to cars, by tilting the balance back toward other users. Officials in Oslo talk of cars being treated as "guests" or "visitors, rather than owning the streets." Cars are not banned entirely, but drivers crawling through the city center are made to feel like interlopers.

Many of these measures draw on an approach called shared space, pioneered by Hans Monderman, a Dutch traffic engineer. In 1968 he designed a residential street in the city of Delft where equal priority is given to cars, bicycles, and pedestrians, forcing road users to pay atten-tion to one another. "When you don't exactly know who has right of way, you tend to seek eye contact with other road users," Monderman told a German broadcaster in 2006. "You automatically reduce your speed, you have contact with other people, and you take greater care." This approach has since been extended to wider areas in several cities around the world, in which items of street furniture such as curbs, traffic lights, road-surface markings, and signs have all deliberately been removed. This reduces the maximum speed of traffic and improves safety by requiring everyone to pay attention to—and negotiate with—other road users. By eliminating traffic lights and keeping traffic moving, it can also reduce travel time for motorists. Perhaps the most striking example of the shared-space philosophy is in the Dutch town of Noordlaren, where a primary school was adjacent to a road where drivers tended to speed. The wall between the playground and the road was removed, and the playground was extended across the road, forcing cars to drive (carefully) through the middle of it. Amazingly, this eliminated speeding without causing any accidents.

Critics of the shared-space model point out some of its drawbacks. In particular, blind and disabled people find it harder to navigate when cross-ings have been removed and there are no longer formal rules about who has right of way. But as the examples of Oslo and Helsinki show, elements of this approach can be applied to make streets safer. Making the streets more human-centric (rather than car-centric) also makes streets cleaner, quieter, and more pleasant for everyone—and reminds visitors from elsewhere that cities do not have to consist of pedestrian islands in the midst of a roaring sea of traffic. Even some American cities have been experimenting with a less car-centric approach. West Palm Beach in Florida has a shared-space zone, and Washington, D.C., is one of fourteen American cities to have set a Scandinavian-style Vision Zero target of zero road deaths by 2024 (though progress has been uneven, prompting a Rally for Streets That Don't Kill People by pedestrians and cyclists in the city in April 2019).

The Vision Zero approach reveals that both approaches taken in the twentieth century—blaming road deaths and injuries entirely on drivers, or on pedestrians—were wrong. Rather than pitting these two overlapping groups against each other, Vision Zero shifts the responsibility somewhere else: to the designers of the road system, who are held accountable for preventing injuries and fatalities. When an accident occurs, it is assumed to be a failure of street design, and measures are then introduced to try to prevent another similar incident. But how likely is it that this approach will catch on globally?

It might seem implausible that a city such as Oslo could provide a model for the world, but the lesson of history is that it has happened before: after all, providing a model for the world is what Los Angeles did a century ago. Deciding that cars ruled the roads was a choice made by political leaders, encouraged by powerful car-industry lobbies, when the supremacy of the car seemed inevitable and inescapable. But no matter how much street space is allocated to cars, it's never enough. So it makes sense to take some of it back and use it for other things, as some cities are now doing. Oslo and Helsinki have shown that it is possible to escape from the car-centric model by investing in public transport and restoring city streets to something closer to their original purpose as shared public spaces—not merely conduits for cars. For those who are not used to it, it feels strangely liberating to be a pedestrian in this kind of environment. But it provides a glimpse of what roads were like before the arrival of the car—and what they could be like again.

The Road to Suburbia

The present relationship between cities and automobiles represents, in short, one of those jokes that history sometimes plays on progress.

—JANE JACOBS, *THE DEATH AND LIFE OF GREAT AMERICAN CITIES*, 1961

DREAMING OF AUTOPIA

It was a vision of the future: 1960, as seen from 1939. The theme of the 1939 New York World's Fair, held at Flushing Meadows–Corona Park in the borough of Queens, was "The World of Tomorrow." The first such exposition with an explicit focus on the future, the fair featured the debut of new technologies including nylon fabric, the View-Master system for viewing stereoscopic color photographs, an early version of Smell-O-Vision, and the first electronic speech synthesizer. But the most popular and influential exhibit of the fair was Futurama, a thirty-six-thousand-square-foot diorama of the America of 1960, depicting it as a suburban paradise built around fast, multilane highways.

More than 5 million attendees saw the exhibit, lining up for hours to take an eighteen-minute ride on benches that moved over the landscape as smoothly and continuously as the model cars seen whizzing through the congestion-free "City of 1960" below. The diorama combined scenes at a variety of different scales and included more than half a million model buildings, a million trees, and fifty thousand cars, including ten thousand moving along a fourteen-lane highway. Speakers built into the benches played a commentary that, as *Business Week* put it, "unfolds a prophecy of cities, towns and countrysides served by a comprehensive road system." For Americans emerging from the Great Depression as a new world war was breaking out in Europe, Futurama offered a hopeful vision of a better future. That future, based on the "free-flowing movement of people and goods," would be built around the car. The exhibit was sponsored by General Motors.

Futurama had been conceived by Norman Bel Geddes, an industrial designer who advocated for building a network of express highways across

The Futurama exhibit at the 1939 New York World's Fair depicted a utopian future built around cars and "magic motorways."

America, both between cities and within them. He called them "magic motorways." Futurama, he wrote, illustrated "how a motorway system may be laid down over the entire country—across mountains, over rivers and lakes, through cities and past towns—never deviating from a direct course and always adhering to the four basic principles of highway design: safety, comfort, speed, and economy."

The exhibit was intended to introduce the general public to the merits of this idea and showcase how highways could solve many problems. They would speed people between suburban homes and downtown shops and offices, address the growing problem of urban traffic congestion, and improve safety by keeping fast-moving cars entirely separate from people. The generic future American city depicted in Futurama was subdivided into industrial, residential, and commercial zones, with some central districts given over to pedestrians. Cars and people could more easily coexist in cities, Bel Geddes believed, if roads were redesigned to keep them apart. "Automobiles are in no way responsible for our traffic problems," he declared. "The entire responsibility lies in the faulty roads." The Futurama exhibit showed what many architects and planners, not to mention the auto industry, expected the car-based urban future to look like. It was a summary, in physical form, of a debate about the shape of cities in the automotive era that had, by 1939, been going on for several decades.

HIGHWAYS TO THE FUTURE

The utopian dream of rebuilding cities around cars dated back to before the first automobiles even existed. In *The Crystal Button*, written in the 1870s, Chauncey Thomas, a Boston carriage-maker, depicted a fictional future city transected by eight double-decker avenues that radiated out from a central plaza. Use of the upper roadway was limited to pedestrians and fast, quiet wheeled vehicles powered by electricity or compressed air. "We do not allow the use of horses in our cities," an inhabitant helpfully explains to a time-traveling visitor from the nineteenth century. "With the continued increase of traffic, it was found that they were a leading source of dust, filth, and unpleasant odors, and they also impeded pedestrian travel unnecessarily." The idea of elevated highways was popular among utopian thinkers of the period, as they imagined how cities might be rebuilt so that they retained their economic vibrancy while eliminating crowding, pollution, and disease. The utopians' imaginary future cities often featured huge skyscrapers (a recent innovation) and apartment blocks set in leafy parks. By the end of the century such visions also included elevated roadways dedicated to cars, with separate walkways, or sometimes moving sidewalks, for pedestrians.

Proposals to remodel existing cities along these lines proliferated in the first decade of the twentieth century, with calls for the construction of urban expressways for the exclusive use of cars. One plan proposed a highway down the center of Manhattan, carved through the second floor of existing buildings. Another proposed the eviction of hundreds of thousands of Manhattanites to construct five new avenues to speed cars across the congested downtown grid. Yet another plan, backed by local business leaders, called for the construction of broad avenues to funnel traffic on and off the Brooklyn Bridge. Drawings accompanying these proposals invariably showed these urban highways being used exclusively by fast-moving, widely spaced automobiles, implying that without horse-drawn vehicles, streetcars, or pedestrians to get in the way, there would be no congestion—a widely held view at the time. But these proposals, with their huge costs and disruption just to make life easier for a few wealthy motorists, proved understandably unpopular and went nowhere.

Even so, many city planners and architects of the time, not just motorists, were enthusiastic about the new ways cars could reshape cities. Members of the City Beautiful movement, a design group that had come together in the 1890s, believed that changing the layout of North American cities could help solve many of their problems. At a national conference held by City Beautiful planners in 1915, attendees were almost unanimous in their view that cars offered opportunities to change the way cities worked for the better (only one architect, visiting from Germany, disagreed and warned that the result would be gridlock). The group's leading light, Daniel Burnham, owned several cars and enjoyed touring Europe in them. Radial avenues inspired by the boulevards built in Paris in the 1860s, cutting through street grids to meet at a monumental civic center, featured in the City Beautiful plans drawn up for several American cities, the most famous of which was Burnham's 1909 plan for Chicago.

He admired both the views made possible by radial avenues, and the way they would speed the flow of traffic, writing of "vistas longer than the eye can reach, in roads of arrow-like purpose that are unswerving in their flight." His plan for Chicago called for Parisian-style avenues that would allow for at least eight lanes of vehicles, from which streetcars would be excluded. Railways, including Chicago's elevated railway loop, were also notably absent from his design; this was a blueprint for a car-based future. Yet the paintings commissioned to promote the plan showed few cars, instead depicting these vast highways as quiet, broad boulevards. In the end, few elements of the City Beautiful group's proposals for American cities were ever implemented. Some cities built monumental civic centers, but the idea of clearing away existing buildings to construct radial avenues proved too unpopular and expensive.

In the few cases where radial avenues were constructed, such as the Grand Concourse (an eight-lane highway in the Bronx), and the Benjamin Franklin Parkway in Philadelphia (a radial boulevard that was driven through the heart of the city's business district), they swiftly filled up with traffic. The theory that replacing horse-drawn vehicles with automobiles would reduce congestion had been disproved, and building new roads for them had not helped either. "The result has appeared to be exactly the opposite," noted the *Municipal Journal and Engineer*. Cities that rejected the idea of building new roads in favor of widening existing ones, by reducing the size of sidewalks, encountered the same problem. New York widened Twenty-third Street in 1910, for example, and then Fifth Avenue and Madison Avenue, adding extra lanes for cars. Baltimore and San Francisco took similar measures. Many cities also improved their road surfaces at the same time, replacing dirt, gravel, or cobblestone paving with smooth asphalt (by 1915 Los Angeles boasted that it had paved all its streets). But the smoother, wider roads just seemed to attract more vehicles. Traffic crossing or joining from side streets impeded steady flow on the grand avenues. And the outermost lanes of these new, wider roads immediately filled up with parked vehicles or delivery trucks. Rather than solving urban problems, cars seemed to be introducing new ones. Perhaps, some visionaries suggested, it was time to design an entirely new kind of city for the automotive age.

A BLUEPRINT FOR SUBURBIA

The suburban-commuter lifestyle is synonymous with car ownership today, but long predates it. The first commuter suburbs grew up along horsecar lines starting in the 1850s. In many cases real estate companies laid rails for horsecars to connect their suburban property developments to the city center. By charging a flat fare, regardless of the distance traveled, horsecar operators got people taking short journeys within the city to subsidize the fares of commuters coming in from the suburbs. Horsecars, running on rails, could travel at about 6 mph, compared with around 4 mph for horse-drawn buses. That meant the distance that could be traveled in a half-hour commute increased from two miles to three miles, allowing people to live farther from the city center while maintaining the same commuting time. This more than doubled the potential residential area around a city and began to affect the layout of some American cities.

Sidney George Fisher, a Philadelphia writer, noted in 1859 that horsecars were a "great convenience" and had almost "displaced the heavy, jolting, slow and uncomfortable omnibus." Instead they were "roomy, their motion smooth & easy, they are clean, well cushioned and handsome, low to the ground so that it is convenient to get in or out and are driven at a rapid pace." He predicted that they would transform urban living because everyone could have a "suburban villa or country home," and downtown would become a "mere collection of shops, warehouses, factories and places of business." But cities soon ran into the limits of horsecars. They became crowded, capacity was limited by the speed and strength of horses, and increasing the frequency of services was difficult on already crowded streets. In 1888, however, the first electric streetcars were introduced, starting in Richmond, Virginia, and spreading to two dozen other cities within a year. These could travel at 12 mph or even 15 mph, extending the half-hour commuting distance from three to at least six miles, and once again hugely increasing the potential residential area around a city as streetcar lines were run to new developments. More people had more choice about where to live.

This half-hour commuting distance may sound arbitrary, but an analysis of urban layouts by Cesare Marchetti, an Italian physicist, suggests that one hour is, on average, how long people are willing to spend traveling to and from work each day and has been for centuries. (Some people's commutes are much shorter or longer; this is an average across a whole city's population.) Marchetti suggested that this time limit defined the size of cities. No ancient walled cities, he found, had a diameter greater than three miles, so assuming a speed of 3 mph, walking to the center from the edge of such a city, or back again, took no more than half an hour. Faster means of transport, starting with horsecars, let cities expand as this half-hour average travel budget allowed people to go farther. Marchetti's analysis found that the city of Berlin increased in size precisely in accordance with improvements to the speed of transport. Before 1800 its radius was about 1.5 miles, and as faster means of transport were introduced, starting with horsecars and streetcars, its radius expanded in direct proportion to their speed.

It was clear to early car enthusiasts that automobiles would expand the potential residential area around cities still further. On November 14, 1896, when Britain's Red Flag act was abolished, allowing motor vehicles to use the roads freely, a group of car enthusiasts drove from London to Brighton in celebration, inaugurating what subsequently became an annual car rally. At a banquet in Brighton that evening, the organizer of the event, Harry Lawson, declared, "The value of property and land will be affected owing to the speed and facility by which we can now travel about the roads of the country. Ground within ten miles of any town will become yet more valuable than the ground inside the town itself, for builders of houses will merely have to put up a stable with a motor in it, and the house will thereby become connected with the town." With its greater speed and flexibility the motor car could, it seemed, usher in a new style of living that combined the best of town and country lifestyles.

Ebenezer Howard, a British social reformer, went further still, proposing not just new suburbs, or the remodeling of existing cities, but a new kind of city altogether. In 1898 he outlined the idea of the "garden city" as a way to mitigate the pollution, overcrowding, disease, and poverty associated with the fast-growing industrial cities of the time, filling in the details in his 1902 book *Garden Cities of To-Morrow*. He advocated the construction of carefully planned networks of garden cities, limited in size and population and surrounded by a green belt of farmland and forest. One of his diagrams shows six "slumless, smokeless cities," each circular in shape, housing thirty-two thousand people and arranged in a hexagonal pattern around a central city of fifty-eight thousand people, with farms, forests, and reservoirs between them. The satellite cities would be linked to the central city, and one another, by a network of canals and railways, as well as roads. This was a very different vision from utopian dreams of skyscrapers interleaved with elevated highways. But in a nod to the utopian tradition, each city would have six radial boulevards running from its center, interspersed with open spaces and public parks.

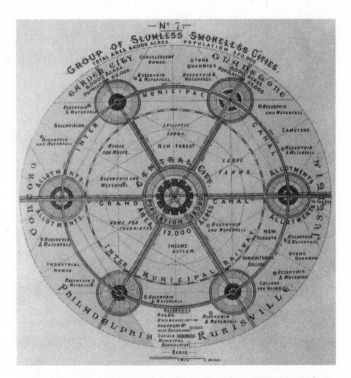

Plan for a group of ideal "garden cities" by Ebenezer Howard, from Garden Cities of To-Morrow *(1902).*

Howard's aim was to re-create an idealized version of a British rural market town, offering working people an alternative to crowded, unhealthy industrial cities. Each town would have designated areas for manufacturing, shopping, housing, schools, and so on and would be self-sufficient, with everyone working in the town where he or she lived. When it came to building the first garden cities, however, Howard had to water down his ideas to win the backing of investors. Letchworth and Welwyn, two garden cities founded just outside London in 1903 and 1920 respectively, did away with his neatly symmetric design. Moreover, the cities failed to become self-sustaining because of their proximity to London and the higher-than-expected cost of their housing, which proved too expensive for blue-collar workers. As a result, the garden cities ended up becoming dormitory suburbs for middle-class residents who commuted to London. Even so, Howard's ideas influenced planners around the world and led to the development of model suburbs, rather than true garden cities, in many other countries. In particular, the inclusion in Letchworth and Welwyn of winding roads to reduce the speed of traffic, and houses arranged on dead-end side streets, or cul-de-sacs, to remove the danger posed by through traffic, were widely copied elsewhere.

The influence of garden-city designs can be seen in Forest Hills Gardens, a residential neighborhood built in Queens, New York, in 1909. But the canonical American example is Radburn, New Jersey, a suburb designed in the 1920s by Clarence Stein and Henry Wright. Stein regarded the traditional American street grid as unsuited to the automobile age and instead created a hierarchy from wide, fast highways to slower, winding roads ending in cul-de-sacs where residents could drive right up their homes. Radburn also borrowed the garden-city ideas of a dedicated network of pathways to separate pedestrian and vehicular traffic, and of arranging groups of homes so that they backed onto roads and faced inward to an interior park or green. The resulting layout was intended as an antidote to the car, which in Stein's view posed "a disrupting menace to city life," though in practice this new approach depended on universal car ownership. Radburn, marketed as "the town for the motor age," would shape postwar suburbs in America and beyond.

At around the same time, the utopian model for the motor-age city was returned to prominence by the Swiss architect Charles-Édouard Jeanneret, better known as Le Corbusier, who declared, "The automobile has killed the great city; the automobile must save the great city." Like Stein, he thought that rather than trying to find ways to incorporate cars into existing street layouts, it was better to segregate cars from people altogether. Having grown up in the pre-car era, Le Corbusier could clearly see the impact automobiles had had on Europe's cities. In 1924 he lamented the way traffic had taken over the grand Champs-Élysées avenue in Paris. "I think back twenty years, when I was a student; the road belonged to us then; we sang in it and argued in it, while the horse-bus swept calmly along." But his dismay was far outweighed by his excitement at the possibilities that cars opened up for cities built around rapid personal transport.

The Ville Contemporaine (Contemporary City), proposed by Le Corbusier in 1922, resurrected the utopian idea of elevated highways threading their way between high-rise office towers and residential blocks surrounded by parks. It also featured pedestrian pathways that were entirely segregated from roadways. In 1925 Le Corbusier proposed the replacement of a large part of central Paris with a version of this plan. It was never adopted. But by this time the idea of car-only highways was growing in appeal both to pedestrians worried about the encroachment of cars on city streets, and to motorists who wanted fast roads free of pedestrians, streetcars, or delivery vehicles. In 1930 Le Corbusier refined his ideas further in his plans for the Ville Radieuse (Radiant City), which once again featured high-rise buildings, situated in parks, with elevated highways running between them. "Suppose we are entering the city by way of the Great Park," he wrote. "Our fast car takes the special elevated motor track between the majestic skyscrapers: as we approach nearer, there is seen the repetition against the sky of the twenty-four skyscrapers . . . the whole city is a park."

On the face of it, this is a very different vision from the semirural idyll of the garden city. But Le Corbusier was trying to solve the same problem as Howard, Stein, and other garden-city planners: the incompatibility of people and fast-moving traffic on city streets. Stein's answer was suburbs with winding roads and cul-de-sacs around village greens; Le Corbusier's was elevated highways, parks, and pedestrian walkways. He declared that "streets are an obsolete notion" and that "normal biological speeds must never be forced into contact with the high speeds of modern vehicles." His rebooting of the utopian city was an attempt to make the garden city work at high densities, packing people into high-rise homes and offices to free up space for parkland. "The garden city is a will-o'-the-wisp," he wrote. "Nature melts under the invasion of roads and houses and the promised seclusion becomes a crowded settlement . . . the solution will be found in the 'vertical garden city.'"

Le Corbusier's proposals coincided with the construction by Robert Moses, New York's parks commissioner and master planner, of the first high-speed, limited-access, car-only "parkways" linking Manhattan with

The Swiss architect Charles-Édouard Jeanneret, better known as Le Corbusier, designed utopian cities transected by fast-moving highways, including the Radiant City, conceived in collaboration with his cousin and business partner, Pierre Jeanneret.

surrounding areas. Despite their name, these were really highways, but the inclusion of a narrow strip (in some cases, just eighteen inches wide) of greenery along their edges meant that adjacent properties could not claim a right of access to the road, because technically a park was in between. Walling parkways off with vegetation in this way ensured that the flow of traffic could not be hampered by vehicles entering or exiting side streets or driveways. Here at last was what car owners had dreamed of: roads built specially to funnel cars in and out of a city quickly. As well as being a pioneer of highways, Moses was also the prime mover behind the 1939 World's Fair. All these strands converged in Futurama, which depicted an American metropolis after a Radiant City makeover, with elevated, car-only superhighways connecting high-rise buildings in the city to new, Radburn-style suburbs. Visitors to the exhibit were given a badge saying I HAVE SEEN THE FUTURE as they left. But the future promised by Futurama was not quite how postwar cities turned out.

THE FUTURE, BROUGHT TO YOU BY GM

The veterans returning to America after the Second World War came home to a severe housing shortage. By one estimate, America had 5 million fewer homes than needed in 1945; in 1947 one third of veterans were still staying with relatives or in shared housing. To address the problem the federal government took steps to encourage construction and home ownership. The Federal Housing Administration arranged loans for builders and low-interest mortgages for buyers, with special terms for veterans. It also set new construction standards for new houses, covering everything from building materials and lot sizes to architectural style and how far back homes should be set from the road. These requirements could most easily be met by building new developments on suburban land, which was cheap and had low property taxes, rather than in existing residential areas. The subsidies were so generous that it became cheaper to buy than to rent, at least for white buyers (the lending rules were heavily discriminatory). Like car ownership before it, home ownership was suddenly within reach of a wider public, not just the rich. The result was a surge in house building that saw home ownership increase from 40 percent of American households in 1940 to 60 percent by 1960. Nearly all of these new homes were in the suburbs.

One of those returning veterans was William Levitt. He had served in the navy and saw how mass-production techniques, honed in the car industry, had been applied to military housing. Returning to civilian life at his family's building firm, he set out to do the same for civilian housing. The company bought a seven-square-mile piece of land on Long Island and began building Levittown, a suburb of more than seventeen thousand homes, in 1947. Standard, prefabricated components were fitted together by teams of workers specializing in one of twenty-six different steps. "We are not builders," Levitt declared. "We are manufacturers." The process was, he noted, the inverse of a Detroit assembly line. "There the car moved while the workers stayed at their stations . . . in the case of our houses, it was the workers who moved doing the same job at different locations." At the peak of construction one house was being completed every fifteen minutes. Levitt called his company "the General Motors of the housing industry," and the comparison was apt: it offered houses at different prices to suit different buyers and even adopted the idea of annual model updates, with improved versions of its houses announced each year. Prices started at $7,990 with 5 percent down (0 percent for veterans), and each house included modern features such as a television and hi-fi system.

Borrowing from Radburn, Levittown had garden-city-style "village greens," and its curving streets and cul-de-sacs were arranged in a maze-like layout to reduce the flow and speed of traffic. Its cycle paths were something of an afterthought: they were not connected to all the houses, and it was often necessary to cross several roads to get to them. This was housing for car-owning commuters. Thanks to Robert Moses's building spree, Levittown had parkway connections to Queens, Brooklyn, Manhattan, and the Bronx. By 1950, 80 percent of the men living in Levittown commuted to Manhattan. As other builders imitated and extended Levitt's approach to construction, Levittown provided the template for suburban developments across America. The mass-production techniques that had made cars affordable had now done the same for housing, the other vital component of what was starting to be called the

American Dream, a term coined in 1931 by the author James Truslow Adams. This new suburban lifestyle was, in other words, doubly indebted to the car.

The explosion of new suburban housing also pulled retailers, company headquarters, manufacturers, and commercial-property developers out into the suburbs during the 1950s. Retailers such as Macy's and Allied Stores led the way, realizing that the highways that carried commuters into cities could also carry shoppers out of them. They built new suburban branches far from traditional downtown retail districts, located instead next to highways and with plenty with parking. (This model first emerged in Los Angeles, where the "Miracle Mile" of Wilshire Boulevard had established itself as a thriving retail center by 1930, and spread to other cities after the war.) Big companies began to build landscaped suburban campuses. Factories also moved out of cities to suburbs, taking jobs with them. The steady shift of white city dwellers into the suburbs, known as white flight, reduced the tax base of cities, prompting city governments to cut back on infrastructure, services, and schools in a cycle of urban decline. Meanwhile, the suburbs boomed. The result was a reshaping of American cities, which became more segregated by race and class; even in the predominantly white suburbs, communities sorted themselves by ethnicity and wealth.

And all of this increased dependency on the car. Before 1920, most American city dwellers had commuted to work on foot or by public transport. But during the 1950s commuting by car became the norm and has been ever since: today eight in ten Americans drive to work, usually alone. Zoning rules contributed to car dependency in the new suburbs by strictly segregating residential areas from office parks, industrial areas, and shops. This separation of activities meant that unlike downtowns or town centers, where a single bus, train, or tram stop can support multiple uses, the new suburbs could not efficiently be served by public transport. The aim was to insulate new suburbanites from noise, pollution, and crime associated with factories or shopping areas, but the outcome was that the office and the shops were only accessible by car.

It is sometimes suggested that GM and other carmakers bought streetcar lines to shut them down and encourage the switch to private cars. But this notion is incorrect. Streetcar ridership had begun to fall in the 1920s as automobiles became more popular, and operators of streetcar lines began to switch over to buses, which had lower running costs because they did not require rails. Passengers preferred buses because compared with streetcars, they were safer (they could pull over to the curb to pick people up and drop them off), more comfortable (with their thick pneumatic tires), and faster (which meant commuters could travel farther in a given time). Streetcars, once the only form of public transport in many American cities, had all but vanished by 1937, remaining in operation in only 4 percent of cities with public transport. It is true that a GM-backed company bought some streetcar operators that were later shut down, but it did so only when the decline of street-cars was already a foregone conclusion, with the aim of ensuring the operators would switch to GM-built buses.

What GM definitely did want, however, was highways. Alfred Sloan, the company's president, had insisted in 1939 that Futurama, which his company had sponsored, was intended "not as a projection of any partic-ular highway plan or program," but the very fact that he denied it was telling. The title of Bel Geddes's companion book to the exhibit, *Magic Motorways*, was another giveaway. Futurama had popularized the notion of superhighways among policymakers and the American public alike, laying the ground for a postwar boom in highway construction. Its center-piece was the Highway Act of 1956, which allocated billions of dollars to construct an interstate highway system. Construction of intercity high-ways was for the most part uncontroversial. But what about where they connected with cities? Planners promised that urban freeways, crossing cities and connecting to interstate highways, would resolve downtown traffic congestion and restore quiet to the streets they bypassed, improving the quality of life in cities. Highway engineers set about determining routes that were as direct as possible, while minimizing costs by choosing the cheapest possible land to build them on.

That often meant disused rail yards, industrial districts, waterfront areas, or parks. But it also included residential areas with low property values, which tended to be predominantly Black neighborhoods. Freeway construction became a tool of deliberate segregation, as white politicians seized the opportunity to demolish Black areas they characterized as "slums." Highways obliterated Black neighborhoods in countless cities, with little or no effort made to rehouse their displaced inhabitants. As a 1956 panegyric to the new highways in the *Saturday Evening Post* put it, "A happy by-product of all these expressway developments is that they invariably do an excellent job of slum clearance as they knife through the poorer sections of the city." Neighborhood organizations decried the construction of "white men's roads through black men's homes," as a slogan of the time put it, but protests and lawsuits had little effect. Only when urban freeways threatened white neighborhoods did the first successful "freeway revolt" take place, in San Francisco. Similar revolts followed elsewhere. In some cases, as in Baltimore and Washington, D.C., they were led by alliances between Black and white community groups who opposed freeway construction.

America's highway-construction boom came to an end in the 1970s, as opposition mounted and the notion of "induced demand"—the realization that new road capacity attracts more cars—became more widely known and accepted, under the mantra "you can't build your way out of congestion." Moreover, the long-held assumption that commuting patterns were from suburb to city center and back again was no longer true as American cities spread out. By the early 1970s suburban jobs outnumbered those in city centers, leading Peter Muller, a geographer, to declare in 1976 that suburbia had become the "essence of the contemporary American city." According to an analysis published in 2016 by Shlomo Angel, an urban-studies expert at New York University, 75 percent of jobs in a typical American city are now outside the urban center. That means commuters mostly spend their time driving from one suburb to another, rather than in and out of the city center. (The average time spent driving to and from work, as predicted by Cesare Marchetti, remains at thirty minutes.)

Modern suburbia may not be the world promised by Futurama, with fast-flowing highways transporting commuters between downtown jobs and leafy suburbs—"healthy uplands between forest and stream," as Bel Geddes put it. But it is the world that most Americans, and an increasing proportion of people elsewhere, now live in. Despite the much-trumpeted resurgence of American cities in recent years, around 70 percent of Americans live in suburbs, and about the same proportion of the population in Canada and Australia, which adopted similar approaches to postwar urban planning. In Europe, with its medieval street layouts, greater population densities, higher land prices, and lower levels of car ownership, the shift to the suburban-commuter lifestyle started later and did not go quite so far. Postwar cities were remodeled to be more car friendly, rather than car dependent. But the phenomenon of suburbanization has occurred, if not to the same extent as in America, wherever people can afford cars, and often on an explicitly American model. Many other countries sent traffic planners to America in the 1950s, hired American consultants and advisers, or adopted American traffic-management standards. Orange County, north of Beijing, is a clone of the California suburb it is named after (it even has the kidney-shaped swimming pools). New commuter suburbs now being constructed around major cities in India are indistinguishable from those in California. In much of the world, urbanization is now more accurately described as suburbanization.

THE FUTURE OF SUBURBIA

Arguments about the pros and cons of the postwar suburban lifestyle began almost as soon as the first residents moved into Levittown. Contented and invariably white families, living in a single-family home with its own yard and garage in a neat suburban neighborhood, were shown in magazine and television advertisements created by real estate developers, carmakers, and manufacturers of domestic appliances, all of whom were avid boosters of the joys of suburban living. Suburbia was depicted as a cozy world of friendly neighbors, healthy families, and domestic bliss. Radio and television sitcoms such as *Father Knows Best* (1949) and *Leave It to Beaver* (1957) reinforced the ideal of the white, middle-class suburban idyll. Suburbia embodied prosperity and patriotism. "No man who owns his own house and lot can be a Communist," declared William Levitt.

Critics of suburbia, by contrast, worried that its dull uniformity would do corrosive damage to the American psyche. In the words of the

American urbanist Lewis Mumford, writing in 1961, suburbia was "a multitude of uniform, unidentifiable houses, lined up inflexibly, at uniform distances, on uniform roads, in a treeless communal waste, inhabited by people of the same class, the same income, the same age group, witnessing the same television performances, eating the same tasteless prefabricated foods, from the same freezers, conforming in every outward and inward respect to a common mold." Suburbia's blandness was blamed for loneliness, alienation, and juvenile delinquency. Novels and films depicted a dark reality beneath the veneer of suburban happiness and conformity. In Joan Didion's novel *Play It as It Lays* (1970), for example, the female protagonist goes for long drives on the freeways of Southern California to try to alleviate her feeling of disconnection from everyone around her.

Versions of these opposing stereotypes about suburbia, born in the 1950s and 1960s, are alive and well today. But contemporary worries about suburbs are rather different. One concern is the toll of commuting. Although the average commute is still around thirty minutes in each direction in America, the number of "super commuters"—those whose commutes exceed ninety minutes—has increased in recent years. A 2018 study found that Stockton, California, was the super-commuter capital of America, with 10 percent of workers taking more than ninety minutes to travel between home and work. The figures were almost as high in Modesto (7.3 percent) and Riverside (7.3 percent). Studies show that commuting is consistently rated as the worst part of people's day, and long commutes are linked to higher levels of stress, anxiety, social isolation, and exhaustion. Some commuters leave home in the predawn hours to avoid the heaviest traffic, then sleep for an hour or two in their office parking lot before starting work. Traffic congestion is getting worse, too, with the average commuter being delayed by forty-two hours a year in 2015, up from twenty hours in 1982. Such delays are much larger for commuters in some cities: around eighty hours a year in Los Angeles, San Francisco, and Washington, D.C.

There are also health impacts from lack of walking. Many modern suburbs no longer have sidewalks, making it dangerous to walk short distances in suburban areas even if you try. About half the car journeys taken in America are of less than three miles; for trips of less than a mile, 62 percent overall are by car, rising to 78 percent in the suburbs. The default is to drive. A study published in 2014 analyzed the density, connectivity, and layout of street networks in twenty-four California cities and related them to local health outcomes. It found that more compact and connected street networks, which promote walking and cycling, were associated with lower levels of obesity, diabetes, and heart disease. Other studies have found that Americans who live in "walkable" neighborhoods weigh, on average, six to ten pounds less than those in less walkable neighborhoods. Those winding suburban streets that are meant to reduce speeds and improve safety, meanwhile, seem to have the opposite effect. Curves encourage faster driving than right-angled turns, and wide streets with houses set far back give drivers a sense of space that also encourages them to accelerate. The most dangerous areas for pedestrians, according to the Centers for Disease Control and Prevention (CDC), are no longer downtown streets but "newer, sprawling, southern and western communities where transportation systems are more focused on the automobile." In short, suburbs.

Perhaps the most serious charge leveled against suburbs is that their households have much larger carbon footprints than those in urban cores, and that suburbs are therefore environmentally unsustainable. A 2014 study from the University of California, Berkeley, found that a household's carbon footprint was chiefly determined by income, vehicle ownership, and home size, "all of which are considerably higher in suburbs." Suburban homes, being larger on average, require more energy for heating and cooling, and their inhabitants are more dependent on cars and less likely to walk, cycle, or use public transport. As a result, the study found, households in far-flung suburbs have as much as twice the average carbon footprint, while those in large, population-dense cities have about half the average. In some counties of California, two thirds of carbon emissions are from vehicles.

Starting around 2006, young Americans seemed to be turning against the suburban lifestyle and flocking instead to city centers. Meanwhile, immigrants and the urban poor were moving out to the suburbs—a phenomenon called the Great Inversion by the urbanist Alan Ehrenhalt.

But then population growth rates in America's suburbs started outpacing those in cities again. "The 'back to the city' trend seen at the beginning of the decade has reversed," noted William Frey of the Brookings Institution in 2019. In retrospect the global financial crisis of 2007–9 may simply have delayed some young Americans' entry into the housing market. The coronavirus pandemic has also increased the appeal of suburbs relative to city centers. One of the chief drawbacks of suburbs—the need to commute—goes away if you can work from home, which about half of American workers can. And staying at home is more pleasant if you have more space. A shift toward working remotely, some if not all of the time, is likely to be an enduring legacy of the pandemic. If workers only go in to the office on certain days or for certain activities, that could reshape commuting patterns and reduce traffic.

There have also been efforts to rethink the way suburbs work, by changing zoning rules to encourage the emergence, either spontaneously or through deliberate redevelopment, of mixed neighborhoods of residential, retail, and office space, and forms of housing other than single-family homes. This typically involves a small, walkable town center with shops, restaurants, offices, and homes mixed together, rather than sorted into separate zones that are only connected by road. In some cases run-down malls, parking lots, or office parks have been redeveloped along these lines, often around a transit stop. Examples of this approach, known as retrofitting, include Mashpee Commons in Massachusetts, a shopping area that has been remodeled to create a walkable downtown connected to a new residential areas, and Belmar, a former mall in Lakewood, Colorado, that has been broken up into twenty-two blocks to create a mixed-use mini-downtown district. Rezoning to allow for the construction of "infill" housing near transit stops, jobs, and services could prove effective in reducing car dependency and carbon emissions, by making suburbs more urban in nature.

Looking further ahead, some urban planners are imagining how suburbs might evolve. Alan Berger, codirector of the Center for Advanced Urbanism at the Massachusetts Institute of Technology, suggests that if efforts to retrofit suburbs and reduce car dependency pay off, the paved area (in the form of roads and parking lots) in future suburbs could be cut in half, as people make greater use of shared vehicles, bikes, and public transport. That could free up space that could be used for agriculture, carbon-storing greenery, or solar panels, helping to sustain both the suburb and nearby urban centers. Artists' impressions of these futuristic, sustainable suburbs show looping roads running through a verdant landscape, while delivery drones fly overhead. It all looks like a high-tech reboot of the garden city. After a century of car-driven suburbanization, the search for the perfect compromise between urban and rural lifestyles may be returning to its pre-automotive roots. Rather than trying to undo suburbanization, Berger's approach is based on interdependence between suburbs and denser urban areas, and trying to imagine ways to make suburbs more environmentally sustainable.

People like living in suburbs. At the moment, it means being dependent on a car to do almost anything, but that is widely considered a price worth paying for a bit more space and privacy, and the opportunity to own your own home. Millions of suburban dwellers have voted with their feet—or, it is more accurate to say, with their cars.

8

Car Culture

The car has become an article of dress without which we feel uncertain, unclad and incomplete in the urban compound.

—Marshall McLuhan, *Understanding Media*, 1964

THE INVENTION OF THE TEENAGER

In December 1944 *Life* magazine introduced its millions of American readers to the customs and culture of a group of exotic creatures, under the headline "Teen-age Girls: They Live in a Wonderful World of Their Own." The word *teen-age* had been around for a few decades. But it caught on in America in the 1940s because it referred to a cohort of young people who were seen, for the first time, as a distinct age group between childhood and adulthood. American teenagers of the 1940s were the first generation to grow up in a world where cars were commonplace; they never experienced a world without them. The cultural tropes that emerged in the 1940s and 1950s, as cars changed the way people socialized, ate, and shopped, went on to spread around the world, reshaping Western popular culture.

The emergence of teenagers was the result of the confluence of three factors. The first was that in America, unlike in other rich countries, sixteen-year-olds were more likely to be in school than employed, thanks to Depression-era laws barring young people from jobs that could be done by adult men. The proportion of American teens attending high school had risen from about 50 percent in 1930 to 70 percent in 1940 and reached 90 percent by 1960. Because teenagers spent most of their day in one another's company at school or in school athletics or other extracurricular activities, they developed their own social rules distinct from those of the home or workplace. Second, labor shortages during the Second World War, and an economic boom after it, ensured that after-school jobs were plentiful—and teenagers in the 1940s were generally allowed by their parents to keep their earnings. This gave them significant spending power.

The third factor was the car. The minimum driving age in most American states was sixteen, and secondhand vehicles were cheap and readily available. The importance of cars in the emergence of teenage culture is evident from *Life*'s 1944 photo story. The lead image is of a group of teenagers gathered around a 1927 Ford Model T. The caption reads, "Gang of teen-agers push boyfriend's Model T to get it started. Car is 17 years old and can hold 12 boys and girls. Favorite ride is out to football game." That brief caption evokes the whole universe of American teen culture in its classic form: hanging out with friends, cruising in cars, footballers and cheerleaders, school proms, and so forth. American teen-agers had the freedom and space to develop a distinctive set of behaviors that subsequently became a potent cultural export. Cars were central to this new teenage culture because they provided independence from parents and a private space beyond their prying eyes.

In particular, cars accelerated a change in the nature of courtship that had been under way since the 1920s. The tradition, in middle-class society at least, had been that young women would invite young men to call on them at home (for a man to call without an invitation was highly improper). The couple would then sit in the parlor for a conversation with the young woman's parents, which would sometimes lead to an invitation to dinner with the whole family. The couple might be granted

GANG OF TEEN-AGERS PUSH BOYFRIEND'S MODEL T TO GET IT STARTED. CAR IS 17 YEARS OLD AND CAN HOLD 12 BOYS AND GIRLS. FAVORITE RIDE IS OUT TO FOOTBALL GAME

TEEN-AGE GIRLS
THEY LIVE IN A WONDERFUL WORLD OF THEIR OWN

Cars, and the freedom and independence they provided, were central to the teenage culture that began to take shape in America in the 1940s.

some time alone together on the front porch after dinner. But only after several such visits would they be allowed to go out for an unchaperoned walk, or perhaps to a dance with a carefully vetted guest list. This tradition of "calling" gave the young woman and her family a great deal of control. Dating, by contrast, which became widespread among middle-class families from the 1920s, generally involved the young man inviting the woman to go out with him. He was expected to pay for entertainment of some kind, while she was expected to provide only her company. (Dating's origins, and indeed the very use of the word *date*, starting in the late 1890s, initially had connotations of prostitution, causing much wringing of hands.) Dating had entirely replaced calling by the outbreak of the Second World War.

In this new model, young men with cars had a distinct advantage. Having transport of their own, they could potentially date a wider circle of girls because they could travel farther and could take them to a wider range of places. Most important, a car was also a destination in its own right: a private space, particularly if parked in a secluded spot, away from parents. In the words of the historian Beth Bailey, courtship had moved "from the front porch to the back seat." Anyone with a car, or access to a family car, would not be short of friends. By the 1930s, a government child-welfare study found, the average urban teen was spending four nights a week going out with friends, in groups or couples. They might go to shows or movies, go out for ice cream and Coca-Cola ("coking"), go to dances—or simply cruise around in cars, stopping to canoodle in a secluded lane (a custom known at the time simply as parking).

Cars provided greater sexual freedom, thrilling youngsters and scandalizing their elders. "Of all the youth who go to parties, attend dances, and ride together in automobiles, more than 90 percent indulge in hugging and kissing," Benjamin Lindsey, a judge from Denver, reported in his 1925 book, *The Revolution of Modern Youth*. Advice on dating etiquette abounded in magazine columns; dating many partners was a way to demonstrate one's popularity, and opting out of this contest by going steady with a single partner was frowned upon. As one boy from Milwaukee told *Senior Scholastic* magazine, "Going steady is like buying the first car you see—only a car has trade-in value later on." But the war changed attitudes. With fewer young men around (except near military bases) and a shift toward earlier marriage in the face of wartime uncertainty, dating went from being a general popularity contest to preparation for the monogamy of marriage. After the war, going steady with one partner became an established part of teenage culture. And teenagers' spending power opened up a lucrative new market, with companies competing to sell them makeup, magazines, and music—and to devise new places for them to go in their cars.

Drive-in theaters had first appeared the 1910s, but became more widespread in the 1930s, in large part because they offered an affordable date-night option. The idea was patented by Richard Hollingshead, whose initial aim was to find a way for his mother, who found wooden cinema seats uncomfortable, to watch films. As a salesman for his family's auto-parts firm, Hollingshead wondered whether there might be a market in letting people watch films from the comfort of their own vehicles. He tested the concept by putting a film projector on the hood of his car in a driveway, hanging a sheet from some trees as a screen, and inviting his neighbors. He patented the idea and opened his first drive-in (though he called it a "park-in theatre"), near Camden, New Jersey, in June 1933. Tickets cost twenty-five cents for each person—and each car. Hollingshead's patented ramp system positioned cars at slightly different heights, to ensure that all of their occupants had a good view of the screen. His invention, he declared, "virtually transforms an ordinary motor car into a private theater box."

The idea was slow to take off. America had only fifteen drive-ins by 1939, and ninety-six by 1945. But everything changed in 1949 when Hollingshead's patent was overturned, allowing other entrepreneurs to open drive-ins without fear of lawsuits. The invention of the in-car speaker, which could be clipped to a car window, also helped. It ensured good sound quality and perfect synchronization with the on-screen image, even for those at the back of the audience. The number of drive-ins jumped to two thousand by 1950 and more than four thousand by 1958. Unlike indoor cinemas, drive-ins could only operate when it was dark, because otherwise the projected image was difficult to see. But this, coupled with the privacy afforded by cars, made drive-ins ideal date venues, for obvious reasons. Hollywood studios saw drive-ins as a threat to their own theater chains and claimed that their best films would be cheapened by being shown outdoors. So drive-ins mostly had to make do with reruns and cheesy B movies. For many customers, however, the quality of the film was often of secondary importance. Press coverage denouncing drive-ins, which earned the nickname "passion pits," only heightened their popularity among frisky teens. But drive-ins were also popular with families, providing a cheap night out without the need for a babysitter because children could sleep in the car.

FROM FAST CARS TO FAST FOOD

As cars were changing how people courted, they were also changing how they ate. If the car could be a private box at the theater, it could also be a private dining room, as the emergence of roadside food outlets demonstrated. Drivers in a hurry wanted to eat quickly, and the car industry provided a model for rapid manufacturing of standardized products. The drive-in restaurants that sprang up along American highways, catering to time-pressed drivers with fast service and the promise of consistency under a nationwide brand, gave rise to the modern concept of fast food. As with so many other aspects of car culture, the first examples appeared in America before the Second World War, and the idea was perfected, and then exported globally, in the postwar period.

The origins of this model can be traced back to 1921, when Jesse Kirby opened what seems to have been the first drive-up restaurant, the Pig Stand, on the highway between Dallas and Fort Worth in Texas. Kirby realized that drivers in a hurry would prefer to eat in their cars and then go. "People with cars are so lazy," he said, "they don't want to get out of them." This insight enabled him to streamline a traditional restaurant, doing away with tables and some waitstaff. Instead, "tray boys," in white shirts and black bow ties, would greet each car as it pulled up outside, sometimes hopping onto its running board as it came to a stop. (They later became known as carhops, a term derived from the bellhops in hotels.) The carhop would take the order and then deliver barbecued-pork sandwiches and Coca-Cola on aluminum trays that could be hooked onto customers' car windows. As well as pioneering the drive-in concept, Kirby and his partners were also early to embrace the idea of restaurant franchises. By 1925 there were six Pig Stands in Dallas, and franchises in several other states. The chain adopted the slogans "America's Motor Lunch" and "A Good Meal at Any Time." By 1927 it had standardized the design of its restaurants, with a red-tiled roof, globe lighting, and a distinctive "sign of the pig," to make them easily recognizable to passing motorists. During the 1930s the globe lights gave way to colored neon, another first attributed to Pig Stand, along with the introduction of deep-fried onion rings and the chicken-fried steak sandwich.

White Castle, a rival fast-food pioneer, launched in the same year, in Wichita, Kansas. It sold ground-beef hamburgers, which many Americans were reluctant to eat, given the poor sanitary practices of the meatpacking industry, highlighted in Upton Sinclair's 1906 book, *The Jungle*. To reassure customers about sanitary standards, White Castle restaurants had spotless interiors, with white enamel tiles and stainless steel. Open kitchens made the food preparation clearly visible to customers, and staff wore clean white uniforms and black bow ties. White Castle's founders, Walter Anderson and Billy Ingram, systematized the production of hamburgers, pre-weighing and pre-shaping them for consistency and serving them with cooked onions in a specially designed bun. Each burger cost five cents, and they were often sold by the bag; a customer who wanted a larger meal simply ordered more identical burgers. Like Pig Stand, White Castle adopted a uniform design for its restaurants. Each had the same floor plan and a distinctive, castle-like exterior that was easily recognized by passing motorists. By 1931 there were 115 White Castle restaurants across several states, and a host of imitators with names including White Tower, Little Tavern, White Tavern Shoppes, and White Hut, all of which copied the formula of selling mass-produced hamburgers in pseudo-medieval surroundings. As a result, hamburgers overtook hot dogs to become the most popular form of fast food in America.

In 1931 a Pig Stand franchise in California seems to have been the first fast-food restaurant to allow customers to order by driving up to a window, rather than parking and waiting for a carhop. But not until 1948 did another chain, In-N-Out Burger, come up with the drive-through model, in which customers placed orders using an intercom and then collected food at a window. With no carhops, no inside seating, and no outside parking, this was fast food stripped to its essentials. Drive-in restaurants competed to serve customers as quickly as possible, equipping carhops with roller skates and experimenting with various ordering systems. But roller skates or intercoms were no use if the kitchen could not keep up with the flow of orders. This insight inspired two brothers, Dick and Maurice McDonald, to reinvent altogether the way fast-food restaurants worked.

The McDonald brothers had set up a drive-in restaurant in Pasadena, California, in 1937, mainly selling hot dogs. When this prospered, they moved to a larger site in San Bernardino and in 1940 opened the McDonald Brothers Burger Bar Drive-In, which, as its name suggested, mostly sold burgers. This new restaurant did better, in part because it was near a high school. Its popularity enabled the brothers to buy a large house with a swimming pool and tennis court. But its success also caused problems. With each order taking, on average, twenty minutes to deliver, cars were backing up outside the restaurant at busy times. The brothers were also frustrated by the constant turnover of short-order cooks, and by their carhops' tendency to waste time chatting with customers. They began to think about ways to slim down and speed up their operation. Eventually, in 1948, they closed their restaurant to overhaul it. When it reopened three months later, it still sold hamburgers. But everything else about it had changed.

The McDonalds got rid of their carhops and required customers to get out of their cars and place orders at a window instead. They also slimmed down their menu, from twenty-five items to nine, having realized that hamburgers accounted for more than 80 percent of food sales. They did away with trays, plates, glassware, and cutlery, all of which could be broken or stolen, and replaced them with disposable paper bags, wrappers, and cups. Most important, they overhauled the making of the hamburgers completely, taking their inspiration from the mass-production techniques of the car industry. They had heard about how these techniques had recently been applied to house building in Levittown—so why not apply them to food? Their new approach required each staff member to specialize in a single task, from taking orders to grilling or wrapping burgers. This made training new hires easier and quicker, ensured that workers did not waste time switching between tasks, and meant skilled cooks were not needed. Much of the food was preprepared, and the same condiments were included in every burger, eliminating the delay of allowing customers to choose. Once assembled and wrapped, burgers were kept warm under heat lamps. And the kitchen was reorganized to ensure workers did not get in one another's way. The two brothers optimized the layout by drawing and redrawing chalk lines on their tennis court, to create and evaluate life-size maps of the different stations in the kitchen.

The brothers dubbed the result the Speedee Service System. With fewer staff and a more efficient production process, they could offer hamburgers for fifteen cents and cheeseburgers for nineteen cents, or about half the price of the same order in a sit-down restaurant. Lines formed outside their restaurant, but moved quickly, because the small, standardized menu meant burgers and fries could be produced continuously, rather than every item having to be cooked to order. The brothers appeared on the cover of *American Restaurant* magazine in 1952 and were deluged with letters from other restaurateurs asking about their system. The McDonalds realized their new approach had great potential and began licensing it to franchisees. When franchisees said they wanted to use the McDonald's name on their restaurants, the brothers devised a standard design, based around two golden-yellow, neon-lit arches that together made an *M*. But as interest in franchises grew, the brothers worried that they would end up spending their time on the road, making deals. They were happy with their single restaurant in San Bernardino, their grand houses and new Cadillacs every year. So when Ray Kroc, a milkshake-machine salesman, offered to become their franchising agent, they eagerly signed him up.

Kroc had come to see the McDonalds in 1954 after they bought two additional "multimixer" machines, each capable of making five milkshakes at a time, for their restaurant, bringing the total to ten machines. How could one restaurant, Kroc wondered, possibly need to make fifty milkshakes at once? He went to visit and was amazed by what he saw. After striking a deal with the brothers, Kroc started opening franchises across America, focusing on fast-growing suburbs, initially in California, because of their high levels of car ownership. By 1960 there were 228 franchises, and Kroc was planning to open 100 more each year. But his aggressive, hypercompetitive tactics alienated the brothers, and in 1961 he bought them out. Having sold the rights to their name, the McDonalds renamed their original restaurant Big M. True to form, Kroc opened a McDonald's around the corner that drove them out of business.

After opening more than a thousand McDonald's restaurants in the United States, Kroc began to expand internationally in 1967. Today there are more than thirty-seven thousand branches in over a hundred countries, making McDonald's the world's second-largest fast-food chain and the golden arches one of the world's best-known corporate logos. The largest chain, with more than forty-two thousand outlets globally, is Subway, and Starbucks, KFC, and Burger King round out the top five. The top fifteen fast-food chains in the world, ranked by number of branches, are all American. Surprisingly, McDonald's was a relatively late adopter of the drive-through model, opening its first drive-through in Arizona in 1975. But drive-through sales soon accounted for 70 percent of its sales in America—an indication of the enduring association between cars and fast food.

FROM FILLING STATION TO SUPERMARKET

Roadside restaurants were not the only way that cars changed how people bought food. An even bigger change was the rise of the supermarket. The idea of customers serving themselves, rather than asking a shopkeeper to assemble their orders for them, had made its debut with the opening of the Piggly Wiggly grocery store in Memphis, Tennessee, in September 1916. It was an instant success and spawned many imitators. But while Piggly Wiggly's founder, Clarence Saunders, pioneered the idea of self-service within grocery stores, it was another entrepreneur, Michael J. Cullen, who devised the concept of the supermarket. In 1930, having worked for many years for Kroger, a chain of self-service grocery stores, Cullen came up with the idea of a much-larger store—as much as forty times the size of a conventional grocery store—that could focus on high volume and low prices.

Supermarkets brought together Piggy Wiggly's self-service model with the roadside-retail approach pioneered by drive-in filling stations, the first of which opened in 1913. Being able to drive a car right up to a fuel pump, rather than buying fuel at a hardware store or blacksmith's shop, was revolutionary. National Supply Stations, which opened a chain of filling stations in California that year, claimed to offer fuel of a more uniform quality and at a lower price, and under a brand that promised motorists consistency. Independent retailers responded to the rise of gas-station chains by opening "super service stations," which, as well as selling gas and oil, also offered other auto supplies, repair services, and cleaning, from retail spaces arranged along the edge of an off-street forecourt. The convenience of being able to pull off the road to access these various services led to the adoption of this model by retailers of food and other goods. Drive-in markets with off-street parking proliferated in Southern California in the 1920s, positioned along main roads in wealthy areas, and away from the congestion of downtown commercial districts. Mix in self-service and scale the whole thing up, and the result, by the late 1930s, was the suburban supermarket, a generally windowless building sitting in a parking lot two or three times the area of the store itself.

This new approach was only possible because of widespread car owner-ship. Locating supermarkets by main roads on urban fringes, rather than in downtown shopping areas, meant rents were lower—so stores could be much bigger and could offer their customers plenty of free parking. By buying produce in larger quantities from suppliers, supermarkets could offer lower prices. Customers who arrived by car could buy goods in quantity at discounted prices—several weeks' worth of coffee or flour or sugar in one go. Supermarkets also acted as their own warehouses, unlike small grocery stores, which could not keep large amounts of stock on-site. This reduced distribution costs, allowing for further price cuts. The first true supermarket, King Kullen, opened in August 1930 in Jamaica, Queens, in New York City. Its slogan was "Pile it high. Sell it low." In Depression-era America, this was a winning formula. By the mid-1930s Kullen had opened seventeen stores, and other retailers with names such as Big Bear, Handy Andy, and Giant Tiger were following suit. By 1941 America had more than ten thousand supermarkets.

"Perhaps no phase of retail distribution has so captured the imagina-tion of the American public as has the supermarket," declared the *Journal of Marketing* that year. "Within a period of less than a decade, approxi-mately 50% of the American consuming public has changed its food-shopping habits." When supermarkets first appeared, it noted,

> so great was the attraction of these food bargains that consumers came from distances of 75 and 100 miles in their cars. This factor has been possible only because of the great growth of the automobile. No longer is the housewife dependent for her food shopping on her own strength or the need of keeping within a narrow radius of

convenience to do her family shopping. Her automobile has made her independent of a particular neighborhood; and so long as there is a parking lot for her convenience, she can go almost any distance she desires for her food buying, if the price attraction is sufficiently great.

This new model changed not just how people shopped, but where. "This projection of the large food market away from the central or main street of a town to its outskirts or to new residential districts away from the business center is changing the physical aspect of cities and of city planning," noted the *Journal of Marketing*. "This also means that we may see greater dispersal of communities and greater merging of rural and urban populations." In other words, suburbia. Supermarkets showed that suburban car owners were willing to travel to get better prices. As supermarkets spread, they gave rise to those archetypal American suburban spaces: shopping centers, in which several stores are grouped around a large supermarket or pharmacist, with space for parking in front.

SEE YOU AT THE MALL

Larger, formally planned shopping centers, often anchored around department stores, had existed since at least the 1920s—the Country Club Plaza, which opened in Kansas City in 1923, was an early example—and a handful of similar developments appeared in the 1930s and 1940s. But a change to America's tax rules known as accelerated depreciation, introduced in 1954 in an effort to boost investment in manufacturing, had the side effect of triggering a surge in construction of large-scale shopping centers. More generous deductions for depreciation enabled property developers to recoup the cost of their investments within five years rather than forty, by allowing even a profitable development to be counted as loss making for tax purposes. As a result, investors piled into American real estate companies.

Building shopping centers was particularly lucrative because they could be constructed on urban fringes, where land was cheap, and where car-owning shoppers were already accustomed to driving to visit supermarkets. The new tax rules, coupled with rising property prices, enabled developers to build one shopping center, exhaust its tax bene- fits, sell it for more than it had cost to build, and then start building another. "Investors seeking the best return on their dollars now looked away from established downtowns, where vacant land was scarce and new construction difficult . . . instead, they rushed to put their money into projects at the suburban fringe—especially into shopping centers," noted Thomas Hanchett, an American historian, in a 1996 paper analyzing the impact of the 1954 tax rules. The total number of shopping centers constructed each year in America immediately tripled from around 50 to 150, and the average number of new, large-scale "regional" shopping centers (greater than three hundred thousand square feet) opening each year jumped from one or two to twenty or thirty. Hanchett's analysis, based on comparisons with Canada, suggests that "federal tax incentives in the United States helped spur the construction of perhaps twice as many shopping centers as would otherwise have been built."

The 1954 rule change also spurred the development of America's first nationwide motel chains, such as Holiday Inn and Howard Johnson's. And it contributed to the decline of drive-in theaters, because the land they occupied was more valuable to property developers as a location for shopping throughout the day, rather than for just showing movies in the evening. Besides, more and more people had televisions at home.

One of the new shopping centers constructed during this boom was Southdale, which opened just outside Minneapolis in 1956. It was designed by Victor Gruen, an Austrian Jewish architect who had fled to America to escape the Nazis in 1938. Gruen later recalled that he arrived in America "with an architect's degree, eight dollars, and no English." He soon made a name for himself designing shop fronts and retail spaces. But as America suburbanized in the 1940s, Gruen disliked what he saw. Suburban roads, he told an architecture conference in the 1950s, were "avenues of horror," "flanked by the greatest collection of vulgarity—billboards, motels, gas stations, shanties, car lots, miscellaneous industrial equipment, hot dog stands, wayside stores—ever collected by mankind." Having grown up in Vienna, a pedestrian-friendly city with grand parks, public squares, and shopping arcades, Gruen was acutely aware of the lack of such communal

The Southdale Center, the first modern enclosed shopping mall, in 1956.

spaces in suburban America, where everyone traveled by car. So when he was asked to design the Southdale shopping center, he saw it as an opportunity to create a new kind of place: an idealized version of a European, walkable city that would, he hoped, displace the sprawl of roadside shopping strips.

His plan placed a shopping center at the heart of a 463-acre development that also included apartment buildings, houses, schools, offices, a hospital, parks, and a lake. His design would prove hugely influential—though not for the reasons Gruen had hoped. The developers ignored his suggestions for housing, schools, and outdoor spaces and simply built the shopping center, surrounded by a huge parking lot. But Gruen's shopping center was different from any that had come before. Inspired by the grand, glass-roofed shopping arcades of Europe's big cities, he made it fully enclosed, with air-conditioning, so that the shops' doors could be kept permanently open. The shops faced inward, arranged on two levels around a large central plaza covered by a skylight. With its benches, plants, and fountains, the plaza was intended to mimic an outdoor town square. This new kind of space, now known as a shopping mall, was hailed by the *New York Times* as a "shopper's dream" and was an instant hit. *Fortune* magazine reported that "this strikingly handsome and colorful center is constantly crowded"; *Architectural Forum* said it was "more like downtown than downtown itself." Southdale became the template for shopping centers, in America and beyond, for the rest of the twentieth century. It was arguably the most influential building of the postwar era.

Gruen imagined Southdale as the antidote to car-based suburbia because it forced shoppers to abandon their cars and walk around in a communal space. As he told an architectural conference in 1964, while evangelizing his ideas, "One technological event has swamped us. That is the advent of the rubber-wheeled vehicle. The private car, the truck, the trailer, as means of mass transportation. And their threat to human life and health is just as great as that of the exposed sewer." But his new malls could only be reached by car, and their proliferation on urban fringes both entrenched car dependency in America and helped extend it to other countries. In 1970, when the 1954 tax loophole started to be closed, America had more than thirteen thousand shopping centers (including enclosed malls), nearly all of which had been constructed in the previous fifteen years in suburban areas, accelerating the decline of traditional downtowns. "Downtown Has Fled to the Suburbs," noted *Fortune* magazine in 1972.

By the 1970s Gruen had come to regret his creation, and in particular what he called "the land-wasting seas of parking" at malls, and their contribution to urban sprawl. He decided to move back to his beloved Vienna. But even there he was horrified to find, just south of the city, a "gigantic shopping machine"—a Southdale-style mall. In 1978, two years before his death, he gave a speech in London entitled "The Sad Story of Shopping Centers," in which he formally renounced shopping malls as a perversion of his original vision: "I am often called the father of the shopping mall. I would like to take this opportunity to disclaim paternity once and for all. I refuse to pay alimony to those bastard developments. They destroyed our cities."

THE RISE AND FALL OF CAR CULTURE

By spawning drive-ins, fast-food joints, and malls, cars reshaped the phys-ical and cultural landscape of America, and then of many other coun-tries, too. But all of these twentieth-century car-centered institutions are now in decline. Admittedly, the few remaining drive-in cinemas saw a revival of interest during coronavirus lockdowns, and in a neat reversal of history, 160 Walmart parking lots were turned into temporary drive-ins in summer 2020. Drive-ins and parking lots around the world have also hosted socially distanced church services, concerts, theatrical performances, and, in Germany, even a drive-in nightclub. But drive-in cinemas cannot compete with the convenience of online streaming, while dating has moved from the front porch, to the back seat, to dating apps. Fast-food chains have also seen slowing demand in recent years, as consumers have become more health conscious, moved upmarket to "fast casual" restau-rants, or switched to ordering food by smartphone from the couch, rather than by intercom from the driver's seat—another trend accelerated by the pandemic.

Although one group did embrace malls as a social space—American teenagers, for whom malls became a place to hang out with friends, go for a meal or a snack, watch a movie, and generally see and be seen—malls are also in retreat. By 2005 around fifteen hundred enclosed malls had been built in America. But hardly any have been built since then, and hundreds of existing malls are either dead or dying. Again, the smartphone is the culprit: it provides a far more convenient venue to chat with friends, flirt with other teenagers, show off one's sense of style, and go shopping. In a strange twist of fate, e-commerce companies are in some cases converting abandoned malls to warehouses and distribu-tion centers. Empty malls are ideal for such purposes because they are generally close to highways, have high ceilings, and are already equipped with loading docks. Again, the decline of the mall and the shift to online shopping is an existing societal shift that has been sped up by the pandemic.

Overall, the significance of the car in American popular culture seems to have peaked in the 1970s and 1980s, just when the first generation of postwar American teenagers found themselves in control of the entertainment industry. Popular TV series of that era, syndicated around the world, included *Starsky & Hutch*, *The Dukes of Hazzard*, and *Knight Rider*, all of which featured cars almost as prominently as the lead actors. The musical *Grease*, which made its debut in 1971, followed by the film version in 1978, presents a nostalgic depiction of 1950s culture, in which cars play a central role ("greasers" were working-class young men with an interest in hot-rodding or motorbikes). And the time machine in the 1985 film *Back to the Future*, which transports the hero to the heyday of teenage culture in the 1950s, takes the form of a DeLorean sports car. In all of these cases cars are symbols of freedom, glamour, and power, for white men, at least; they are shown driving on open, empty roads and never find themselves stuck in traffic, unable to find parking, or subject to unjust police stops. The DeLorean grants its driver freedom to travel at will through time, as well as space.

But cars are no longer associated with freedom in the same way. Instead it is now the smartphone that grants users previously unimaginable freedom to socialize, shop, and transport themselves to exciting new spaces, out of sight of parents. Just as the teenagers of the 1940s had never known a world without cars, today's teens have never known a world without the internet and are establishing their own cultural norms around smartphones and online communication. As with cars, it may be that the first generation to grow up with a new technology defines its social and cultural impact—or perhaps it just takes a generation for new technologies to bed in. Either way, just as the norms established by car-driving teenagers in the 1940s, and the new institutions that sprang up to serve them, ended up dominating popular culture for decades, the cultural norms now being established around smartphones—online dating, food delivery, e-commerce—could prove surprisingly long-lasting. It may be that Chinese teenagers are playing the same role for the smartphone that American teenagers did for the automobile, as Chinese smartphone apps and business models are exported to the rest of the world. Meanwhile, just as technology has undermined the most visible emblems of car culture, it is also redefining the car itself—which is undergoing the most fundamental transformation since its debut.

9

The Fall and Rise of the Electric Car

Ever since the small electric runabouts were introduced, about ten years ago, they have always been popular with women. In the early days of motoring the little electrics were about the only kind of motor car a woman could handle easily, as the early gasoline cars required more strength to crank than most women possess.

—*NEW YORK TIMES*, JANUARY 20, 1911

THE GOLDEN AGE OF THE ELECTRIC VEHICLE

Much of the early enthusiasm for the automobile stemmed from its promise to solve the problems associated with horse-drawn vehicles, including noise, traffic congestion, and accidents. The fact that cars failed on each of these counts was tolerated because they offered so many other benefits, including eliminating the pollution—most notably, horse manure—that had dogged urban thoroughfares for centuries.

But in doing away with one set of environmental problems, cars introduced a whole set of new ones. The pollutants they emit are harder to see than horse manure, but are no less problematic. These include particulate matter, such as the soot in vehicle exhaust, which can penetrate deep into the lungs; volatile organic compounds that irritate the respiratory system and have been linked to several kinds of cancer; nitrogen oxides, carbon monoxide, and sulfur dioxide; and greenhouse gases, primarily carbon dioxide, that contribute to climate change. Cars, trucks, and buses collectively produce about one fifth of global carbon dioxide emissions. Reliance on fossil fuels such as gasoline and diesel has also had far-reaching geopolitical ramifications, as much of the world became dependent on oil from the Middle East during the twentieth century.

None of this could have been foreseen at the dawn of the automobile age. Or could it? Some people did raise concerns about the sustainability of powering cars using nonrenewable fossil fuels, and the reliability of access to such fuels. Today, electric cars, charged using renewable energy, are seen as the logical way to address these concerns. But the debate about the merits of electric cars turns out to be as old as the automobile itself.

In 1897 the bestselling car in the United States was an electric vehicle: the Pope Manufacturing Company's Columbia. Electric models were outselling both steam- and gasoline-powered ones. By 1900 sales of steam vehicles had taken a narrow lead: that year 1,681 steam vehicles, 1,575 electric vehicles, and 936 petrol-powered vehicles were sold. Only in 1903 did petrol-powered vehicles take the lead for the first time, with the success of the Oldsmobile Curved Dash. In Europe, petrol-powered vehicles had swiftly established their dominance in the late 1890s, prompting one American observer to declare that the "rest of the world appears to have gone daft on gasoline." In America, by contrast, the debate about the relative merits of the different forms of propulsion went on well into the first decade of the twentieth century. "It must be remembered that the electric motor, the steam engine, and the gas engine have all been proven successful, and that an automobile made by a well-known concern and fitted with any one of these three types of motive power is a practical motor vehicle," noted an American writer in 1901. So how close a race was it really, and why did gasoline-powered vehicles ultimately prevail in America, too?

Articles assessing the merits of the three technologies generally agreed that electric vehicles were cleaner, quieter, and more reliable than the alternatives and were also simpler to operate. But their range was limited to around thirty miles on a single charge, recharging was slow, and they had trouble negotiating rough roads outside big cities. Steamers had a longer range than electrics and had no difficulty climbing hills or carrying large loads. But their long-term prospects were limited. They were complicated to operate (requiring special licenses in some states), needed refilling with water every twenty or thirty miles, produced clouds of steam that hampered visibility, and were slow to start because they needed to build up a head of steam first. (They could at least use existing roadside troughs that supplied water to horses.) Gasoline-powered vehicles based on internal combustion engines were noisy and smelly, difficult to start, and less reliable than the alternatives, at least to begin with. Albert Pope, founder of Pope Manufacturing and maker of the bestselling Columbia electric vehicle, insisted, "No one will buy a carriage that has to have all that greasy machinery in it." But although they were complicated and temperamental, gasoline vehicles had the advantage of greater range because gasoline was widely sold at general supply stores, initially as a cleaning solvent, and then as a fuel. Each technology had pros and cons, but given the considerable disadvantages of steam power, it came down to a contest between electric- and gasoline-powered cars.

Electric vehicles had a clear edge in fleets. Their cleanliness, quietness, and reliability made them ideally suited for urban use, and their limited range was not a problem because most urban trips were short, and they could be recharged at a central depot overnight. Accordingly, electric vehicles found use as taxicabs in several cities, including New York, Berlin, and Amsterdam, around the turn of the twentieth century. Berlin's fire-department chief, deeming internal combustion engines too unreliable, replaced horse-drawn fire engines with electric ones in 1908, prompting his counterparts in several other German cities to follow suit. Electric buses and delivery trucks were adopted in parts of America, France, and Germany. "Growth of Electric Commercial Trucks: Efficiency and Economy of Vehicles Forcing Business Men to Supplant Horse-Drawn Wagons," declared a *New York Times* headline in 1910. "Business men are no longer sentimental about the horse and are now more sensitive about their better friends, dollars and cents," the paper reported. Electric vehicles, it noted, could reduce haulage costs by 15–40 percent compared with horse-drawn wagons.

Perhaps the most remarkable example, to modern eyes, of how things might have worked out differently for electric vehicles is the story of the Electrobat, an electric taxicab that briefly flourished in the late 1890s. The Electrobat had been created in Philadelphia in 1894 by Pedro Salom and Henry Morris, two scientist-inventors who were enthusiastic proponents of electric vehicles. In a speech in 1895, Salom derided "the marvelously complicated driving gear of a gasoline vehicle, with its innumerable chains, belts, pulleys, pipes, valves and stopcocks . . . Is it not reasonable to suppose, with so many things to get out of order, that one or another of them will always be out of order?" The two men steadily refined their initial design, eventually producing a carriage-like vehicle that could be controlled by a driver on a high seat at the back, with a wider seat for passengers in the front. In 1897 Morris and Salom launched a taxi service in Manhattan with a dozen vehicles, serving a thousand passengers in their first month of operation. But the cabs had limited range and their batteries took hours to recharge. So Morris and Salom merged with another firm, the Electric Battery Company. Its engineers had devised a clever battery-swapping system, based at a depot at 1684 Broadway, that could replace an empty battery with a fully charged one in seconds, allowing the Electrobats to operate all day.

In 1899 this promising business attracted the attention of William Whitney, a New York politician and financier, who had made a fortune investing in electric streetcars. He dreamed of establishing a monopoly on urban transport and imagined fleets of electric cabs operating in major cities around the world, providing a cleaner, quieter alternative to horse-drawn vehicles. Instead of buying cars, which were still far beyond the means of most people, city dwellers would use electric taxis and streetcars to get around. But realizing this vision would mean building Electrobats on a much larger scale. So Whitney and his friends teamed up with Pope, maker of the bestselling Columbia electric vehicle. They formed a new venture around the Electrobat operation, called the Electric

Vehicle Company, and embarked on an ambitious expansion plan. EVC raised capital to build thousands of electric cabs and opened offices in Boston, Chicago, New Jersey, and Newport. In 1899 it was briefly the largest automobile manufacturer in America.

But its taxi operations outside New York were badly run and failed to make money. Repeated reorganizations and recapitalizations prompted accusations that EVC was an elaborate financial swindle. The industry journal the *Horseless Age*, a strong advocate of petrol-powered vehicles, attacked the firm as a would-be monopolist and said electric vehicles were doomed to fail. When news emerged that EVC had obtained a loan fraudulently, its share price plunged from $30 to $0.75, forcing the firm to start closing its regional offices. The *Horseless Age* savored its collapse and cheered its failure to "force" electric vehicles on a "credulous world." But other observers saw things differently. In 1902 *Electrical World and Engineer* noted "The dismal failure of public electric automobiles in several cities tended to give the motive power a black eye irrespective of its real merits." In retrospect, EVC's business model might have worked, and urban transport might have taken a very different path. But instead the dubious behavior of EVC's bosses discredited electric vehicles at the height of their popularity.

In the years that followed, as more people bought private cars, electric vehicles took on a new connotation: as women's cars. This association arose because they were suitable for short, local trips, did not require hand cranking to start or gearshifting to operate, and were extremely reliable by virtue of their simple design. (It is tempting to ask what Bertha Benz would have made of this logic.) As an advertisement for Babcock Electric vehicles put it in 1910, "She who drives a Babcock Electric has nothing to fear." The implication was that women, unable to cope with the complexities of driving and maintaining petrol vehicles, should buy electric vehicles instead. Men, by contrast, were assumed to be more capable mechanics, for whom greater complexity and lower reliability were prices worth paying for powerful, manly petrol vehicles with superior performance and range. It was the medieval arrangement of horse-riding men and carriage-riding women all over again.

Advertisements for the Baker electric depicted women at the wheel of its vehicles, with one driver dropping her husband off at a golf course.

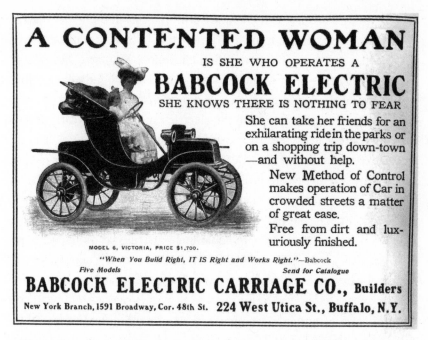

A CONTENTED WOMAN

IS SHE WHO OPERATES A

BABCOCK ELECTRIC

SHE KNOWS THERE IS NOTHING TO FEAR

She can take her friends for an exhilarating ride in the parks or on a shopping trip down-town —and without help.

New Method of Control makes operation of Car in crowded streets a matter of great ease.

Free from dirt and luxuriously finished.

MODEL 6, VICTORIA, PRICE $1,700.

"When You Build Right, IT IS Right and Works Right."—Babcock

Five Models   *Send for Catalogue*

BABCOCK ELECTRIC CARRIAGE CO., Builders

New York Branch, 1591 Broadway, Cor. 48th St.   224 West Utica St., Buffalo, N.Y.

Electric cars were advertised as being particularly suitable for women, because they were clean, reliable, and did not require any mechanical expertise to operate.

Cole, another manufacturer, claimed its electric cars were "the choice of American womanhood." Two manufacturers, Detroit Electric and Waverly Electric, launched models in 1912 that were said to have been completely redesigned to cater to women. As well as being electric, they were operated from the back seat, with a rear-facing front seat, to allow the driver to face her passengers—but also making it difficult to see the road. For steering they provided an old-fashioned tiller, rather than a wheel, which was meant to be less strenuous but was less precise and more dangerous. Henry Ford bought his wife, Clara, a Detroit Electric rather than one of his own Model Ts. Some men may have liked that electric cars' limited range meant that the independence granted to their drivers was tightly constrained.

By focusing on women, who were a small minority of drivers— accounting for 15 percent of drivers in Los Angeles in 1914, for example, and 5 percent in Tucson—makers of electric cars were tacitly conceding their inability to compete with petrol-powered cars in the wider market. That year, Henry Ford confirmed rumors that he was developing a low-cost electric car in conjunction with the inventor Thomas Edison. "The problem so far has been to build a storage battery of light weight which would operate for long distances without recharging," he told the *New York Times*, putting his finger on the electric car's primary weakness. But the car was repeatedly delayed, as Edison tried and failed to develop an alternative to the heavy, bulky lead-acid batteries used to power electric cars. Eventually the entire project was quietly abandoned.

The failure of electric vehicles in the early twentieth century, and the emergence of the internal combustion engine as the dominant form of propulsion, has much to do with liquid fuel providing far more energy per unit mass than a lead-acid battery can. But the explanation is not purely technical. It also has a psychological component. Buyers of private cars, then as now, did not want to feel limited by the range of an electric vehicle's battery, and the uncertainty of being able to recharge it. A 1902 article, "The Problem of the Automobile," published in *Electrical World and Engineer*, argued that even if charging points or battery-swapping stations were available across America, "one does not wish to limit his country tour to lines of travel along which he can strike charging facilities . . . [one] wants to have a certain liberty of action which a journey fully prearranged cannot give." In the words of the historian Gijs Mom, private cars in this period were primarily seen as "adventure machines" that granted freedom to their owners—and an electric vehicle granted less freedom than the petrol-powered alternative. "To possess a car is to become possessed of a desire to go far afield," wrote one city-dwelling car enthusiast in 1903. Sales of electric cars peaked in the early 1910s. As internal combustion engines became more reliable, they left electric vehicles in the dust.

ANOTHER ROAD NOT TAKEN

The story of the electric vehicle provides an intriguing glimpse of a parallel universe in which shared electric vehicles, rather than privately owned gasoline-powered ones, might have come to dominate road transport, at least within cities. The first decades of the twentieth century also witnessed another automotive might-have-been. What if the primary fuel for cars had been renewable ethanol, derived from crops, rather than gasoline, derived from oil? The modern world would look very different without the geopolitical and environmental consequences of twentieth-century oil dependency. But could that alternative reality have come to pass?

When the Ford Model T was launched in 1908, it was capable of running on either gasoline or ethanol; it was, to use the modern term, a flex-fuel vehicle. Controls mounted by the steering wheel let the driver adjust the carburetor and the spark-plug timing to work with either fuel, both of which were readily available in the United States. Indeed, an active debate was under way about which was the better long-term bet as an automotive fuel. Ethanol and gasoline, both hydrocarbons, are slightly different in their chemical makeup. Ethanol burns more cleanly but has a lower energy density: a given volume of the fuel contains about one-third less energy than the same amount of gasoline.

Ethanol, otherwise known as ethyl alcohol or simply alcohol, had widely been used as a fuel, chiefly for lighting, in the early nineteenth century. In the United States, rather than buying whale oil for fuel, farmers would use a still to produce ethanol from crop waste. By the early 1860s, thousands of distilleries were producing around 90 million gallons of alcohol a year for lighting. The alcohol was mixed with camphor oil, extracted from trees, to improve the way it smelled when burning. This also rendered fuel alcohol undrinkable. But in 1862 a tax on alcohol of $2.08 per gallon was introduced to fund the Civil War. This tax was intended to apply to beverage alcohol, but there was no exemption for alcohol produced for use as fuel. As a result, another hydrocarbon product—kerosene derived from crude oil—became the dominant fuel for lighting almost overnight, and many of the small distilleries that had produced fuel alcohol went out of business. The tax on alcohol was left in place after the Civil War as a temperance measure. Kerosene sales reached 200 million gallons a year by 1870, and by the 1880s one oil company, the Standard Oil Trust, controlled 85 percent of the supply. Kerosene was the oil industry's primary product. But it, too, was about to suffer a reversal of fortune.

Crude oil, also known as petroleum, is a complex and variable mixture of hydrocarbon compounds, ranging from light, clear liquids that evaporate easily, also known as spirits, to heavy oils. It can be separated into its lighter and heavier components, each of which evaporates at a different temperature, by judicious use of heating and recondensation, a process known as fractional distillation. Extracting kerosene from oil produced a lighter by-product, gasoline, which was initially considered almost worthless. It was sold in small quantities in paint or general supply stores for use as a solvent and cleaning agent. But oil producers would often simply dump it on the ground and leave it to evaporate or flush it into rivers. (It was said that if hot coals were thrown overboard from a steamboat on the Cuyahoga River in Ohio, a major oil-producing region, the water would catch fire.) In the 1880s and 1890s, however, electrification reduced the demand for kerosene as a lighting fuel. At the same time, gasoline's suitability as an engine fuel caused demand for it to increase, as the first automobiles appeared, and as stationary gasoline engines were installed on farms and in factories. The price of gasoline rose from around seven cents a gallon in 1899 to twenty cents in 1902, and by 1910 it had displaced kerosene as the oil industry's primary product.

The reliance of automobiles on gasoline prompted two concerns. The first was that gasoline was a finite, nonrenewable resource. In 1899 *Motor Age* printed an article by Gustave Chauveau, a French engineer. He was worried that discoveries of new oil wells were becoming "daily more rare, and the old wells gradually being exhausted." *Motor Age's* editors added their own suggestion that "even conservative engineers think it the part of wisdom to look around for a substitute for gasoline." Another concern was that in America the gasoline supply was under the control of Standard Oil. To the leaders of the automobile industry, that it was "entirely dependent upon a fuel the supply of which is in the hands of a monopoly, and is also limited by natural conditions, must be somewhat disquieting," noted the *Horseless Age* in 1905. "In view of the possible limitation of supply it would be highly important if only a tolerably satisfactory substitute for gasoline could be found or developed."

Alcohol was the obvious alternative, being a renewable fuel that could be made from grain crops or farm waste. Engines built to run on gasoline could be adjusted to run on alcohol instead. Fuel alcohol appealed to countries with no oil reserves of their own, and in particular to

Germany, which led the way in fuel-alcohol research, subsidizing domestic alcohol production while taxing imports of foreign oil. In France, the Automobile Club of Paris arranged long-distance rallies to compare the effectiveness of alcohol, gasoline, and mixtures of the two in different types of vehicles. Between 1901 and 1904, exhibitions and conferences on fuel alcohol took place in France, German, Italy, and Spain. (Britain, with its extensive foreign empire, was less worried about access to oil.)

American engineers also concluded that alcohol was the most promising substitute for gasoline. "This fuel, far from being controlled by a monopoly, is the product of the tillers of the soil," noted the *Horseless Age* with approval. Government agencies agreed: alcohol could potentially create a valuable new market for American farmers, by allowing them, in effect, to produce feed for cars instead of horses. Furthermore, noted *Motor* magazine in 1904, alcohol "is much cleaner, less odorous, and freer from danger of explosion" than gasoline. Admittedly, because of its lower energy density, "slightly more alcohol is required for the development of a given power than is required of gasoline, but this is more than offset by the lower cost—13 cents a gallon in Germany at the present time."

In the United States, however, alcohol cost far more: around fifty cents a gallon, or more than twice the cost of gasoline. And that cost did not include the excise tax on alcohol, which was still in place, and which raised the price to around $2.50 a gallon. The United States was unusual in not exempting fuel alcohol from such excise taxes; many other countries did so, provided it had been rendered undrinkable by mixing it with poisonous, bad-tasting, or foul-smelling additives. But in America, all efforts to exempt such "denatured" alcohol, or to repeal the excise altogether, starting in the 1880s, had failed. In part this was because Standard Oil and its allies, keen to protect their own sales, argued that a repeal would cause an increase in drunkenness. But in 1906 proponents of repeal finally achieved a breakthrough. A series of articles about the anti-competitive practices of Standard Oil published by Ida Tarbell, a muck-raking journalist, prompted the government to investigate. And President Theodore Roosevelt indicated his support for repeal as a means of weakening the oil monopoly. The "Free Alcohol" law passed in May 1906 abolished the excise on denatured alcohol from January 1, 1907.

Hopes were high that this would lead to a surge in alcohol production. "It is only the heavy tax imposed by the United States that has prevented the use of a large number of vegetable products for the manufacture of exceedingly cheap and available alcohol," noted the *New York Times*. With the excise removed, the price of alcohol fell dramatically, to around forty cents a gallon. But it was still twice as expensive as gasoline. And the price of gasoline was starting to drop as new oil fields were found in Texas, Oklahoma, and California, to replace the declining output of those in Pennsylvania, Ohio, and Indiana. Training programs to stimulate alcohol production, and attempts to encourage farmers to form cooperatives, came to nothing. Many farmers were reluctant to compete against Standard Oil, even though it had formally been accused of being an illegal monopoly in a federal suit filed in November 1906. Standard Oil had an efficient national distribution system (based on its ownership of pipeline networks and discounts illegally negotiated with railway companies) from oil wells to shopkeepers. But no such network existed for alcohol.

"It will be some time before denatured alcohol will be more economical than other fuels," the *Horseless Age* gloomily conceded in 1908. More oil reserves were being discovered, and chemical engineers were figuring out how to break down heavier hydrocarbons into lighter compounds using heat and pressure. This technique, called cracking, allowed as much as 45 percent of each barrel of oil to be converted into gasoline, up from about 13 percent before. Concerns about scarcity of gasoline diminished as the supply increased; worries about Standard Oil's stranglehold on production dissipated, too, after the company was declared an illegal monopoly and broken up into thirty-four separate regional firms in 1911. All this meant that alcohol was unable to compete with gasoline in America. And even in countries that heavily promoted alcohol production, notably Germany, it failed to catch on as a full replacement for gasoline. Instead the two fuels were blended, to reduce dependence on oil imports.

Interest in fuel alcohol picked up in the 1920s for a technical reason, as carmakers developed engines with higher compression ratios, to deliver more power. Such engines suffered from "knocking," a pinging noise indicating uneven combustion that can damage the engine. Engineers discovered that fueling engines using pure alcohol, or a mixture of alcohol and gasoline, solved the problem. Charles Kettering, the head of research at General Motors, instructed his team to investigate the feasibility of switching totally to alcohol. As well as solving knocking, it would also insulate carmakers from the long-term risk of future oil shortages. One GM researcher concluded that alcohol was the "most direct route . . . for converting energy from its source, the sun, into a material that is suitable for a fuel."

But GM's researchers identified a key limiting factor on the adoption of fuel alcohol, given widespread car ownership: the availability of farmland. One GM study estimated that replacing gasoline would require 46 percent of all food crops produced in America to be turned into alcohol. In a speech in 1921, Kettering observed, "To take the place of gasoline, over half of the total farm area of the United States would be needed to grow the vegetable matter from which to produce this alcohol." That would either cut into the food supply or make the country dependent on food imports.

A potential solution to this problem was to make "cellulosic" alcohol from agricultural waste, wood, and various shrubs, rather than food crops such as corn. Such cellulosic matter "is readily available, it is easily produced and its supply is renewable," noted a GM researcher. But the chemical processes to break down cellulose into fermentable sugars were inefficient or expensive. Using a cheap "weak acid" process on a ton of wood produced only twenty gallons of alcohol; a "strong acid" process could produce three times that quantity, but at a much higher cost. Even so, for a while it was widely assumed that using a mixture of alcohol and gasoline, and eventually moving to cellulosic alcohol, was the way forward. Henry Ford told the *New York Times* in 1925 that alcohol was "the fuel of the future" because "there is fuel in every bit of vegetable matter that can be fermented."

However, GM's engineers discovered another way to prevent knocking: by adding lead to gasoline. Adding three grams of lead to every gallon of gasoline had the same antiknocking effect as mixing in 15 percent alcohol, but was much cheaper. This allowed GM to build larger cars with more powerful engines, without the risk of engine damage from knocking. General Motors teamed up with Standard Oil of New Jersey to produce and promote leaded gasoline, which (unlike alcohol as a fuel additive) could be patented. By 1936, 90 percent of all gasoline sold in America was leaded, despite evidence of its health risks. Alcohol was abandoned as a fuel additive in America, though it continued to be used in Europe, at concentrations up to 25 percent, until the Second World War.

Despite a resurgence of interest in fuel alcohol in recent decades in some countries, notably Brazil, it ultimately played only a supporting role to gasoline and diesel as a transportation fuel during the twentieth century. Engineers focused on developing and improving engine technologies based around gasoline and diesel, rather than alcohol. Might things have worked out differently? As a fuel, alcohol's fatal weakness is the large amount of land that would be required to grow the crops needed in its production. In a world without oil, in which all vehicles ran on alcohol, that might have limited their adoption and encouraged fuel economy. But it might also have led to food shortages and higher prices. Moreover, the availability of cheap oil meant alcohol could not compete. Perhaps a breakthrough in cellulosic-alcohol production could have led to a different world; but despite renewed efforts in the twenty-first century, such a breakthrough has yet to occur. And even if it had done so, oil would probably have remained a cheaper option—financially, at least. But relying on oil turned out to have other costs.

OIL SHOCKS AND ELECTRIC DISAPPOINTMENTS

Overproduction of oil, not scarcity, was the main concern in 1930s as the Depression reduced demand, even as new reserves were discovered. At one point a barrel of oil could be bought in Oklahoma for a mere forty-six cents. With the backing of the government, American oil companies were also expanding overseas, and by the mid-1930s they had won concessions in countries including Bahrain, Iraq, Kuwait, Saudi Arabia, and Venezuela. The best time to strike such deals, oil executives reckoned, was when oil was plentiful and prices were low. At the outbreak of Second World War the United States accounted for more than two thirds of world oil production and was producing about 30 percent more than it consumed. So it was able to support its allies with exports to Europe; Germany and Japan, by contrast, lacked secure access to oil, which proved to be a significant factor in their defeat. But by the end of the war America's role as the world's leading oil producer was under threat, as cheaper sources of oil came onstream. "The center of gravity of world oil production is shifting from the Gulf-Caribbean region to the Middle East—and is likely to continue to shift until it is firmly established in that area," noted a report written for the U.S. government in 1943. As the Cold War began and America established military bases around the world to contain the Soviet Union, access to oil was a vital part of its strategy, prompting America to take much more interest in the security of the Middle East.

In 1948 James Forrestal, America's secretary of defense, warned that without access to oil from the Middle East, "American motorcar companies would have to design a four-cylinder motorcar sometime within the next five years." Most American cars had six- or eight-cylinder engines. Either they would have to become more sparing in their use of gasoline, Forrestal implied (for example, by switching to four-cylinder engines), or America would find itself dependent on Middle Eastern oil. America chose the latter path, though most motorists were initially unaware of it. The United States was the world's most enthusiastic adopter of the automobile, particularly in the postwar rush to the suburban, car-dependent lifestyle. The number of cars and other light vehicles on American roads increased from 25 million in 1945 to more than 100 million in 1973—equivalent to five hundred vehicles per thousand people, or twice the level in Europe. American cars were not simply more numerous; they were also much bigger than cars in other countries. On average, they were three quarters of a ton heavier than those made in Europe and Japan, and their V-8 engines had more than twice the engine capacity of the four-cylinder engines most prevalent elsewhere. As a result, they used a lot more fuel.

An increasing proportion of that fuel came from imported oil. Imports, mostly from the Middle East, accounted for 27 percent of America's supply by 1973. In December that year the Middle Eastern members of the Organization of Petroleum Exporting Countries (OPEC) cut off oil exports to the United States in protest at its support for Israel in the Yom Kippur War. The price of oil surged, and the sudden reduction in supply resulted in higher gasoline prices, the introduction of rationing, and long lines at gas stations. (To complicate matters, in America at the time gasoline was subject to price controls, and refiners were reluctant to sell fuel for less than it cost to produce, further constraining supply.) For the first time, American drivers realized they could not take the supply of gasoline for granted. The oil shock led the government to introduce a national speed limit of 55 mph, and fuel-economy standards that required American manufacturers to achieve an average fuel economy, across their entire product lines, of 18 miles per gallon by 1978 and 27.5 by 1985.

But American carmakers did little to change their products. By the late 1970s, 80 percent of American-made cars still had V-8 engines. In 1979, in a second oil shock, oil supplies from the Middle East were once again disrupted, this time as a result of the Islamic revolution in Iran and the outbreak the following year of the Iran-Iraq War. The actual production of oil barely fell, but prices soared and panic buying ensued. This second oil shock stimulated the demand for smaller cars. Sales of small hatchbacks increased in Europe, while in America, more buyers were turning to imported cars, 80 percent of which came from Japan. As well as being more economical to run than much-larger American cars, models from Japanese brands such as Datsun, Toyota, and Honda also proved to be more reliable. By 1980, Japanese cars accounted for 16 percent of the American market, up from 3.5 percent in 1970.

Electric cars might also have been expected to benefit from the concerns over the sustainability of gas-guzzlers. But electric-car technology had made little progress since the 1920s. The biggest problem remained the battery: lead-acid batteries were still heavy and bulky and could not store much energy per unit of weight. Other sorts of rechargeable batteries based on different materials, such as nickel metal hydride, were barely any better and were generally more expensive. The most famous electric vehicles of the 1970s, the four-wheeled lunar rovers driven by American astronauts on the Moon, were powered by nonrechargeable batteries because they only had to operate for a few hours. On Earth, attempts to revive electric cars as commercial products failed to get off the ground.

The Sebring-Vanguard CitiCar, a tiny electric car shaped like a wedge of cheese, was launched in 1974 in response to the first oil shock. Its six-horsepower motor was powered by lead-acid batteries under its seat, giving it a range of about forty miles and a top speed of about 30 mph. Around twenty-three hundred were sold before production ceased in 1977. Sales of another tiny electric car, the Zagato Zele, produced in Italy and marketed in America as the Elcar, totaled around five hundred. It, too, relied on lead-acid batteries, with a fiberglass body to reduce weight. *Consumer Reports* reviewed both vehicles in 1975 and was unimpressed by their flimsy construction, lack of basic features (the CitiCar's doors had no locks), and poor crash protection. A rollover or side impact, the magazine warned, "would imperil the lives of persons inside these tiny, fragile, plastic-bodied vehicles. A rollover or a severe crash holds the further threat of sulfuric acid pouring from ruptured batteries." The magazine observed that "a practical, safe, economical electric car might be just right as a second car limited to short commutes and shopping trips. But neither the CitiCar nor the Elcar is practical, safe, or economical." It concluded, "It would be foolhardy to drive either car on any public road."

THE RETURN OF THE ELECTRIC CAR

The reemergence of the electric car in the twenty-first century can nevertheless be traced back to the era of the oil crisis. In 1972 Stanley Whittingham, a researcher at the oil company Exxon, was investigating a new battery design based on lithium. The lightest metal on the periodic table of elements, lithium can store fifteen times as much electrical charge per kilogram of weight as lead when used in a battery. Nonrechargeable lithium batteries came into use in the 1970s as a way to power watches, calculators, and medical implants. Whittingham's breakthrough was to show how lithium could be used as the basis of a rechargeable battery—at least in theory. In practice, however, batteries made using his design tended to catch fire, as the highly reactive lithium, used as the battery's negative electrode, assumed an unstable form after several charge-discharge cycles. This problem was solved in the 1980s, when researchers in Britain and Japan, working independently, found a way to avoid using solid lithium as the negative electrode. Instead, they used latticelike structures, one made of carbon, and the other of cobalt oxide, as the electrodes. The lithium in such a battery exists in ionic rather than metallic form, making it much safer and more stable. As a result, such batteries are known as lithium-ion batteries.

The first commercial lithium-ion battery was launched by Sony in 1991, for use in portable electronic devices such as camcorders. Sony's engineers further improved the design by adding safety features. If lithium-ion batteries are overcharged, they can overheat, disintegrate, and catch fire. Sony added a porous polymer that would melt if the battery overheated, shutting it down. It also developed a "smart" charger that stops a battery from charging when it is full. By the early 2000s lithium-ion batteries had become the preferred power sources for laptops and mobile phones. But they were still considered too expensive for electric cars: a lithium-ion battery pack capable of powering an electric car cost around $10,000 in 2002. Lead-acid batteries were five times heavier, four times larger, and stored less energy, but they were also much cheaper.

That was why the EV1, an electric vehicle briefly produced by General Motors in the late 1990s, used lead-acid batteries. The EV1 was not sold, but was made available via lease agreements to drivers in Los Angeles, Tucson, and Phoenix, starting in 1996. A second-generation model, introduced in 1999, used a nickel metal hydride battery, which increased its range from about 90 to about 120 miles. The EV1 attracted a loyal following, but only eleven hundred vehicles were ever made. In 2002 GM announced plans to shut down the program, and the following year it recalled the vehicles and crushed nearly all of them. (A few were preserved, with their drivetrains deactivated, for display in museums.) GM's decision prompted an outcry from the EV1's fans, many of whom had offered to buy their vehicles outright. The company insisted that the EV1 had shown that battery technology was still too immature to make electric cars commercially viable. But critics claimed that GM had always wanted the EV1 to fail because electric vehicles, having few moving parts, would eat into its profitable market for spare parts. A viable electric vehicle might also have led to tighter regulation of gasoline-powered vehicles.

Outrage at the cancellation of the EV1 had an unanticipated side effect. In the late 1990s Alan Cocconi and Tom Gage, two electric-car enthusiasts, had built an electric roadster called the tzero by fitting an electric drivetrain, powered by lead-acid batteries, into a fiberglass kit car called the Piontek Sportech. They hoped to put the tzero into production and sell it for around $80,000. In 2003 they decided to switch the battery pack in one of their prototype vehicles from lead acid to lithium ion. They assembled the new battery pack from sixty-eight hundred small lithium-ion cells, of the kind used in laptops, power tools, and camcorders. Small lithium-ion cells were much cheaper than larger ones because they were produced in greater volume for use in consumer-electronics products. The new battery pack weighed a quarter of a ton less than the old one, but could store three times as much energy and extended the tzero's range from about 90 to about 250 miles. The car was also capable of accelerating from 0 to 60 mph in less than four seconds.

In late 2003, just as GM began reclaiming and crushing its fleet of EV1s, the tzero came to the attention of two American technology entrepreneurs and car enthusiasts, Martin Eberhard and Elon Musk. Impressed by the tzero's performance, and angered by the demise of the EV1, both men separately urged Cocconi and Gage to put the tzero into production, to prove GM wrong. This led Gage to introduce Eberhard to Musk. The two men decided to team up to commercialize the tzero's technology through a new company, Tesla Motors. Its first vehicle, the Tesla Roadster, combined the tzero's drivetrain and battery with the chassis of a Lotus Elise sports car. Unveiled in 2006, the Roadster changed the perception of electric cars by emphasizing performance and speed and illustrating the potential of lithium-ion batteries to deliver reliability and long range. Unlike previous electric cars, with their poor performance, limited range, and odd body shapes, the Roadster did not require drivers to compromise; indeed, it could outperform a gasoline-powered Porsche or Ferrari in some respects. But it did require drivers to be wealthy: it cost about $100,000.

From the beginning, however, the aim of Tesla's founders was to commercialize electric vehicles on a large scale. The Roadster was the first step in what Musk (who replaced Eberhard as Tesla's CEO in 2008) called the "Tesla Motors master plan" in a blog post in 2006:

> Our long term plan is to build a wide range of models, including affordably priced family cars. This is because the overarching purpose of Tesla Motors (and the reason I am funding the company) is to help expedite the move from a mine-and-burn hydrocarbon economy towards a solar electric economy, which I believe to be the primary, but not exclusive, sustainable solution . . . The strategy of Tesla is to enter at the high end of the market, where customers are prepared to pay a premium, and then drive down market as fast as possible to higher unit volume and lower prices with each successive model . . . Without giving away too much, I can say that the second model will be a sporty four door family car at roughly half the $89k price point of the Tesla Roadster and the third model will be even more afford-able . . . When someone buys the Tesla Roadster sports car, they are actually helping pay for development of the low cost family car.

In subsequent years Tesla has broadly followed through on this plan, with the introduction of the "sporty four-door" Model S in 2012 and the Model 3 in 2017 (though even the cheapest Tesla model, at about $40,000, cannot yet be described as affordable). It has become the world's leading maker of electric cars, and in July 2020 it overtook Toyota to become the world's most valuable carmaker—despite shipping far fewer cars. In 2019 Tesla delivered 367,200 vehicles, compared with Toyota's 10.5 million. Its valuation reflects investors' optimism that electric cars are the future of the industry, and that Tesla is several years ahead of estab-lished carmakers. Among other things, it has built a series of enormous factories, in partnership with Panasonic, a Japanese electronics giant, to maximize production and minimize cost of the battery packs needed for its vehicles. And as lithium-ion battery technology has improved and production has expanded, the price per kilowatt hour has fallen by 90 percent between 2010 and 2020. In 2019 the Nobel Prize in Chemistry was awarded to Stanley Whittingham, John Goodenough, and Akira Yoshino for their work on the development of lithium-ion batteries. "This lightweight, rechargeable and powerful battery is now used in everything from mobile phones to laptops and electric vehicles," the prize committee declared. "Lithium-ion batteries have revolutionized our lives since they first entered the market in 1991. They have laid the foundation of a wireless, fossil fuel–free society, and are of the greatest benefit to humankind."

ELECTRIC CARS AND CLIMATE CHANGE

Lithium-ion batteries have made it possible. But the switch to electric cars seems inevitable because of tightening regulation of combustion-powered vehicles in order to address climate change. The automobile, having been introduced in part to address one pollution problem, has contributed to another one: carbon dioxide emissions from the burning of fossil fuels. Limiting global warming to less than 2°C above its preindustrial average will clearly require drastic cuts in carbon dioxide emissions in the coming decades. Indeed, emissions will not simply have to be reduced, but eliminated altogether by the middle of this century to meet that goal. The governments of several countries have pledged to achieve "net-zero emissions" by 2050, and in support of that goal they have introduced carbon-trading systems and restrictions on many industries. That has included setting dates for ending the sale of new vehicles with internal combustion engines. Britain, Iceland, Ireland, Israel, the Netherlands, and Sweden will not allow such sales from 2030; Canada, France, and Singapore have opted for 2040. More than twenty major cities around the world, including Amsterdam, Barcelona, London, Seattle, and Vancouver, have set their own similar or even more ambitious targets. The writing is on the wall for the internal combustion engine.

To what extent will electrifying road vehicles help address climate change? Globally, transport (including land, sea, and air) accounts for 24 percent of carbon dioxide emissions from burning fossil fuels. Road vehicles (both freight and passenger vehicles) account for 72 percent of those emissions. Overall, then, emissions from road vehicles are responsible for 17 percent of the global total. Of those emissions, about one third are produced by heavy-duty, mostly diesel-powered vehicles (such as trucks and buses), and two thirds by light-duty, mostly gasoline-powered vehicles (such as cars and vans). So electrifying road vehicles, or reducing their use, could make a significant contribution toward mitigating climate change.

But even if all vehicles could magically be turned into electric ones overnight and thus stopped burning fossil fuels, there would still be the challenge of providing the electricity needed to charge them. Electricity generation, which still relies heavily on burning coal and natural gas in many countries, is the single largest contributor to carbon dioxide emissions, accounting for 40 percent of the total. Electric vehicles will only be truly green, zero-emission vehicles if they are charged using zero-carbon sources of electricity such as wind, solar, nuclear, or hydropower. (That said, electric vehicles are greener than those powered by fossil fuels even when charged with electricity from nonrenewable sources. That is because power stations burn fuel far more efficiently than car engines do and therefore produce fewer emissions per unit of energy produced. This remains true even when transmission losses are taken into account.)

Can existing power grids cope with a switch to electric vehicles? The problem is more one of timing than capacity. The additional capacity needed to charge electric vehicles is thought to be no more than 10 percent of current electricity demand. Electricity demand in many countries is falling, as a result of more energy-efficient lights, appliances, and buildings. So grid delivery capacity should not be a problem. The challenge will be to coordinate intermittent supplies of renewable energy, such as wind and solar, with demand from charging vehicles. Electric vehicles may be able to help, if they are adopted on a large scale, by acting as grid-connected storage batteries (so-called vehicle-to-grid models). And variable electricity tariffs could encourage people to charge their vehicles at off-peak times and spread the extra demand throughout the day.

Switching to electric cars would make a big dent in global emissions, then, though the challenges of switching large trucks, ships, and planes away from fossil fuels would remain. But it would not address other problems associated with cars, such as traffic congestion, road deaths, or the inherent inefficiency of using a one-ton vehicle to move one person to the shops. And just as the rise of the automobile led to worries about the sustainability and geopolitical consequences of relying on oil, the electric car raises similar concerns. The supply of lithium and cobalt needed to make batteries, and of the "rare earth" elements need to make electric motors, are already raising environmental and geopolitical questions. Lithium is quite abundant, but cobalt is not, and the main source of it is the Democratic Republic of the Congo, where around a quarter of production is done by hand, using shovels and torches. Conditions for miners are grim, and the industry is dogged by allegations of corruption and use of child labor. Once mined, cobalt is mostly refined in China, which also has the lion's share of global lithium-ion battery-production capacity and dominates production of rare-earth elements, too. Geopolitical tensions have already led to disputes between China and Western countries over the supply of computer chips and related manufacturing tools. So it is not hard to imagine similar disagreements breaking out over the minerals and parts needed to build electric vehicles. (This explains why Tesla has struck a deal with Glencore, a mining giant, to guarantee its supply of cobalt and also operates its own battery factories, both inside and outside China. It also explains why some companies are looking to deep-sea mining as an alternative source of cobalt.)

Moreover, history suggests that it would be naive to assume that switching from one form of propulsion to another would mean that things would otherwise continue as they were; that is not what happened when cars replaced horse-drawn vehicles. Some people say it's time to rethink not just the propulsion technology that powers cars, but the whole idea of car ownership. The same technology that enabled Elon Musk to succeed where Thomas Edison failed a century earlier—the lithium-ion battery—underpins the smartphone as well as the electric car. And thanks to the smartphone, the early twenty-first century has seen lots of experimentation around new modes of transport that explore the space between privately owned vehicles and public transport. As with electric cars, some of these ideas have deeper roots than you might think.

10

All Hail the Ride

There was a little man
Had a wooden leg; hadn't any money,
Didn't want to beg. So he took four spools,
And an old tin can, called it jitney
And the blamed thing ran.

—A RHYME ABOUT JITNEYS, 1915

THE DEEP HISTORY OF RIDE SHARING

On July 1, 1914, an enterprising motorist named L. P. Draper picked up a man waiting at a streetcar stop in Los Angeles, took him a short distance in his Ford Model T, and charged him a nickel for the ride. At the time, streetcars in most American cities had a flat fare of five cents, so Draper's passenger was simply paying the going rate. But Draper had invented a new model for urban transport: offering short rides in private cars for a flat fare. Draper had determined that this was entirely legal, provided he had a chauffeur's license, which was easily obtained from the city authorities. Once word got around, a few other drivers in Los Angeles began doing the same thing. Cars offering rides in this way came to be known as jitneys, after a slang term for the nickel. Some drivers picked up a few riders while driving to or from their places of work. But an economic slowdown, which had begun in 1913, made operating a jitney an attractive option for those who had lost their job but owned a car and wanted a quick way to make a little money. A jitney driver, often in a Ford Model T, would typically cruise the main street of a city, looking for three or four passengers to ferry to or from the central business district.

At first, the phenomenon was limited to Southern California. In Los Angeles, the police department had issued an average of six chauffeur's licenses a day for the first eleven months of 1914. But on December 2 it issued sixty of them. The *Electric Railway Journal*, the trade journal of the streetcar industry, noted "an enormous increase in the number of privately owned automobiles that solicit fares at 5-cents each on the streets of Los Angeles." The local streetcar system was said to be losing $600 a day in revenue, forcing it to lay off eighty-four workers and withdraw twenty-one streetcars on six lines. By this time the idea had spread to San Francisco, where at least six jitneys were operating on Market Street. The jitney craze spread rapidly as newspapers across America wrote about it, instantly prompting drivers and riders in new cities to try it. In Kansas City, for example, the number of jitneys went from zero to two hundred in two weeks, carrying twenty-five thousand passengers a day—and twice that number two weeks later. By the summer of 1915, sixty-two thousand jitneys were operating in cities across the United States. One contemporary report referred to "The Jitney Invasion." Because most cars were open bodied, jitneys were most popular in warm, dry parts of the country.

Jitneys offered convenience for riders, giving many people their first experience of car travel. With multiple fare-paying riders, they were much cheaper than cabs and offered an alternative to overcrowded streetcars for people who could not afford to buy a car of their own. Jitneys could be as much as twice as fast as streetcars because they did not make so many stops and, not running on rails, could maneuver around blockages. Some offered door-to-door service for regular customers on specific routes. Jitneys also provided service to popular destinations, such as shopping districts or sports venues, that were not served by streetcar routes.

A car being used as a jitney in New York, 1915.

And they continued to run late at night, when streetcars and conventional taxis had stopped operating. Streetcar companies in many cities were resented for prioritizing high returns for their investors over service to riders. So jitneys were hailed, like omnibuses before them, as emblems of freedom. They represented "a new page in the history of locomotion when convenience and economy came together," declared one jitney enthusiast in the *Independent* newspaper in May 1915. "Nothing can stop the jitney now, no corporation, no legislation. The era of extortion and of corruption is over."

That prediction proved to be wide of the mark. Streetcar companies lobbied furiously against jitneys. The *Electric Railway Journal* denounced them as "a menace," "a malignant growth," and "this Frankenstein of transportation." The journal argued that jitneys should be licensed in the same way as taxicabs and subject to the same insurance requirements, it and suggested that jitneys should have fixed routes and rigid schedules. Municipal governments took the side of streetcar companies. One reason was that streetcar companies were often required to maintain pavements and provide street lighting along their routes, and to pay city taxes, typically 1–2 percent of receipts. So if they were put out of business by jitneys, that would increase costs and reduce revenues for local governments. Second, streetcars' flat-rate pricing meant that short-distance riders were subsidizing long-distance ones, making it more affordable to live in streetcar suburbs farther from city centers. Municipal governments liked this model because it allowed cities to expand by making commuting cheaper, thus increasing the taxable population. Jitneys, which generally provided short rides of two miles or so, could not offer long-distance journeys without raising their prices. That would make commuter suburbs less attractive places to live and hamper cities' growth. Finally, jitneys caused an increase in traffic congestion, and in the number of road accidents. In Los Angeles in 1915, the number of accidents went up by 22 percent, and a quarter of all accidents involved jitneys. Jitney drivers were also accused of robbery, rape, and providing getaway vehicles for criminals. The lack of regulation of jitney drivers made such problems difficult to police.

Some of the suggestions for regulating jitneys, such as requiring them to have proper insurance, and outlawing the dangerous overloading of vehicles, made sense. But for the most part the rules were designed to protect streetcars by putting jitneys out of business. The jitney drivers had the backing of some newspapers. But they had little collective clout because the turnover of drivers was so rapid. A survey of jitneys in one city found that 1,308 jitneys operated on its streets in eighty-nine days. Of these, around one third operated for only one day, one third for less than fifteen days, and only one third for more than fifteen days. In short, few jitney drivers were doing it full-time; the appeal of jitney driving was that it was flexible, letting drivers work when they wanted to. But this meant that jitney drivers, as a group, were no match for the well-connected streetcar firms and their business and political supporters. As a result new regulations were imposed on jitneys in every city and state where they operated, inflating their costs and restricting their operation in various ways. In some states, a jitney license cost the equivalent of half a full-time jitneyman's earnings. Because such licenses had to be purchased annually, part-time jitney driving was effectively outlawed. Other rules prevented jitneys from driving on streets with streetcar rails, picking up passengers from streetcar stops, or passing streetcars or buses. In some cities, groups of jitney drivers mounted legal challenges. But by the end of 1915, anti-jitney rules had been introduced in 125 of the 175 cities where jitneys operated; the remaining cities followed suit the next year. Some jitney drivers switched to become taxi drivers, but most did not. The jitney experiment was over less than three years after it had begun.

Banning jitneys did nothing to alleviate traffic congestion because some riders responded by buying their own cars, rather than going to back to streetcars. Nor did suppressing jitneys prevent streetcars from being replaced by buses, which were cheaper to operate, in the 1920s. These buses, like the streetcars before them, were operated by monopolies and ran on fixed routes with rigid schedules (unlike jitneys, which adjusted their routes in line with passenger demand). The rigidity of urban bus systems made car ownership a more attractive option, for those who could afford it. Buses went into decline, requiring many municipalities to take over and subsidize their operation during the 1950s. The decline pushed people toward private car ownership, generally with low occupancy, which is a recipe for congestion. An analysis of the jitney craze published in 1972 by two American academics, Ross Eckert and George Hilton, concluded, "The policy of putting down the jitneys led directly to much of what is looked upon as most unsatisfactory in contemporary urban transport."

THE ROAD TO CIVIL RIGHTS

African Americans living in the American South were particularly affected by the demise of the jitneys. All-Black jitney routes, operated by Black drivers for Black riders, had briefly flourished in several Southern cities, providing a way for riders to avoid discriminatory Jim Crow rules on buses and trains. On buses, these rules required Black riders to sit at the back, to enter and leave the bus via the back door if white passengers were on board, and to give up their seats to white passengers for whom no seat was available. On trains, Black passengers were required to ride in separate carriages that were more crowded, less clean, and less comfortable than those provided for white passengers. Waiting rooms in bus and train stations were also segregated. As a result, the freedom and autonomy offered by the automobile was of particular value to African Americans. Cars enabled them to avoid the indignity of having to conform to the racist system of segregation, and to go where they wanted, when they wanted, with privacy and security.

Writing in the magazine of the National Association for the Advancement of Colored People in 1932, the civil rights activist (and editor of the magazine) W. E. B. Du Bois noted the growing number of Black car owners: "All over and everywhere the colored people are traveling in their automobiles." He himself often drove long distances to meetings and conferences. On one occasion he drove all the way from New York to Kentucky and was pleased at the way that car ownership was undermining businesses that supported segregation. "The only discrimination that we chanced upon was one at which we heartily laughed," he wrote. "A filling station on the Jacksonville–Daytona road had a sign 'For white trade only.' We passed it four times and saw no single car there."

As car ownership became more widespread among African Americans, a new genre of guidebooks emerged in the 1930s. The most famous of these was *The Negro Motorist Green Book*, by Victor Green, a Black travel writer, who took his inspiration from similar books that helped Jewish travelers avoid discrimination. These books listed hotels, restaurants, and resorts that welcomed Black customers, along with Black barbershops, beauty parlors, and shops across the country. "The White traveller for years has had no difficulty in getting accommodations, but for the Negro it has been very different," he wrote in the book's first edition, published in 1937. "He, before the advent of a Negro travel guide, had to depend on word of mouth, and many times accommodations were not available. Now things are different. The Negro traveller can rely on the 'Green Book' for all the information he wants." Because not many hotels were open to Black customers in the 1920s and 1930s, many of the accommodations listed were rooms in the private homes of Black families.

Such guides mostly avoided direct references to the racism and discrimination they aimed to enable their readers to avoid. "We have not sought
and shall not seek to create or solve problems of communities," declared
the introduction of The Travelers Guide: Hotels, Apartments, Rooms, Meals,
Garage Accommodations, etc. for Colored Travelers," published in 1931. "We
have found directly opposite conditions existing in adjoining cities of one
State regarding racial attitudes and relations . . . in many places transformation of sentiment is going on, forward or backward, the causes of
which are easily traceable." The guide's authors said their aims, given the
rise in car ownership among African Americans, were to enable Black
motorists to learn more about the country, to help college and club groups
stay in touch by meeting up, and to encourage leisure travel. Helping
travelers avoid harassment and discrimination, the main reason why the
book existed in the first place, was the last item on the list. Green and
his staff, similarly, avoided explicitly political language, only referring in
oblique terms to the reason the guide was necessary. "It has been our
idea to give the Negro traveler information that will keep him from
running into difficulties and embarrassments, and to make his trips more
enjoyable," stated the 1951 edition. Black readers knew exactly what this
meant, but keeping the politics implicit made it easier to attract advertisers (such as car manufacturers) and to promote and sell the book more
widely.

As well as avoiding discrimination, traveling by car was a way for Black
motorists to deny custom and funding to segregated transport systems.
But cars could also play a more direct role in the struggle for civil rights,
as African American drivers showed in 1956, when they used their cars to
support the Montgomery Bus Boycott. Planning for a citywide bus
boycott had been under way for several months by the time Rosa Parks
was arrested for refusing to give up her seat to a white passenger on a
Montgomery bus, on December 1, 1955. "I only knew that, as I was being
arrested, that it was the very last time that I would ever ride in humiliation
of this kind," she later recalled. The following Sunday, plans for a one-day
boycott, to take place the following day, were made public through
announcements at Black churches in the area, and the distribution of
flyers. The boycott coincided with Parks's appearance in court for refusing

to give up her seat. "We are, therefore, asking every Negro to stay off the buses Monday in protest of the arrest and trial," read the flyer announcing the boycott.

> Don't ride the buses to work, to town, to school, or anywhere on Monday. You can afford to stay out of school for one day if you have no other way to go except by bus. You can also afford to stay out of town for one day. If you work, take a cab, or walk. But please, children and grown-ups, don't ride the bus at all on Monday. Please stay off all buses Monday.

The organizers of the boycott had a plan to help those who would be forced to walk. Black taxi drivers agreed to carry passengers on the day of the boycott for ten cents, the same price as a bus fare. In addition, the organizers arranged a volunteer car-pool system, with vehicles borrowed from or driven by Black car owners. These drove up and down the bus routes, carrying those least able to walk to their destination for no charge. The boycott was widely observed, and given that 75 percent of bus riders in Montgomery were Black, the action had an unmistakable effect, as near-empty buses plied the streets. The organizers decided to continue the boycott and established a new body, the Montgomery Improvement Association (MIA), to oversee it. Martin Luther King Jr., a young local minister, was elected as its leader.

In the weeks that followed, city officials issued an order forbidding licensed taxi drivers from carrying passengers for any less than forty-five cents. The MIA responded by establishing its own fleet of vehicles, using funds sent in by supporters across the United States. It bought a station wagon for each Black church in Montgomery, to be used to transport members of its congregation to and from work. These cars, registered as the property of each church, came to be known as "rolling churches." They, and other cars provided by volunteers, picked up riders from eighty-six designated dispatch stations, including Black churches, funeral parlors, and shops, with one departure every ten minutes from five A.M. to ten A.M. The cars, which numbered more than three hundred, ran until eight P.M. every day. Riders made donations to the MIA, which could then reimburse drivers for fuel and other expenses. The MIA also raised money through bake sales and food sales. White customers who bought sandwiches, cakes, and pies had no idea that they were helping fund the boycott. When white-owned insurance companies withdrew coverage for the vehicles, the MIA arranged to have them insured directly by Lloyd's of London instead.

As revenues for the bus system collapsed and officials were forced to cut routes and lay off drivers, opponents of the boycott tried to shut down the car-pool system by intimidating its drivers. Police officers would pull them over and claim they had committed traffic offenses. King himself was arrested on January 26, 1956, after picking up three passengers in his own car from an MIA station; the police claimed he had been driving at 30 mph in a 25 mph zone. He was one of more than one hundred car-pool drivers charged with traffic offenses that week. The homes of MIA leaders, including King's, were firebombed. But still the boycott continued. The following month King was one of eighty-nine participants, twenty-four of them ministers, to be indicted under a 1921 anti-boycott law. The first to be brought to trial, he was fined $500 and spent two weeks in jail. By this time, the MIA had launched a federal lawsuit against bus segregation.

Finally, on November 5, 1956, eleven months after the boycott had started, the City of Montgomery found a way to shut down the car-pool system: a judge ruled that it was operating without a legal permit. But that same day the Supreme Court issued its ruling on the MIA's federal lawsuit, declaring bus segregation in Alabama to be unconstitutional. The bus boycott ended in victory. A month later buses in Montgomery were once again carrying Black passengers, who could now sit wherever they liked. The boycott brought King to national prominence, and the same tactic was adopted in other cities. Noting the subsequent significance of the automobile in supporting civil rights campaigns, a writer in the *Pittsburgh Courier* declared, "The key to the movement was a key to an automobile."

FROM JITNEYS TO UBER

In the early twenty-first century, the idea of offering rides to strangers in private cars has reemerged in a new guise: through ride-sharing or ride-hailing apps. The new model had its origins in America, before being widely copied elsewhere. It would not have been possible without smartphones, mobile internet access, and satellite-positioning systems that can pinpoint the positions of both riders and drivers. But it also draws on the earlier traditions of the jitney and of the shared minivan taxis found in many parts of the world. In Eastern European countries a shared taxi is known as a *marshrutka*; in Turkey, as a *dolmus*; in Trinidad and Tobago, as a maxi taxi; in West Africa, as a *kia kia*, which means "quick quick"; in Thailand, as a *songthaew*; and in the Philippines, as a jeepney, a combination of *jeep* and *jitney*. Such shared taxis generally operate on particular routes, but not on a fixed schedule, waiting until they have enough passengers before setting out.

In 2008 two American entrepreneurs, Logan Green and John Zimmer, started an intercity carpooling service for students. While studying at the University of California, Santa Barbara, Green had used car-pool rides, arranged via online message boards, to visit his girlfriend in Los Angeles. Zimmer had also used carpooling services, while studying at Cornell University, to travel to and from his home in upstate New York. Both men were interested in how the internet could make carpooling more efficient and more widespread. After being introduced by a mutual friend, they hit on the idea of using Facebook, which was quickly emerging as America's dominant online social network, to connect riders and drivers and allow them to find out more about each other before a ride. They hoped this would increase trust and encourage greater usage of carpooling for intercity trips. They called their new company Zimride—not a play on Zimmer's surname, but a reference to the shared taxis that Green had ridden in during a trip to Zimbabwe in 2005. By 2012, Zimride had thousands of users at 150 participating universities and companies. This success prompted Green and Zimmer to wonder if the pairing up of drivers and riders could be extended from long, intercity journeys to shorter ones within cities.

Meanwhile another start-up, called Uber, had launched a car-hailing service in San Francisco in 2011. Its founders, Garrett Camp and Travis Kalanick, were technology entrepreneurs who saw the potential of the smartphone to link drivers with riders. To begin with, Uber's smartphone app only allowed users to hail black town cars, and rides were more expensive than in a taxi. But the convenience of hailing a ride with a few taps on a smartphone, coupled with the difficulty of finding an ordinary taxi in San Francisco, meant some people were happy to pay extra. In 2013, Uber expanded its service to allow drivers to offer rides in ordinary cars through the app. Zimride's founders had by this time hit upon the same idea and launched their own ride-hailing service, also accessed via a smartphone app, called Lyft. Starting in 2014, both companies introduced the option of shared trips, for riders willing to trade convenience for cost.

Uber's subsequent expansion into other countries around the world pitted it against local rivals using the same model: Ola in India, Didi Chuxing in China (itself the product of a merger between two Uber clones), Careem in the Middle East, and Grab in Southeast Asia. The ride-hailing market became fiercely competitive, prompting Uber to team up with local rivals in many parts of the world to avoid expensive price wars. It ended up merging its regional operations with those of Didi Chuxing in China, Grab in Southeast Asia, and Careem in the Middle East.

The ride-hailing model pioneered by Uber has proved hugely popular—and hugely controversial. As with jitneys a century earlier, ride-hailing firms have faced opposition from taxi drivers, public-transport firms, and city authorities who say the firms fail to comply with existing regulations, do not vet drivers properly, and increase traffic congestion. As ride-hailing firms have expanded into new cities and raced to attract customers, they have fought bitter price wars, undercutting existing taxi providers and drawing riders away from public-transport systems. Ride-hailing platforms also insist that drivers are contractors, not employees, and therefore are not subject to rules on minimum wages, holiday pay, unemployment insurance, and so forth. Uber in particular has fought a series of legal battles with regulators around the world over the employment status of its workers, the level of background checks on drivers, and other issues. In many cases ride-hailing firms end up being granted licenses to operate in a particular city, but regulators can threaten to withdraw the license if certain conditions are not met.

Ride-hailing firms say their model offers benefits to both drivers and passengers. Once enrolled with a ride-hailing platform, drivers can work when they want to, supplementing their income when needed. Riders benefit from the convenience of smartphone-based hailing, competitive pricing compared with taxis, and the option of even cheaper rides if they share a vehicle with other passengers. There may be broader societal benefits, too: the availability of ride-hailing in a city appears to reduce the level of drunk driving (though it may increase the amount of heavy drinking). Ride hailing can also help with "transit deserts"—urban areas where large numbers of people (typically the poor or elderly) depend on public transport lacking in sufficient capacity or adequate service. Several American cities have collaborated with ride-hailing firms in experimental plans to carry passengers over the "last mile" between their homes and nearby transit hubs. But perhaps most important, ride-hailing offers some people a viable alternative to the hassle and expense of car ownership. "Owning a car means monthly car payments, searching for parking, buying fuel, and dealing with repairs," wrote Zimmer, now the president of Lyft, in a blog post in 2016. He has often said that his company's goal is "a world built around people, not cars," by reducing car ownership and car dependency, and allowing the space and resources allocated to cars to be used for other things, such as parks, playgrounds, or housing.

Many of today's arguments over ride hailing are similar to those that raged over jitneys a century ago. Once again, entrepreneurs are trying to define a new, more responsive form of transport in between private car ownership, which is expensive but flexible, and public transport systems, which are cheaper for riders, but operate on fixed routes and schedules. Once again, opponents claim—with much justification—that corners are being cut on insurance, safety, and tax rules. But there is an important difference. The jitney drivers were unable to speak with a collective voice and stood little chance against regulators, streetcar trusts, and taxi companies. The ride-hailing platforms, by contrast, have deep pockets and have become skilled lobbyists. They will not always get their way, nor should they. But their emergence means a much-better prospect now than a century ago of a new, more flexible transport service that provides bene-fits for drivers, riders, and cities alike.

ON YOUR BIKE (AND SCOOTER)

Just as the smartphone has rebooted the old idea of the jitney, it has also put a new spin on another mode of transport: the bicycle. In recent years it has boosted the popularity of bike sharing—the short-term rental of bicycles for short trips in urban areas—by resolving many of the prob-lems that had prevented bike sharing from working well.

The first bike-sharing program, launched in Amsterdam in 1965, was called Witte Fietsen, which is Dutch for "white bikes." Luud Schimmelpennink, a designer and political activist, collected a few dozen bicycles, painted them white, and left them around the city, unlocked, so that anyone could use them and then leave them for the next rider. But the bicycles were soon stolen, thrown into canals, damaged, or confis-cated by the police, so the experiment was short-lived. The idea lay dormant until the 1990s, when a second wave of bike sharing began in Denmark. Bikes were locked into storage racks and could be released by inserting a coin. Slotting the bike into another storage rack at the end of a journey released another coin, repaying the small deposit. The bicycles had a distinctive design, including advertising panels intended to subsi-dize the cost of the service and discourage theft. But riders were anon-ymous, and many of the bikes ended up being stolen or vandalized anyway.

The next move came from France, where a program launched in the city of Rennes in 1998 relied on smart cards, rather than coins, to release bikes from storage racks, lock them up again after use, and charge for rides. Because users had to register for a smart card and were personally liable for bicycles unlocked using their card, theft plummeted. The Rennes program led to a larger one in Lyon—and then, in 2007, to an even larger one in Paris. Called Vélib', a combination of the French words for "bicycle" and "freedom," it offered 10,000 bicycles and 750 docking stations at launch and soon doubled in size. Within five years Vélib' had more than 224,000 users who had collectively made over 130 million trips. Vélib' inspired similar programs around the world: globally, the number of cities with bike-sharing systems went from around seventy when it launched to more than seven hundred in 2013.

Since then, smartphones have boosted the prospects of bike-sharing even further, in two ways. Smartphone apps mean there is no need to sign up for a smart card to use bike sharing. And incorporating a smartphone with satellite-positioning capability into each bicycle means its position can be tracked at all times. That opened the way to "dockless" bike-sharing, a model popularized by two Chinese start-ups, Ofo and Mobike. (Mobike was cofounded by Wang Xiaofeng, who was the general manager of Uber's Shanghai office at the time.) Dockless bikes are unlocked by scanning a bar code on the frame using an app. Riders are then charged according to the distance and duration of their ride and lock the bicycle up again at their destination to await the next rider. Satellite positioning makes it easy for riders to see if a bike is nearby.

An explosion of more than thirty dockless bike-sharing programs in China in 2017 led to unsightly piles of bicycles on street corners and under trees in major cities. As rival operators fought for market share, they offered heavily subsidized or even free rides for several months. (Tracking the bikes' locations lets operators offer location-specific advertising, such as a discount at a nearby coffee shop, to riders at the start or end of each journey.) The market has since settled down, with many operators going out of business. Meanwhile, the dockless model has quickly spread around the world because the lack of docking infrastructure means no planning permission is needed to launch a new service. But authorities in many cities have confiscated bikes that are improperly parked and imposed restrictions on the operators of dockless programs. As with the early days of ride hailing in private cars, dockless bike sharing has gone from a Wild West free-for-all, in which rival start-ups compete to sign up customers, to a steadily more regulated environment. The latest twist on bike sharing is the option to rent electric bikes, which use a motor to assist the rider and make longer journeys less strenuous.

The dockless bike-sharing model, combined with improvements in batteries and electric propulsion, has also led to a flowering of start-ups offering electric scooters, or e-scooters, for short trips. This model was pioneered by Bird and Lime, two American start-ups, in 2017. Uber and

Lyft launched their own scooter-sharing services the following year. Since then the model has spread around the world, though not as quickly as dockless bike sharing because laws in some cities do not allow e-scooters. As with dockless bicycles, e-scooters have raised concerns about clutter on pavements, as well as the safety of riders and pedestrians. To address the problem of clutter, many cities have adopted a model pioneered by San Francisco, which limits the number of scooter-sharing firms that are licensed to operate in the city, and the number of vehicles they can provide. Competing firms bid for licenses when they become available, allowing local authorities to set the rules around e-scooters. Among other things, the maximum speed of e-scooters is usually limited to 8–10 mph. That may not sound like much, but it is comparable to the average speed of traffic in many cities, and taking an e-scooter, when one is available, is often quicker.

One complication with dockless e-bikes and e-scooters is that they need to be recharged regularly, but obviously cannot rely on docking stations to top up their batteries. Instead, operators of such sharing systems offer payments to people who go out into the city, collect vehicles in need of recharging, charge them up at home, and then return them to the streets. Bonuses are offered for collecting vehicles from particularly out-of-the-way locations, and coordination is via an app that shows the locations of vehicles in need of charging. In Paris people can commonly be seen riding an e-scooter with two or three other e-scooters stacked on top of it, as they carry them off to be recharged. This model also allows vehicles to be redistributed across a city each morning so that supply can be matched with demand. And satellite positioning allows faulty bikes, e-bikes, and e-scooters to be located and picked up for maintenance when necessary.

Collectively, these new modes of transport, based on small vehicles that can be accessed when needed using smartphone apps, have come to be known as micromobility, a term coined by Horace Dediu, a technology analyst, in 2017. He and other advocates of micromobility point to its environmental benefits compared with using cars—including electric cars. In America, China, and the European Union, around 60 percent of car journeys cover less than five miles. Why use a vehicle that weighs one or two tons to carry one person on a short trip? For many car journeys micromobility can offer an attractive alternative. McKinsey, a consultancy, estimates that the global micromobility market will be worth $300 billion to $500 billion by 2030.

Of course, the weather may be unsuitable, or the trip may be being made by several people, or with heavy or bulky items. And what if you need a car for a day trip, or a weekend? For such cases, the smartphone has made possible a new twist on car rental. Car-sharing services such as Zipcar let drivers rent a car by the minute, hour, or day. A smartphone app shows cars available nearby, often parked in specially designated bays. Users unlock the vehicle using their phone, use the car for as long as needed, return it to another bay, and are billed accordingly. For urbanites who rarely use cars, such services mean they no longer need to own one, but still have access to one when needed.

The combination of new technology and new business models is providing an ever-expanding range of transport options. Collectively, ride hailing, micromobility, and on-demand car rental offer new approaches to transport that provide the convenience of a private car without the need to own one, for a growing fraction of journeys. Dediu calls this "unbundling the car," as cheaper, quicker, cleaner, and more convenient alternatives slowly chip away at the rationale for mass car ownership. This process has begun, but how far will it go? And while electric propulsion makes vehicles cleaner and smartphone technology opens up new modes of transport, another potential breakthrough is waiting in the wings: the possibility that cars will soon be able to drive themselves.

11

From Horseless to Driverless

One day your car may speed along an electric super-highway, its speed and steering automatically controlled by electronic devices embedded in the road. Travel will be more enjoyable. Highways will be made safe—by electricity! No traffic jams . . . no collisions . . . no driver fatigue.

—Advertisement for America's Electric Light and
Power Companies, *Saturday Evening Post*, 1957

THE DRIVERLESS RACE BEGINS

The idea of cars that drive themselves has been around for decades. The Futurama exhibit of 1939, with its grand, fast-flowing highways, depicted a vision of 1960 in which cars drove themselves on "magic motorways." Futurama's designer, Norman Bel Geddes, thought this would have many benefits. "Human nature itself, unaided, does not make for efficient driving," he argued. "Human beings, even when at the wheel, are prone to talk, wave to their friends, make love, day dream, listen to the radio, stare at striking billboards, light cigarettes, take chances." He proposed that cars be controlled like trains, with their speed and steering handled automatically, under the oversight of operators in towers, akin to locomotive engineers. "It would be impossible for a drunk or sleeping motorist to leave the road," noted *Business Week* with approval. "Drivers could bowl along with their hands off the wheel, free to enjoy the scenery or hug their girls." With self-driving cars there would be no traffic and no accidents—claims that are once again being made by proponents of autonomous vehicles today. Are they right? We may soon find out because driverless cars are no longer the figment of a designer's imagination.

Fittingly, just as the modern automotive era began with the Paris–Rouen race of 1894, recent efforts to build autonomous cars also began with an unusual competition. Known as the Grand Challenge, it was organized by DARPA, America's main military-research agency, and took place in March 2004 in the Mojave Desert. Where *Le Petit Journal*, the sponsor of the Paris–Rouen race, wanted to accelerate the development of horseless vehicles, DARPA hoped to foster the emergence of driverless ones. Announcing the contest in January 2003, it called for "pioneers in a wide range of fields to become part of Grand Challenge teams, including advertisers and corporate sponsors, artificial intelligence developers, auto manufacturers and suppliers, computer programmers, futurists, inventors, motor sports enthusiasts, movie producers, off-road racers, remote-sensing developers, roboticists, science fiction writers, technology companies, universities, video game publishers, and other trailblazers." The first vehicle to complete an off-road course within a specified time would win a $1 million prize.

DARPA wanted autonomous vehicles for use in military convoys in Iraq and Afghanistan, where roadside bombs were the largest cause of American casualties. In experiments with self-driving cars, dating back to the 1950s, wires or magnets had been placed in the road for guidance (Bel Geddes envisaged a similar approach). But DARPA wanted vehicles that could, like human-driven ones, work anywhere, without the need for any special infrastructure. It hoped that by offering a prize it would encourage innovators from a wide range of backgrounds, rather than just the usual military suppliers, to find ways to build the vehicles. Sure enough, more than one hundred teams—some based at leading universities, engineering companies, robotics firms, and start-ups, and others

ELECTRICITY MAY BE THE DRIVER. One day your car may speed along an electric super-highway, its speed and steering automatically controlled by electronic devices embedded in the road. Travel will be more enjoyable. Highways will be made safe—by electricity! No traffic jams . . . no collisions . . . no driver fatigue.

A 1957 advertisement for America's Electric Light and Power Companies depicts
a driverless car. "One day your car may speed along an electric super-highway,
its speed and steering automatically controlled by electronic devices embedded in the road.
Travel will be more enjoyable. Highways will be made safe—by electricity!
No traffic jams . . . no collisions . . . no driver fatigue."

made up of enthusiasts tinkering in their garages—applied to take part in the contest. After a rigorous selection, vehicles from twenty-one teams assembled for five days of qualifying tests. The vehicles were required to navigate a mile-long obstacle course on a closed racetrack, to ensure they could avoid hazards and follow a predetermined route without human assistance. Fifteen vehicles made it through to the race itself, which was held on March 13, 2004. Just as in Paris in July 1894, the lineup of vehicles at the starting line was a motley assortment of very different-looking machines.

Sandstorm, built by Red Team, from Carnegie Mellon University, was a bright red Humvee, its upper half sheared off and replaced by a metal frame supporting a collection of cameras and sensors. Other vehicles were lightly modified but still recognizable dune buggies, pickup trucks, or sport utility vehicles, bedecked with various gadgets to sense their surroundings. These vehicles faced the challenge of navigating a 142-mile course on an unsurfaced desert road, running from Barstow, California, to Primm, Nevada, and closed to all other traffic. Vehicles were scheduled to depart every few minutes, starting at six thirty A.M. Each team was provided with a set of two thousand waypoints that specified the route. But having a map is not the same as being able to drive. Completing the course would require much more than simply using the GPS to drive from one waypoint to the next, because GPS is only accurate to within a few feet, making it insufficient on its own to guide autonomous vehicles. Hence the need for cameras, radar systems, laser scanners, and other sensors to identify the edges of the road and avoid bushes, rocks, and any other obstacles. Each vehicle would be followed by a control vehicle occupied by DARPA officials, equipped with an emergency "e-stop" button that could halt the vehicle remotely. Any vehicle that strayed off the route would be disqualified.

The race did not start well. Some vehicles withdrew with mechanical problems or because they behaved strangely in the starting area, where one immediately drove into a wall, and another had to be remotely stopped when it veered away from the starting line toward the spectator grandstand. Even vehicles that made it onto the course soon ran into problems, including running off the road, flipping over, getting stuck on rocks, being unable to climb hills, or becoming tangled in wire marking the edge of the course. One vehicle came to a halt because its vision system was confused by its own shadow. Only six vehicles traveled more than one mile along the course, and only four traveled more than five miles. The vehicle that did best was Red Team's Sandstorm, which traveled 7.4 miles before going off course and getting caught on an embankment. As the vehicle tried to free itself, its front wheels caught fire, an inglorious end to a race that seemed only to have demonstrated the difficulty of building a self-driving vehicle. Television news reports showed montages of the various vehicles going wrong. *Popular Science* called it "DARPA's debacle in the desert." It seemed that the agency had set the bar too high, and the technology was simply not up to the job. But DARPA was undaunted. It announced a follow-up challenge, to be held the following year.

This time around 195 teams entered, again from a wide range of backgrounds. Of these, 43 teams were invited to take part in a qualifying round at a racetrack, and 23 made it through to the main event, which was held on October 8. As in 2004, the vehicles traversed an unpaved desert road, a 132-mile loop that began and ended in Primm, Nevada. Many of the teams from 2004 took part in 2005, returning with upgraded versions of their vehicles. They were joined by some newcomers, including teams from Cornell, Princeton, and Stanford universities, and a team backed by Gray, an insurance company. Sebastian Thrun, a former colleague of Red Whittaker's at Carnegie Mellon, led the Stanford team. Its vehicle, Stanley, was based on a blue Volkswagen SUV with a cluster of laser scanners mounted on its roof.

Given the contestants' poor showing in 2004, DARPA might have been forgiven for making the 2005 course a little easier to navigate. Instead, it made it harder. The road was narrower and had more curves. It included three narrow tunnels where vehicles would lose their GPS signal, and the last section of the route ran through Beer Bottle Pass, a winding mountain road with sheer drop-offs. The teams were given the GPS coordinates of waypoints along the route just two hours before the start, to ensure they could not preprogram their vehicles with information about the course.

The results of this second race, coming so soon after the debacle of the first challenge, were astonishing. Of the twenty-three participants in the competition, five completed the entire 132-mile course, and all but one beat the 7.4-mile record from the previous year. Stanley, built by the team from Stanford, came first; Carnegie Mellon's Sandstorm finished second. In just eighteen months, autonomous driving had gone from impossible to feasible. A third DARPA contest two years later, in

November 2007, set the bar higher still. It required vehicles to complete tasks in a simulated urban environment, coping with road signs, traffic signals, and other vehicles. Six teams completed this far more complex challenge, with the laurels going to Carnegie Mellon. Stanford came second.

Just like the early road races of the 1890s, the DARPA contests provided a public demonstration of a new technology and offered a showcase for daring engineers. And like the French races, they brought together a group of people who would go on to define a new field built around a new technology. As Thrun later told *Wired* magazine, "None of what is happening in self-driving today would have happened without the original challenge—it created a new community."

Encouraged by this rapid progress, Google established a self-driving car program in 2009, led by Thrun, who hired people he had met during the DARPA challenges, including Chris Urmson (a member of the rival Carnegie Mellon team) and Anthony Levandowski (who had built a self-driving motorcycle). "There was an incredible sense of camaraderie, and that community fostered the folks who are leading a lot of the technology today," Urmson told *Wired*. Since then they and other participants in the various DARPA contests have gone on to work on autonomous-vehicle technology at Google, Uber, Tesla, and a host of start-ups, from Aurora to Zoox. Prototype self-driving cars first took to America's public roads in 2012; they have since traveled millions of miles. Just as the Paris–Rouen race provided a glimpse of the future of horseless carriages, the DARPA challenges did the same for driverless cars.

But predictions that self-driving "robotaxis" would be ubiquitous by 2020 proved overly optimistic. Autonomous vehicles (AVs), as self-driving cars are known in the industry, can do extraordinary things, such as navigating busy downtown streets and handling complex junctions with multiple traffic lights. But they seem to be stuck in perpetual testing, never quite being considered safe or reliable enough to be allowed out onto the roads without the supervision of one or two on-board safety drivers. An AV that can handle 90 percent of real-world situations safely is an impressive piece of engineering, but of little practical use. Building one that can handle that final 10 percent has turned out to be far more difficult than expected.

HOW AUTONOMOUS CARS WORK

Building a fully autonomous car can be broken down into three separate problems: perception (figuring out what is going on in the world), prediction (determining what will happen next), and driving policy (steering left or right, accelerating or braking). The last part, driving policy, is considered relatively simple. Perception and prediction pose the biggest challenges.

Autonomous cars perceive the world using a combination of sensors including cameras, radar, and lidar—a radar-like technique that uses invisible pulses of light, rather than radio waves, to create a high-resolution 3D map of the surroundings. (The small domes or cylinders seen on top of self-driving cars are spinning lidar scanners.) Each of these sensors has its pros and cons. Cameras are cheap and can see road markings, but cannot measure distance reliably; radar can measure distance and velocity, but cannot see in fine detail; lidar provides fine detail but is expensive and gets confused by snow. Most people working on autonomous vehicles believe that using a combination of sensors is the best way to ensure safety and reliability. Tesla is a notable exception: it thinks cameras and radar are enough, and that costly lidar is not needed. High-end lidar systems cost tens of thousands of dollars, though new solid-state designs being devised by start-ups promise to reduce the price to a few hundred dollars.

Having gathered and combined the data from its sensors, the car needs to work out what everything is. In particular, it must identify other vehicles, pedestrians, cyclists, road markings, traffic lights, road signs, and so forth. Humans find this easy, and machines used to find it difficult. But machine vision has in recent years improved enormously, thanks to the use of deep learning, an artificial-intelligence technique in which systems learn to perform particular tasks by analyzing thousands of labeled examples. For autonomous cars, this means getting hold of thousands of images of street scenes, with each element carefully labeled, so that a perception system can be trained to recognize them. The simplest way to obtain such images is to pay people to label

How an autonomous vehicle sees the world. Combined inputs from sensors and cameras are analyzed to identify and label nearby vehicles, pedestrians, and landmarks (such as traffic lights).

street scenes manually, by drawing boxes around cars, pedestrians, and so on. (Tesla employs several hundred expert labelers, according to Elon Musk; other companies farm the job out.) The hardest things for a perception system to identify are rarely seen items such as debris on the road, or plastic bags blowing across a highway. According to Sebastian Thrun, in the early days of Google's AV project, its perception system misidentified a plastic bag as a flying child. Puddles on the road also caused problems, too. AVs have also been confused by bicycles mounted on racks on the backs of cars and by a man dressed in a chicken suit to promote a restaurant (who should have been classified as a pedestrian, but was not).

Once a vehicle has identified everything around it, it faces the challenge of predicting what will happen in the next few seconds—and deciding how to respond. Will nearby people and vehicles continue moving on their current trajectories? Road signs, traffic lights, brake lights, and turn signals also provide information about how the situation is likely to evolve.

But human drivers are used to dealing with a lot of unusual exceptions to the normal flow of traffic, such as roadworks, broken-down vehicles, delivery trucks, emergency vehicles, fallen trees, or bad weather. Local exceptions and driving customs, such as the "Pittsburgh left" (where the first left-turning vehicle at a traffic light is allowed to take precedence over oncoming traffic), further complicate matters. Human drivers communicate by flashing their lights and using other nonverbal cues. Edging forward at a four-way stop signals to others that you intend to proceed; when changing lanes on a highway, you must take into account how much other drivers will have to speed up or slow down in response, and whether that is reasonable. Getting AVs to do these things is hard.

Driving relies a lot on common sense, and an understanding of how the world works (children cannot fly, for example). Humans take these things for granted, but computers do not. One way to make perception and prediction easier, while the technology is still being developed, is to restrict the testing of AVs to urban areas that have been mapped in detail and have good weather, little traffic, and simple road layouts. This explains why Phoenix, Arizona, with its sunshine and regular grid system, is a popular place to test AVs—as are business parks, university campuses, and retirement communities. Pittsburgh is regarded as a step up in difficulty because of its harsher weather; both Ford and Uber have tested AVs in the city (which is also home to Carnegie Mellon University, a source of AV expertise). Cruise, an AV start-up, now mostly owned by GM, has demonstrated some impressive autonomous driving on the complex streets of downtown San Francisco, as has Zoox, another start-up. The city's steep hills pose an extra challenge to AVs' vision systems because when descending a steep hill, the AV may misinterpret the road in front of it as an impassable obstacle. Other firms favor Boston as a test location, where both the weather and the local driving style are considered particularly challenging.

HOW AUTONOMOUS CARS GO WRONG

When an AV gets confused and does not know how to respond or is about to make the wrong decision, the safety driver in the driving seat takes over, which automatically switches off the autonomous-driving system. This is known as a disengagement, and the number of disengagements per thousand miles traveled provides a crude measure of how the companies developing AVs are progressing. Disengagements can be seen not as failures but as learning experiences that help AV systems improve. Analyzing data from the lead-up to a disengagement can reveal what the car got wrong. It is then possible to simulate how it should have responded with various modifications to its software. After being tested in simulation, the improved software is then rolled out in real vehicles. This process has been going on since 2012, when Google's self-driving car unit—since renamed Waymo—was granted a license to begin testing in Nevada. The first journey took place on May 1 that year, with Grand Challenge veterans Chris Urmson and Anthony Levandowski in the front seats of a modified Toyota Prius, and two state officials in the back. The car passed its self-driving test, the world's first, despite two disengagements, one of which happened when the vehicle was confused by construction work on the road and halted.

Disengagements are to be welcomed if they occur when the car realizes that it cannot handle the situation. AVs that misunderstand their surroundings and then fail to disengage can be deadly. That happened on March 18, 2018, when an Uber AV, being tested in Tempe, Arizona, struck and killed a pedestrian, Elaine Herzberg, as she wheeled her bicycle across a four-lane road. Although it was dark, the car's radar and lidar detected her six seconds before the crash. But the perception system got confused: it classified her as an unknown object, then as a vehicle, and finally as a bicycle, whose path it could not predict. Just 1.3 seconds before impact, the self-driving system realized that emergency braking was needed. But the car's built-in emergency braking system had been disabled, to prevent conflict with the self-driving system: confused AVs have in the past been rear-ended (by human drivers) after slowing suddenly. Instead, a human safety driver in the vehicle was expected to brake when required. But the safety driver, who was watching a video on a smartphone, failed to brake in time. Herzberg became the first pedestrian to be killed by an autonomous vehicle.

Four people have also died while traveling in Tesla cars under the control of the company's Autopilot software. This is not a full self-driving system because it can only be used for highway driving and is meant to be used under the supervision of the driver, who can resume control at any time. As well as maintaining a safe distance from the car in front, Autopilot steers the car to keep it in the center of its lane and can execute lane changes if the driver taps the indicator (turn-signal) stalk. It is an advanced form of cruise control. But drivers who use it regularly may come to believe that it is more capable than it really is and may not pay sufficient attention. The four fatal crashes, one in China and three in America, occurred when Autopilot's vision system failed to identify an obstacle in the vehicle's path: either a stationary truck, a highway divider, or, in two cases, a semitruck with a trailer that was crossing the roadway. In the two cases involving a semitruck, the roof of the Tesla was sheared off as it passed underneath the trailer. The vision system appears to have mistaken the white side of the trailer for the sky.

Tesla claims that when used properly, Autopilot increases safety, and that its cars have logged more than 1 billion miles with Autopilot engaged. With its system deployed in thousands of its cars, Tesla can refine its technology by gathering data in real-world situations, and asking its fleet to collect examples of specific things (such as Stop signs partly hidden by trees). Tesla hopes, in this way, to make steady progress from Autopilot, a semiautonomous system, to full autonomy. But many engineers working on self-driving cars believe that semiautonomous systems are inherently dangerous because of the risk that drivers will come to trust them too much and fail to supervise them. Opponents of semiautonomy, including John Krafcik, the chief executive of Waymo, believe that it is safer to focus on building fully autonomous vehicles where passengers are never required to intervene, as his firm is doing. But such vehicles need to be able to handle absolutely any situation without human intervention, and that is a tall order. By 2020 Waymo's fleet of autonomous cars had driven more than 20 million miles on public roads in twenty-five cities, and billions more miles in simulation. The company says its vehicles drove 1.45 million miles in California in 2019, with a disengagement rate of 0.076 per 1,000 miles (equivalent to one disengagement every thirteen thousand miles).

As impressive as that is, fully autonomous vehicles seem to be stuck in limbo. The number of miles driven by prototypes continues to increase, and the frequency of disengagements continues to decline, but such vehicles do not seem to be getting any closer to actual deployment. In 2018 Waymo launched a ride-hailing service for around fifteen hundred selected customers in the Phoenix area using autonomous minivans with safety drivers on board. In late 2019 it began to operate some minivans without safety drivers on some routes. (If a vehicle gets confused, it can stop and ask a remote operator how to handle the situation.) This was the first truly driverless robotaxi service, but is still only available to a small number of customers in a small area and falls short of Waymo's goal of having tens of thousands of driverless robotaxis on the road by 2020. Other firms' robotaxi plans have also been delayed. GM said its self-driving unit, Cruise, would launch a driverless robotaxi service by the end of 2019, but delayed it to 2021. Elon Musk has talked about a Tesla robotaxi service since 2016 and said in 2019 that it would launch in 2020, but failed to meet that deadline. Several AV start-ups provide rides in autonomous vehicles on university campuses, in retirement communities, and in business parks, invariably with human supervisors on board. But full autonomy on public roads, with no safety driver, still seems a distant dream. Perhaps the industry will steadily inch its way toward fully driverless vehicles. But without some kind of breakthrough, self-driving cars are still not quite safe enough to be let loose on public roads without supervision.

THE DREAM OF THE DRIVERLESS CAR

Proponents of driverless cars have not given up on the dream. They argue that if AVs could be deployed in large numbers, they would offer enormous benefits. Mary Barra, the chief executive of General Motors, has declared that her company's goal "is a future with zero crashes, zero emissions, and zero congestion" made possible by "autonomous, electric shared and connected vehicles." In an interview in 2019, she highlighted the "enormous opportunity to eliminate the human error that causes more than ninety percent of all fatalities in the U.S." As has been pointed out ever since the days of Futurama, AVs would potentially be much safer than fallible human drivers. Globally, around 1.25 million people die on the roads each year, according to the World Health Organization; road deaths are the leading cause of death among people aged fifteen to twenty-nine. Another 20 million to 50 million people are injured. Cars have become much less deadly in recent decades due to safety features such as seat belts and airbags, but road deaths in America have risen since 2014, seemingly as a result of distraction by smartphones. AVs have superhuman, 360-degree vision, theoretically enabling them to anticipate dangers and detect hazards human drivers cannot. Self-driving cars would let riders text, drink, or sleep without endangering anyone. If AVs become wide-spread, future generations may look back on the era of human-piloted vehicles, and the associated death toll, in astonishment. Even with modern safety features, about 700,000 Americans died on the roads between 2000 and 2020—more than the number of Americans killed in combat in the twentieth century (about 630,000).

As well as being safer, AVs could grant independence and freedom to people who cannot drive cars: the very old, the very young, and the disabled. Already, AVs are ferrying people in retirement communities, whose residents may not feel confident behind the wheel or may wish to avoid the hassle of car ownership. In 2016 Google released a video in which Steve Mahan, a blind man, was shown doing errands in an auton-omous car in a quiet neighborhood in Austin, Texas. He was the first non-Google employee to ride alone in one of its AVs, without a safety driver. "It is like driving with a very good driver," Mahan told the *Washington Post.* "These cars will change the life prospects of people such as myself." Using AVs summoned via ride hailing as a "last mile" solution to move people to and from bus and train stations could also make public transport more viable in less densely populated areas, or in poorly served "transit deserts." Some cities might even operate their own robotaxi fleets, subsidizing rides in poor neighborhoods using fares collected in rich ones. Fleets of shared AVs could blur the distinction between private cars and public transport. In this way, say advocates of AVs, they could increase transport equity, by making cheap, convenient transport more widely available.

City dwellers will flock to embrace AVs, analysts predict, because calling a robotaxi when needed will be cheaper than owning a car. The logic runs as follows. Today, ride-hailing services cost riders around $2.50 per mile, compared with about $1.20 per mile to own and operate a private car. Paying the driver accounts for about 60 percent of the cost of ride hailing. So removing the driver and switching to electric vehicles will cut the cost of ride hailing by 80 percent, to about $0.50 per mile, predicts UBS, an investment bank. (Other analysts put the cost even lower.) A typical Western household, driving ten thousand miles a year, could therefore reduce its annual transport costs from $12,000 to $5,000 by switching to robotaxis. As a UBS analyst puts it, "Once the car becomes autonomous, the relevance of car ownership drops materially." The possibility that cheap robotaxis could undermine car ownership explains why both ride-hailing firms, such as Uber and Lyft, and carmakers have been investing billions of dollars in autonomous-driving research. Any firm that develops a viable robotaxi would potentially be able to undercut both ride-hailing companies that rely on human drivers, and carmakers whose business model depends on selling people cars. Fear of this outcome has resulted in a constantly shifting web of alliances between AV start-ups, ride-hailing firms, and carmakers, as everyone tries to hedge bets. Waymo, for example, has partnerships with Lyft, Fiat Chrysler, and Jaguar Land Rover, while Toyota has invested in Uber's AV unit. GM's AV unit, Cruise, has dallied with both Lyft and Uber. And so on.

If AVs do undermine the case for car ownership, that would have dramatic implications for urban planning. Fewer vehicles would mean that less space would be wasted on parking for private cars, which are unused 95 percent of the time. A study modeling the use of AVs in Lisbon, Portugal, found that the city's 203,000 cars could be replaced with a fleet of 26,000 robotaxis. In effect, cities have banked a large amount of valuable real estate in the form of parking spaces and garages, notes Peter Norton, a historian at the University of Virginia, and could decide how to spend the resulting windfall. Housing is one obvious option; parks or playgrounds are another. Streets could also be reconfigured to allow more room for pedestrians and cyclists. And because AVs are expected to be electric, there would be much less noise and pollution. There might also be less traffic. Widespread sharing of robotaxis would make more efficient use of road space; computer-controlled vehicles can be smart about route planning, to avoid jams; and once they are widespread, AVs could travel closer together than existing cars, increasing the effective capacity of roads. Whether or not AVs reduce congestion, riders will at least be able to do other things while traveling. Not having to drive would free up enormous amounts of time that can be used to work, play, socialize, or sleep. "Americans can take back a total of 30 billion hours per year that they now spend driving, sitting in traffic, or looking for a parking space," predicts the consulting firm BCG. Morgan Stanley bank, calculates that if all vehicles in America were driverless, the resulting productivity gains would be worth $507 billion a year.

AVs could also make possible new kinds of suburbs, the latest twist on the twentieth-century dream of garden cities. Alan Berger, a professor of urban studies at the Massachusetts Institute of Technology, suggests that much of the land that has been devoted to cars, the roads, and parking, could be reclaimed for ecological functions. That would mean more space for plants, more biodiversity, and more scope for food production. It would also improve water retention, reducing the risk of flooding in the urban core. City centers do not have enough space to generate solar power or grow food, but the suburbs do. In short, cities could function much better, Berger predicts, "once autonomous vehicles allow us to design different kinds of suburbs."

NOT SO FAST

Many of the predictions made about driverless cars sound eerily familiar to those made in the early days of the horseless carriage. That suggests they should be taken with a large pinch of salt. Automobiles were expected to be safer than horse-drawn vehicles because unlike horses they could not bolt, kick people, or be scared by sudden noises. But because of their greater numbers and higher speeds, cars proved to be far more deadly. It seems unlikely that AVs will be widely deployed unless they are dramatically safer than human drivers (those in the industry suggest that AVs would have to be a thousand times safer, reducing annual road deaths in America from around forty thousand to around forty). But they raise new safety concerns that do not apply to human-piloted vehicles, such as cybersecurity. Some prototype AVs can ask for help from a remote operator when they get confused. What if an AV is remotely hijacked and deliberately crashed into another vehicle, for example?

Similarly, cars were expected to reduce traffic congestion because they would take up less space on the road than horse-drawn vehicles. Again, the opposite proved to be the case. The lesson of the twentieth century is that when more road capacity is added to ease congestion, it encourages more car journeys. Likewise, if robotaxis are much cheaper than owning a car, people may want to use them more. But how much more? In 2017 a group of researchers led by Mustapha Harb, at the University of California, Berkeley, conducted an ingenious study that aimed to find out. A group of volunteers in the San Francisco Bay Area agreed to have their car usage tracked via GPS for a week. Then they were given a chauffeur for a week to drive their cars for them, including on trips in which the participants were not in the vehicle. They could send their cars to collect groceries, for example, take a friend home after a dinner party, or pick up children from school. By simulating the effect of having a self-driving vehicle, the researchers could see how this changed the participants' usage.

They were shocked by the results. The subjects took 58 percent more trips, and the distance traveled by their vehicles, whether or not they were in them, increased by an average of 83 percent. All of the subjects sent their cars to do errands, as expected. But not having to drive also encouraged participants in the study to make longer journeys. Several retirees in the study group, for example, opted to be driven upstate to Napa Valley for wine tastings, which they would not otherwise have done, because of the distance (a couple of hours each way) and because drinking large amounts of wine precludes driving. For one participant, the total "vehicle miles traveled" (VMT) during the experiment increased by 341 percent.

This is the flip side of the observation that AVs will grant people more freedom: the result may well be more trips, and more traffic. The roads could also fill up with autonomous delivery vehicles, with nobody on board, because if AVs make deliveries cheaper, that could encourage more online purchases. As the example of e-scooters shows, rival fleet operators might flood the roads with AVs and offer heavily subsidized rides as they fight for market share, worsening congestion. Another nightmare scenario is that commuters who own their own AVs might ask their cars to drop them off at work, then order them to go home or spend the day circling the office, before picking them up in the evening. AVs might also undermine public transport systems. A study by the University of California, Davis, found that among Uber and Lyft riders in America, bus use had fallen by 6 percent and light-rail use by 3 percent. Cheap AV rides could draw even more people away from public transport and onto the roads. This might discourage further investment in public transport, which could in turn expand, rather than diminish, the size of transit deserts. AVs could, in short, just as easily reduce transport equity as increase it.

The obvious answer is to use pricing to encourage some kinds of behavior and discourage others. Some cities already have congestion-charging programs of various degrees of complexity, or rules to encourage vehicle sharing, such as dedicated carpooling lanes. AVs would allow far more subtle forms of per mile road tolling and congestion charging—adjusting prices depending on time, place, vehicle type, number of riders, traffic levels, and so forth—to maximize sharing, minimize congestion, and improve transport equity. A "zombie tax" could be imposed on empty AVs, charging them more per mile when traveling without occupants, for example. City authorities could decide whether to penalize or encourage long-distance AV commuting, or to subsidize rides in poorer neighborhoods. Fine-tuning of pricing would promote equality of access to mobility, as well as control of congestion. Some cities may wish to micromanage this, operating their own AV fleets and integrating them with other forms of public transport.

Yet the same tolling plans that let city planners minimize congestion or subsidize robotaxi services in underserved areas would have a darker side. Choices about who goes where and when, and at what cost, are inescapably political. Systems that monitor where AVs go and adjust prices for different trips and different users would provide an extraordinarily subtle policy tool that could transform cities. But in the hands of an authoritarian government, it would be a powerful means of social control. Robotaxi operators will know an enormous amount about their riders, chronicling their every move. Ride-hailing firms already do. Some taxis already record riders for security reasons. Robotaxis will surely surveil both their passengers (parents will demand live video feeds from cars taking their children to gym class) and their surroundings (in the event of an accident, video evidence will be crucial). Video cameras and facial-recognition technology mean that each AV will be a moving camera platform. Police investigating a crime will ask cars that were in the vicinity what—and whom—they saw.

And in a world where people rely on autonomous transport, new forms of segregation and discrimination become possible. Access to some locations might be restricted to certain networks of driverless cars, just as some websites have paywalls that provide access for subscribers only. The equivalent of "network neutrality" rules might be required in phys-ical space, with a requirement that all locations be equally accessible by all AV fleets. Couldn't you just take a bicycle, or walk? Not if some roads or lanes are designated for exclusive use by AVs. In authoritarian coun-tries, robotaxis could restrict people's movements. China's "social credit" system, which awards points based on various aspects of people's behavior, already restricts train travel for those who step out of line. Just because AVs have the potential to increase freedom does not mean they will.

These problems may never arise because AV technology may never be deemed safe enough for widespread use. But it is worth thinking about them anyway. More generally, it is helpful to recognize that predictions about AVs, like those about cars more than a century ago, are likely to be wide of the mark, and there are sure to be other consequences that nobody foresees. As historian Peter Norton puts it, "Autonomous vehi-cles will open a Pandora's box of unintended effects." But not just yet. Widespread deployment of robotaxis is now not expected until 2025 or 2030 at the earliest. As they look for nearer-term opportunities, AV firms are shifting their focus. Some are working on autonomous trucks, on the principle that highway driving is less complicated than driving on city streets. Others, particularly in China, are working with city authorities to make urban environments more AV friendly, for example by installing dedicated infrastructure to support AVs, restricting access for other vehicles in some districts, and limiting AV firms' legal liability in the event of accidents. Should they eventually materialize, robotaxis seem likely to be part of the answer to what comes after the automotive age— but only part of it. So what does the postcar world look like?

12

The Road Ahead

Technology is neither good nor bad; nor is it neutral.

—MELVIN KRANZBERG, AMERICAN HISTORIAN (1917–95)

THE LONG HISTORY OF THE END OF THE CAR

People have been predicting the end of the automotive era for decades. In 1958, a time that is now remembered as the height of American car culture, John Keats, an American satirist, published *The Insolent Chariots*. A humorous broadside against the excesses of the American car industry and car culture, it was the sequel to *The Crack in the Picture Window*, an attack on the sprawl of suburbia. *The Insolent Chariots* came out during an economic downturn, one cause of which was a sudden drop in car sales, which had fallen by 31 percent compared with 1957. Keats blamed the recession squarely on American carmakers, saying the public had seen through their glitzy marketing, with its promises of freedom and social status, and was no longer interested in what they had to offer. (Ford had just launched the Edsel, a notorious flop.) Instead of serving the needs of the economy, the overmighty car industry was, Keats complained, now driving it off a cliff. Many of his criticisms sound familiar today: he lamented the way that highways and suburbs, built around the car, had homogenized the landscape. "It is now possible to drive across the face of the nation without feeling you've been anywhere or that you've done anything," he wrote. But his claim that Americans had finally fallen out of love with the automobile turned out to be incorrect. Car sales, and the economy, rebounded later in the year.

The anti-car books in the 1960s, most famously Ralph Nader's *Unsafe at Any Speed: The Designed-In Dangers of the American Automobile* (1965), focused on safety problems, and the industry's failure to address them. Rather than calling for the end of the car, though, these books (with titles including *Highway Homicide* and *Licensed to Kill*) took for granted the central place of the automobile in modern life and demanded action to make it safer.

By the early 1970s, however, critics of the car were arguing that it was time to move on from car dependency altogether. In *Autokind vs. Mankind: An Analysis of Tyranny, a Proposal for Rebellion, a Plan for Reconstruction* (1971), Kenneth Schneider, a city planner, explained how he had realized that cities were prioritizing cars and carmakers over people: "The social malignancy underlying automobility draws men into inescapable dependence. Dependence arises from a vicious circle in which the charm of the car and the remaking of the environment reinforce each other. Automobility gradually permeates the daily behavior of people, the purpose of institutions, and the structure of the cities and countryside. This tyranny has been promoted under the cunning popular myth of expanding freedom and affluence. The current reality of auto tyranny is cultural power, social blackmail, physical deprivation, injury, and death." He called for cities to be redesigned around people.

Perhaps the most surprising critique of the car came from John Jerome, former managing editor of *Car and Driver* magazine, in his book *The Death of the Automobile* (1972). "The premise of this book is that the automobile must go," he declared, listing the many problems it had caused:

> Automobiles kill almost sixty thousand of us per year and injure 4 million more, pollute the environment more outrageously than any other industrial source, gobble natural resources like cocktail

peanuts, destroy the cities, choke off development of more efficient or serviceable transit systems, spread squalor on the land . . . exacerbate our unsolved problems of poverty and race, shift patterns of home ownership and retail trade as casually and whimsically as natural disasters, alter sexual customs, loosen family ties, elbow their way into living space despite our best efforts to keep them out, rearrange the very social and moral structure of the nation, and dominate the economy to the point of subverting the hallowed capitalist system.

Pollution, in particular, would bring people to their senses and enable them to see, "finally, that the automobile is the enemy," Jerome predicted, and would lead them to accept the need to "phase the automobile out of the economy and our lives." And this was before the oil shock of 1973 gave American critics of the car even more reason to believe its supremacy was coming to an end. Yet enthusiasm for cars was undimmed. "Some day Americans will admit that the automobile is socially and economically obsolete," lamented Catherine Marshall, an academic, in the *Michigan Quarterly Review* in 1980. She called for a switch to walkable neighborhoods, greater emphasis on walking and cycling, and fewer, smaller cars for essential or emergency trips—all familiar prescriptions today. "Of course there's an automobile in our future. But the way we use it, and the extent to which we allow it to dictate the pattern of our lives, will have to change," she predicted. Nothing changed.

Instead, sales of cars continued to reach new peaks, both in America and globally. And rather than getting smaller and more fuel efficient, cars did exactly the opposite in the 1990s, with the emergence of sport utility vehicles, which emerged to exploit an American regulatory loophole. Because they were classified as light trucks, SUVs could sidestep the emissions, fuel-economy, and safety standards imposed on passenger cars. The rise of the SUV coincided with another wave of commentary hailing the imminent end of the automotive era, not just in America but in Europe.

Once again, these announcements of the death of the car proved premature. In 2000, total light-vehicle sales hit record highs of more than

17 million in America and 55 million worldwide. After plunging during the financial crisis of 2008–9, sales swiftly resumed their upward climb, and global light-vehicle sales hit an all-time high in 2017 of 95 million vehicles—driven by booming sales in China, which had become the world's largest car market in 2010, and by the global popularity of SUVs. So much for the idea that concerns over traffic, safety, pollution, climate change, or "peak oil" would lead to a change of heart. Despite decades of predictions to the contrary, there was no sign of consumers turning away from the automobile. In his 2008 book *Autophobia*, the historian Brian Ladd concluded, "Change seems both inevitable and vitally necessary. Yet it does not appear imminent . . . Individual decisions have consistently favored greater car use, whether in spite of public policies to discourage it, or because of policies that encourage it. There is, then, good reason to conclude that the car has triumphed, and that its opponents are spitting into the wind."

THE EVIDENCE FOR "PEAK CAR"

But in the 2020s there are clear signs that enthusiasm for cars is finally waning. Even some people within the industry now acknowledge that the world is now at, or has passed, "peak car"—the point at which car ownership and use level off and start to decline. Car production may never exceed its level in 2017. "It could well be that we passed the peak in global automotive production," said Volkmar Denner, chief executive of Robert Bosch, the world's largest maker of car parts, in January 2020. And that was before the coronavirus pandemic whacked car sales.

China has been the driver of car sales in the early twenty-first century, with the number of vehicles sold rising from 5 million in 2004 to 29 million in 2017. But sales have since slowed, spurred in part by a switch to ride hailing, which is an enormous industry in China. Didi Chuxing, the country's ride-hailing giant, provides twice as many rides each day within China as Uber does in the rest of the world. (In 2018 Didi provided 10 billion rides within China, or about 30 million per day, compared with 14 million Uber rides a day globally.) A survey in 2016 by the consulting firm McKinsey found that 60 percent of Chinese consumers no longer considered owning a car to be a status symbol, and 40 percent said that owning a car seemed less important, because of the proliferation of alternatives, such as ride hailing, bike rental, and so on. Car ownership has become steadily less attractive in China because of the relatively high level of taxes, insurance costs, and parking fees, while lower labor costs make ride hailing more affordable than in Western countries. And car ownership has not developed to the same extent as in Western countries—there are around nineteen cars per hundred people, compared with eighty-four in the United States and sixty-one in Europe—and may now never do so. Instead, the growing Chinese middle class, which has shown itself to be receptive to new services and products, seems happy to skip the hassle of car ownership in favor of on-demand mobility services arranged via smartphone. If so, the motor that had been driving global car sales has been switched off.

Evidence for peak car in Western countries, meanwhile, has been accumulating for some time. In America, the total number of vehicle miles traveled has continued to increase. But it has been growing more slowly than both the total number of vehicles and the population. The number of miles driven per vehicle, and per person of driving age, both peaked in 2004 and have since fallen to levels last seen in the 1990s. The average distance driven per person per year peaked in the 2000s or earlier in many Western cities including London, Stockholm, Vienna, Houston, and Atlanta. In Australia, Belgium, Britain, France, Germany, Italy, Japan, New Zealand, and Spain, distance traveled per person has been flat or falling since the early 2000s (in Britain, the average motorist drove seventy-six hundred miles in 2018, down from ninety-two hundred in 2002). Miles traveled by car per annum per capita in Italy, Britain, the Netherlands, and Sweden peaked in 2000, 2002, 2004, and 2005 respectively.

In America the proportion of the population with a driving license declined between 2011 and 2014, across all age groups. Young people are either qualifying to drive at a later age or not doing so at all. Since the 1980s, the proportion of Americans with a license has fallen from 46 percent to 25 percent among sixteen-year-olds, 80 percent to 60 percent among eighteen-year-olds, and 92 percent to 77 percent among those aged twenty to twenty-four, according to researchers at the University of Michigan. Young people are also qualifying to drive later than they used to in Britain, Canada, France, Norway, South Korea, and Sweden. Even in car-loving Germany, the share of young households without cars increased from 20 percent to 28 percent between 1998 and 2008. "That car-driving rates have stopped growing and in many cases are declining in most economically developed nations is unquestionable," noted a European Union report in 2017. "Furthermore, it is accepted that the greatest change in driving rates is amongst the young, especially young men, who also are increasingly not learning how to drive." Perhaps this is due to a wider trend of young people delaying life choices. But it seems unlikely that they will take to driving later. Evidence from Britain suggests. that those who learn to drive in their late twenties drive 30 percent less than those who learn a decade earlier.

What has caused this change of heart? Peak-car theorists attribute it to several overlapping factors. Most people now live in cities, most vehicle miles are driven in cities rather than rural areas, and the decline in driving is chiefly a decline in urban driving. The cost and hassle of car owner-ship has increased as traffic congestion has increased and cities have intro-duced congestion charging zones and pedestrianized parts of city centers and made parking scarcer and more expensive. For many urbanites, but particularly the young, cars are no longer regarded as essential, as smartphones let them shop and socialize online. The steady shift toward e-commerce also means cars are needed for fewer shopping trips. And when a car is needed, for a weekend away or to help a friend move house, car-sharing and rental services are readily accessible.

In recent years restrictions on car use in cities have become more severe, with the closure of some roads, or some areas, to private cars alto-gether. This has even been the case in car-loving America, as shown by the closures to private cars of Market Street in San Francisco and Fourteenth Street in Manhattan, to make more room for public trans-port. Some cities have announced that they will ban nonelectric cars alto-gether in the 2030s or 2040s, to improve air quality and reduce carbon emissions. Such moves are sometimes decried as a "war on the car." But even many motorists now support them: a survey of ten thousand people carried out in 2017 in ten European capital cities, for example, found that 63 percent of residents owned a car, but 84 percent said they would like to see fewer cars on the roads in their city. And just as car ownership has become less convenient, alternatives to car use—ride-hailing, bike-sharing, and other mobility services—have proliferated. Travel-planning apps also make public transport a more attractive option, by showing when buses, trains, or trams will arrive, and how to combine them to complete a journey. But the arrival of those alternatives seems merely to have accelerated what was, in Western countries at least, an existing trend that had been going on for some years.

The coronavirus pandemic seems likely, on balance, to accelerate it further. Fear of contagion has discouraged use of public transport and prompted some people to commute by car instead. But this seems unlikely to herald a global boom in car sales. Evidence from Asia suggests that the risk of transmission on public transport can be managed with appropriate use of masks, thermal scanners, and staggering of journeys to reduce crowding. The pandemic has also encouraged more people to adopt e-commerce and teleworking, which substitute for car journeys and are likely to persist, to some extent, after the pandemic has passed. KPMG, a consultancy, predicts that the pandemic will result in a world of "fewer trips, fewer miles, and fewer cars." Commuting and shopping, the company notes, account for 40 percent of miles driven in America, and the pandemic-induced boosts to e-commerce and teleworking will have "powerful and enduring" effects, reducing the number of vehicles on American roads by 7 million to 14 million. And cities have taken the opportunity provided by lockdown to reclaim street space from cars, with road closures, the creation of new bike lanes, and the introduction of wider sidewalks. In many cases these changes are expected to become permanent. That may encourage more people to try bikes, scooters, and walking, while further discouraging the use of cars. More generally, the pandemic has provided a glimpse of a world that is less dependent on cars and shown that dramatic changes to living and working habits are possible and can quickly be implemented.

In short, the tide would seem to be turning against the car, in particular in cities, where the cost of car ownership is increasingly onerous. A further shift is about to tip the scales still further, by making alternatives—from buses and trains to ride hailing and bike sharing—even more attractive. Because for the first time, thanks to the smartphone, they can now all be stitched together to create a far more compelling alternative to the car.

THE INTERNET OF MOTION

What will be dominant mode of urban transport in the postcar era? Will it be buses, trains and trams, taxis, ride hailing, car clubs, bike sharing, or scooters? The answer is yes—to all of the above. Individually, they may be less convenient than using a private car for a specific trip, with different coverage areas, ticketing systems, apps, membership requirements, and billing systems. But combine them into a single product accessed and paid for via a single app, and that complexity goes away. For any given trip, users are offered a range of options, with different prices and journey times, across multiple modes of transport. They can then choose on the basis of cost (lowest price), convenience (fewest changes), or speed (quickest arrival). In effect, multiple transport networks are connected to form a single, seamless, and more powerful network. This is what happened with computer networks, with the establishment of a "network of networks"—the internet. The same interconnection is now happening in transport, to create what might be called the internet of motion.

This approach, known in the industry as mobility as a service (MaaS), can be seen in action in Helsinki, where trains, trams, buses, bike rental, taxis, e-scooters, and car rental can all be accessed through a single app. (The term *MaaS* was popularized by Sonja Heikkilä, a Finnish graduate student, who used it as the title of her master's thesis in 2014.) The app, called Whim, lets users plan a route, see the price up front, make payments, and buy tickets. As well as "pay as you go" access, Whim also offers monthly subscription plans, akin to mobile-phone contracts, that provide bundles of different options for different users. A package for students includes unlimited bike rental and public transport, for example, while a "weekend" package also throws in unlimited use of rental cars on weekends. The Finnish company behind the app, MaaS Global, says its aim is "to make the biggest change in transport since cars became widely affordable." Its launching similar services in Antwerp, Birmingham, Singapore, and Vienna. It is just one of many start-ups competing to provide cities around the world with the means to stitch together different modes of transport. Ride-hailing firms (such as Uber) and large carmakers (such as Ford and Daimler) are also moving into this area, because they, too, regard it as the future of urban mobility.

All this is feasible because of smartphones with built-in satellite-positioning and payment features, the emergence of new transport options, and one other crucial element: the decision by cities to open up access to real-time data from their public-transport systems. This lets mapping apps (such as Google Maps) show how to get from one place to another using a range of public-transport options, as well as driving, cycling, or walking. Other providers of transport services, such as ride hailing or bike sharing, provide similar data interfaces, making it possible (for example) to summon an Uber car from a Google Maps search. And providers of transport services, such as Uber, are also trying to turn their apps into general-purpose transport portals. Uber's app, for example, can be used to find and pay for Lime e-scooters and also shows routes on public transport, alongside the option to hail a car. In some cities, the Uber app can also be used to buy tickets for public transport. The company's chief executive, Dara Khosrowshahi, has said, "The goal of reducing private car ownership is one we share with cities across the globe." He wants Uber to be "the Amazon of transportation"—in other words, a one-stop shop.

It is not alone. Start-ups including Transit, Citymapper, Moovit, and Trafi are also pursuing the transport-aggregator model, hoping to become the go-to option for travel in the cities they cover, or to provide the technology for cities to launch their own Helsinki-like bundles. Jelbi, a MaaS program in Berlin powered by Trafi's technology, claims to be the biggest in the world, combining buses, trams, trains, ferries, and shared mobility options such as bikes, e-scooters, shuttles, car sharing, and taxis. Moovit has links with more than 4,000 public-transport operators and 360 ride-hailing and micromobility providers in 3,200 cities in 106 countries. Citymapper is live with directions and ticketing in more than 50 cities, and Transit in more than 200. "We use the power of open data, mobile and payment technology to make transport sustainable and hassle free," says Citymapper on its website. Transit is more explicit about its aim of moving cities into a postcar future. "We dream of happier communities, where multiple modes work together and getting from A to B with Transit is simpler than climbing into a car," says its website. "Our cities came long before the car, and will still be around after all the cars are gone."

Given that such programs explicitly aim to provide an alternative to car ownership, it may seem odd that carmakers are also moving into the field. After all, a future in which different modes of transport can seamlessly be combined will involve fewer cars and less private ownership. But carmakers hope to provide vehicles (and later autonomous vehicles) for ride-hailing and car-sharing fleets. In some cases they are also dabbling with providing mobility services themselves. Ford briefly operated Chariot, a ride-hailing service, and owns Spin, an e-scooter start-up. BMW and Daimler operate a joint car-sharing program that allows Smart, Mercedes-Benz, BMW, and Mini vehicles to be rented by the minute, via an app, in several European cities. Carmakers claim that the new model provides an opportunity for them to shift from selling cars into the potentially more profitable business of selling rides. Total car sales each year add up to around $2 trillion; but the personal transport market, which includes vehicles, services, and software, is worth more like $10 trillion, according to industry estimates.

The stage is therefore set for a brutal fight between carmakers, ride-hailing giants, and mobility start-ups in the coming years, as the emphasis shifts from car ownership to mobility services. To succeed, the internet of motion will have to overcome several challenges. Not every city dweller has or can afford a smartphone. People who have owned cars all their lives may be reluctant to give them up. New funding sources will be necessary as car-related tax revenues decline. Roaming will need to be enabled between services in different cities. But perhaps the biggest challenge is the need for cooperation—between public transport systems and city governments, and providers of ride-hailing and micromobility services. They have incentives to cooperate: an e-scooter company that is included in a city's MaaS app, for example, is likely to see greater usage because users do not need to sign up for it separately. But the two sides do not always see eye to eye, to say the least, and in some cases are in open conflict over pricing, safety, workers' rights, and data sharing, among other things. For Uber to become an integral part of the transport infrastructure in the cities where it operates, as it hopes, it is likely to have to accept higher levels of taxation and regulation than it does today.

Combining multiple transport systems into a single service would allow cities to subsidize rides for some users (the elderly, or those on low incomes), in some neighborhoods (such as those poorly served by public transport), or to encourage some behaviors—a free ride if you cycle, rather than taking a shared taxi, for example. In Berlin, some users of the Jelbi app are being offered discount vouchers to encourage adoption of bikes and scooters. By adjusting prices and incentives, cities would be able to make progress on their health and environmental goals, undoing some of the harmful consequences of car dependency.

But possibly the greatest merit of the internet of motion is that it is flexible. It can adapt to different mixtures of transport modes in different cities, depending on the local circumstances, and can monitor and cater to changing usage and travel patterns as cities evolve. It allows for exper-imentation and iteration, for example by testing pop-up bus lanes or bike lanes, reclaiming parts of residential streets through small green areas called parklets, or creating pedestrian plazas, and measuring their impact on street use and travel patterns—an approach called tactical urbanism. Experiments that work can be made permanent, and those that do not can be reversed. The internet of motion also provides a framework that can accommodate new modes of transport in the future, such as auton-omous vehicles, drone-like flying taxis, or whatever is invented in the decades to come. Although it currently makes most sense in cities, this model could be extended to cover rural areas, or entire countries or regions, as new transport technologies emerge. Weaving multiple public and private services together into a transport tapestry should make it easier to ensure that a single mode of transport does not become unduly dominant, as happened with cars. Meanwhile, the car can gradually be unpicked from the urban fabric, allowing streets and parking areas to be reclaimed for other uses. In the twentieth century, cars granted people independence. In the twenty-first century, the internet of motion promises to grant them independence from their cars.

THE LESSONS OF HISTORY

The future of urban transport will not be based on a single technology, but on a diverse mixture of transport systems, knitted together by smartphone technology. The smartphone, rather than any particular means of transport, is the true heir to the car. Like the car before it, it gives users the freedom to socialize, shop, and explore—and not just in the virtual realm. Steve Jobs, the cofounder of Apple, once observed that computers were like "bicycles for the mind." It turns out that smartphones can also be used to deliver transport for the body. The resulting internet of motion provides a way to escape from the car-based transport monoculture that exists in many cities. That should be welcomed because the experience of the twentieth century suggests that it would be a mistake to replace one transport monoculture with another, as happened with the switch from horses to cars—and would happen again if, say, autonomous cars became the dominant mode of transport in the future. A transport monoculture is less flexible, and its unintended consequences become more easily locked in and more difficult to address. With a mixed, flexible system there is much less danger of path dependency—where decisions made in the past make subsequent change harder to bring about—and more scope for experimentation. That is the first of three lessons that the history of motion offers for the future.

The second lesson is to expect the unexpected nevertheless. All technologies have unintended consequences, and in the case of transport technologies, which by necessity span the physical world, those consequences can be particularly far-reaching, as the history of the car demonstrates. In the early years, some people foresaw highways and suburbs. But mostly they imagined the world largely as it was, just with fewer horses and less pollution. The ways in which cars would transform aspects of everyday life, from mass production to dating to fast food to shopping malls, were entirely unanticipated. So the shift away from cars, with the adoption of new approaches to transport, is sure to have unexpected consequences, both big and small. Might autonomous vehicles, for example, heighten inequality and lead to new forms of segregation? Will fewer cars mean less smoking, given that more than half of tobacco sales in America take place at gas stations? How will new forms of transport affect urban layout, population density, and property prices? We do not know the answers to these questions. But, mindful of the history of the car, we do at least know to ask them—and to watch out for other unintended consequences, too. Autonomous vehicles have yet to be widely deployed and may never be, but debate is already lively about their possible social, cultural, and economic impacts.

The third lesson is that, among unintended consequences, one particular aspect of transport technologies merits close scrutiny: their exhaust, which has a nasty habit of taking everyone by surprise with unanticipated long-term impacts. Nobody worried about horse manure clogging city streets when the first carts and wagons began rumbling along in the Bronze Age. Similarly, the idea that invisible carbon dioxide emissions from combustion engines would contribute to a global environmental crisis did not gain purchase until a century or so after the first cars took to the roads. Instead, initial concerns about pollution focused on "smoky exhaust" and, later, on smog created by sunlight acting on the exhausts from vehicles and factories. By the time the problems caused by their exhausts had become apparent, both horses and cars were firmly entrenched. Could the same thing happen again?

As combustion engines are phased out, and cars, trains, and other forms of ground transport go electric, direct exhaust products should not be a problem. (Electric transport will only be truly emission-free when it is powered by renewable power from a zero-carbon grid.) But transport systems will produce another form of potentially problematic exhaust: data. In particular, they will produce reams of data about who went where, and when, and how, and with whom. They already do. In an infamous (and since deleted) blog post from 2012, entitled "Rides of Glory," Uber analyzed its riders' behavior to identify the cities and dates with the highest prevalence of one-night stands, for example. The post caused a furor and was seen as symptomatic of the unrestrained "tech bro" culture that prevailed at Uber at the time. But it highlights a broader point. Shared bikes and e-scooters also track who went where, and when, for billing purposes. The companies that operate mobility services are keen to keep this data to themselves: it helps them predict future demand, can be useful when preparing to launch new services, and can also be used to profile riders and target advertising. Someone who takes a shared bike or a hailed car to a sporting-goods shop is probably interested in sporting goods, for example. Bike-sharing services in China already offer riders discount coupons for use at nearby stores at the end of each ride. And so on.

Cities, also, want to track the position and usage of shared bicycles and e-scooters so they can adjust the provision of bike lanes, compare levels of usage in low-income and high-income neighborhoods, check that vehicles are not being used in places where they should not be, and inform mobility-service providers of such things as road closures or special events such as festivals that might lead to shifts in demand. For this reason, dozens of cities around the world have adopted a system called the Mobility Data Specification (MDS), which was originally created by the Los Angeles Department of Transportation and is now managed by an independent body called the Open Mobility Foundation. At present, MDS only covers bicycles and e-scooters, though it could be expanded to cover ride-hailing, car-sharing, and autonomous-taxi services in the future. Many cities consider MDS to be a building block in their future mobility strategies because it allows for the interchange of data between mobility providers, city authorities, and regulators.

But mobility-service providers and privacy groups are concerned that MDS lets cities track individuals and could, for example, allow the police to identify people who attend a demonstration or visit a particular location. They also worry that the foundation that oversees MDS will not store the data securely. It is not difficult to imagine the sort of things that an authoritarian regime might do with such data. The American Civil Liberties Union and the Electronic Frontier Foundation filed a lawsuit against the City of Los Angeles in June 2020. In its response, the city insisted that all records are anonymized and aggregated before being shared with other MDS participants. To further complicate matters, a coalition set up to oppose MDS, Communities Against Rider Surveillance

(CARS), did not disclose Uber's role in its initial establishment and funding, prompting some members to withdraw in protest.

All of this suggests that personal-mobility data is likely to become as much of a flash point in the future as internet-browsing data, its online counterpart, already is. This may seem like an esoteric concern, but the same could have been said of worries about carbon dioxide emissions, which are just as invisible, at the dawn of the automotive era. And unlike the people of that time, those building and using new mobility services today have the chance to address such concerns before it is too late.

The wheel has turned full circle. It is 1895 again, and cities and their inhabitants, concerned about traffic, safety, and an environmental crisis, must make decisions about new transport technologies. The future is not predetermined. It will be shaped by the choices citizens, entrepreneurs, and regulators will make in the coming years. Cars will not go away anytime soon. But we now have an opportunity to learn from history and choose a way forward in which the world is no longer built around the automobile. As we consider the road ahead, it is worth taking a careful look in the rearview mirror.

ACKNOWLEDGMENTS

Researching and writing this book has been a wild (and sometimes bumpy) ride; for one thing, autonomous vehicles make no attempt to avoid Pittsburgh potholes. I am grateful to the historians, urbanists, and technologists who have helped me along the way by sharing their expertise and knowledge so generously; any errors are of course entirely my fault. Thank you to Richard Bulliet, Eric Morris, Joel Tarr, Kassia St. Clair, Stephen Davies, Tom Wheeler, Tony Hadland, Peter Norton, and Brian Ladd; to Joel Kotkin, Donald Shoup, Shlomo Angel, Alan Berger, Jarrett Walker, William Riggs, Richard Florida, and Chenoe Hart; and to Sebastian Thrun, Elon Musk, Chris Urmson, Sterling Anderson, Oliver Cameron, Stan Boland, and Karl Iagnemma. Finally, I wish to express my gratitude to my parents for indulging my obsession with cars from a young age, to my son, Miles, for all the car hunts in the automotive jungles of Knightsbridge and Goodwood, to my daughter, Tate, for her classical expertise and sharp eye as an editor, and finally, for putting up with all the horse manure stories, to my wife, Kirstin, to whom this book is dedicated.

NOTES

INTRODUCTION

Cities' dependence on horses in general, and the problem of horse manure in particular, are discussed by Tarr, *The Search for the Ultimate Sink*; Thompson, "Victorian England: The Horse-Drawn Society"; and McShane, *Down the Asphalt Path*. The lurid descriptions of "pea soup" can be found in Jacobs, *The Death and Life of Great American Cities*. The horse-manure problem had been exacerbated by another form of excrement: guano (mineralized seabird droppings), which was adopted as an agricultural fertilizer starting in the 1840s because it had a much higher nitrogen content than manure. The value of horse manure gathered from city streets dropped, making disposal more expensive. It is telling that in London, the authorities went from charging contractors for the right to remove manure from the streets in 1846 to paying them to do so in 1851. There are many references in online articles to "The Great Horse Manure Crisis of 1894," though I can find no evidence that this term was used at the time, or that anything in particular happened in 1894. The claim that the *Times* of London predicted in the 1890s that the city would be buried under nine feet of horse manure by 1950, also widely cited online, seems to be apocryphal.

CHAPTER I

The best two recent discussions of the history of the wheel are Bulliet, *The Wheel: Inventions & Reinventions*, and Anthony; *The Horse, the Wheel, and Language*, which supersede earlier works by Tarr, *The History of the Carriage*, and Piggott, *The Earliest Wheeled Transport*. The account of the emergence of the wheel, and the earliest wheeled vehicles, draws on those works and on papers by Burmeister, Shishlina et al., Horváth et al., Morgunova et al., and Parpola. For the history and development of the chariot, including the invention of spoked wheels, see Anthony and Vinogradov, "Birth of the Chariot," and Chondros et al., "The Evolution of the Double-Horse Chariots." For Roman roads and Pompeii's one-way systems, see Poehler, *The Traffic Systems of Pompeii*.

CHAPTER 2

The equestrian statue of Marcus Aurelius is now in the Capitoline Museums in Rome; the version on display in the Piazza del Campidoglio is a replica made in 1981. The original survived into modern times because it was wrongly thought to depict the emperor Constantine, who made Christianity the state religion of the Roman Empire, and whose images were therefore spared in later Christian purges of Roman statues. For princess carriages and the rise of the coach, see Bulliet, *The Wheel*. For the history of the *cours*, see Wrigley, *The Flâneur Abroad*, and Gerbino, *François Blondel*. For the influence of wheeled vehicles on architecture and city layout, see Kostof, *The City Shaped* and *The City Assembled*. For the history of the horsebus/omnibus, see Vuchic, *Urban Transit Systems and Technology*, and McShane, *Down the Asphalt Path*. Modern readers will note the similarity between John Taylor's condemnation of carriages and modern taxi drivers' denunciations of Uber and other ride-hailing firms. Similarly, Samuel Pepys's evident pride in his new carriage will be familiar to anyone who takes pleasure in "new-car smell" or enjoys the envious glances of their neighbors after acquiring a fancy new vehicle.

CHAPTER 3

The account of the history of early steam-powered vehicles, both on and off rails, draws primarily on Maggs, *Great Britain's Railways*, and Dickinson and Titley, *Richard Trevithick*. For the increased dependence on horses brought about by steam trains, see Thompson, "Victorian England: The Horse-Drawn Society." For the impact of trains on city planning, see Mumford, *Designing the Modern City*. The origins and history of the bicycle are discussed in Herlihy, *Bicycle*; Guroff, *Mechanical Horse*; and Hadland et al., *Bicycle Design*. Many bike historians dispute the Tambora hypothesis, advanced by Hans-Erhard Lessing. It is true that there is no direct documentary evidence for it, but the timing is highly suggestive. For a considered account, see Townsend, "Year Without a Summer." Incidentally, the supposed drawing of a bicycle by Leonardo da Vinci, which depicts strikingly modern-looking pedals and chain, is a recent forgery that seems to have been added to one of Leonardo's manuscripts by an unknown hand in the 1970s. The original draisine, meanwhile, lives on in the form of the "balance bikes" now used as starter bicycles for children, which focus on teaching them how to balance, not how to pedal. The account of the development of the first automobiles draws on Dell, Moseley, and Rand,

Towards Sustainable Road Transport; Rhodes, *Energy*; Volti, *Cars and Culture*; and Albert, *Are We There Yet?*. For the bicycle's crucial role in paving the way for the car, see Reid, *Roads Were Not Built for Cars*.

CHAPTER 4

For Bertha Benz's road trip, see Dell, Moseley, and Rand, *Towards Sustainable Road Transport*. The account of the Paris–Rouen race draws on contemporary newspaper reports in the *Petit Journal*, *Pall Mall Gazette*, *New York Times*, and *New York Herald*. For an exhaustive account of the American debate about what to call these new vehicles, see Lipski, "The Introduction of 'Automobile' into American English." The confusion about naming has a modern echo in the debate over the best nomenclature for autonomous vehicles, also known as driverless cars, self-driving cars, or robotaxis. They, too, may end up simply being called cars. For early reactions (and objections) to the automobile, see Ladd, *Autophobia*, and McShane, *Down the Asphalt Path*.

CHAPTER 5

The account of the creation of the Model T, and the Ford–GM rivalry, follows Wells, "The Road to the Model T"; Tedlow, "The Struggle for Dominance in the Automobile Market"; Sloan, *My Years with General Motors*; Cormier and Bisley, "Cars: Accelerating the Modern World"; and Volti, *Cars and Culture*. Henry Ford does not actually seem to be on record as having said "any color, as long as it's black," but that was definitely his policy. To modern drivers, the success of the Model T seems even more astonishing when you consider how complicated it was to drive. It had three pedals, like a modern manual-transmission car, but they were used to switch between high and low gear; engage reverse; and brake. The throttle was controlled by hand, and the handbrake also released the clutch. The thousand-fold growth in American car sales over twenty years is equivalent to doubling every two years (because $2^{10}=1,024$), which is, of course, one formulation of Moore's Law, which has long been used to map the steady increase in microprocessor transistor density, and hence computing performance at a given price. Both are in fact examples of a deeper law known as Wright's Law, also known as the experience curve, which states that for every doubling of the cumulative production of a particular item, costs fall by a constant percentage. This turns out to apply to a wide range of manufactured goods.

CHAPTER 6

The account of the death of Henry Bliss draws on contemporary newspaper reports in the *Alton Evening Telegraph, New York Times, Washington Evening Times*, and *New York World*. For the history of road safety (or lack thereof), see Norton, *Fighting Traffic*; McShane, *Down the Asphalt Path*; Ladd, *Autophobia*; O'Connell, *The Car and British Society*; and Schlich, "Trauma Surgery and Traffic Policy in Germany in the 1930s."

For a detailed history of traffic lights see McShane, "The Origins and Globalization of Traffic Control Signals." The use of red to mean "stop" (or "danger") is often attributed to the fact that it is the color of blood, but there is a less gory explanation. When a lighthouse was constructed at Flamborough Head in England in 1806, the engineer, Robert Stevenson, was required to give its lamp a different color, so that it could be distinguished from an existing lighthouse nearby, which had a white light. He experimented with different colored pieces of glass and found that the red glass available at the time was the most transparent and gave the brightest light. A red light therefore came to be associated with a warning. Red lamps were then adopted as warning lamps on ships. In Japan, traffic lights indicating "go" are sometimes noticeably blue. The reason is linguistic, not technical; local regulations require the lamps to be *ao*, a word that signifies a wide range of colors that includes those known as green and blue in other languages.

CHAPTER 7

The account of the debates over utopian cities and garden cities draws on Shelton, "Automobile Utopias and Traditional Urban Infrastructure"; Fotsch, "The Building of a Superhighway Future at the New York World's Fair"; Buder, *Visionaries and Planners*; Ladd, *Autophobia*; McShane, *Down the Asphalt Path*; and Jacobs, *The Death and Life of Great American Cities*. For the history and future of suburbanization, see Weaver, "The Suburbanization of America," and Gallagher, *The End of the Suburbs*. On General Motors and streetcars, see Slater, "General Motors and the Demise of Streetcars." For retrofitting of suburbs, see Williamson, "Retrofitting Suburbia."

CHAPTER 8

The account of the history of dating and drive-ins follows Peiss, "Charity Girls and City Pleasures"; Bailey, "From Front Porch to Back Seat: A History of the

Date"; Cohen, "Forgotten Audiences in the Passion Pits"; and Luther, "Drive-In Theaters: Rags to Riches in Five Years." For the rise of fast food, see Schlosser, *Fast Food Nation*; Jakle and Sculle, *Fast Food*; and Halberstam, *The Fifties*. For the rise of supermarkets and then shopping malls, see Longstreth, "The Drive-In, the Supermarket, and the Transformation of Commercial Space in Los Angeles, 1914–1941"; Jackson, "All the World's a Mall"; Hanchett "U.S. Tax Policy and the Shopping-Center Boom of the 1950s and 1960s"; Davison, "Super City: Los Angeles and the Birth of the Supermarket"; and Zimmerman, "The Supermarket and the Changing Retail Structure."

CHAPTER 9

For the early history of electric vehicles, see McShane, *Down the Asphalt Path*; Albert, *Are We There Yet?*; and Volti, *Cars and Culture*. For the emergence of gasoline, rather than alcohol, as the main automotive fuel and America's resulting dependence on foreign oil, see McCarthy, "The Coming Wonder?"; Rhodes, *Energy*; and Painter, "Oil and the American Century." It is worth noting that the British term "petrol" is simply an abbreviation of "petroleum ether" or "petroleum spirit," another name for gasoline. The word petrol only came into general use in the 1930s, however, before which the fuel was referred to as "motor spirit." Ligroin, the fuel used to power the original Benz Motorwagen, was yet another name for gasoline. It, too, was sold in pharmacies as a cleaning fluid, and was also known as petroleum benzine, or simply benzine or benzin. This name was not, as is sometimes suggested, derived from Carl Benz's family name, but was in wide use from the mid-ninteenth century, and is why gasoline is known as *benzin* in German and *benzina* in Italian. To further complicate matters, benzine is not the same as benzene, which is a specific hydrocarbon compound (whereas benzine is a mixture of several different hydrocarbons). Modern electric cars, with their many different types of plug and charger, are only marginally less confusing.

CHAPTER 10

For the history of the jitney, see Eckert and Hilton, "The Jitneys"; Schwantes, "The West Adapts the Automobile"; McShane, *Down the Asphalt Path*; and Norton, *Fighting Traffic*. For green books and the role of cars in the civil rights movement see Sorin, *Driving While Black*, and Blakemore, "How Automobiles Helped Power the Civil Rights Movement."

CHAPTER 11

The account of the DARPA Grand Challenges draws on contemporary media reports in *Popular Science*, *Wired*, and other periodicals. The history of the development of autonomous vehicles draws on my research and interviews for "Reinventing Wheels," a special report published in the *Economist* in January 2018. Prototype robotaxis such as the VW Sedric and the bidirectional Zoox vehicle, with their face-to-face bench seats and lack of steering wheels, look a lot like carriages, but without horses. You might even call them horse-less carriages.

CHAPTER 12

For the long history of predictions of the end of the car, see Ladd, *Autophobia*.

SOURCES

Albert, D. M. *Are We There Yet?: The American Automobile, Past, Present, and Driverless*. New York: W. W. Norton & Company, 2019.

Anthony, D. W. *The Horse, the Wheel, and Language: How Bronze-Age Riders from the Eurasian Steppes Shaped the Modern World*. Princeton: Princeton University Press, 2010.

Anthony, D. W., and Vinogradov, N. B. "Birth of the Chariot." *Archaeology*, vol. 48, no. 2 (1995): 36–41.

Bailey, B. L. "From Front Porch to Back Seat: A History of the Date." *OAH Magazine of History*, vol. 18, no. 4 (July 2004): 23–26.

Berger, M. L. *The Automobile in American History and Culture: A Reference Guide*. Westport: Greenwood Publishing Group, 2001.

Blakemore, E. "How Automobiles Helped Power the Civil Rights Movement." Smithsonianmag.com, February 28, 2020

Bondár, M., and Székely, G. V. "A New Early Bronze Age Wagon Model From the Carpathian Basin." *World Archaeology*, vol. 43, no, 4 (2011): 538–553.

Buder, S. *Visionaries and Planners: The Garden City Movement and the Modern Community*. Oxford: Oxford University Press, 1990.

Bulliet, R. W. *The Camel and the Wheel*. Cambridge: Harvard University Press, 1975.

Bulliet, R. W. *The Wheel: Inventions & Reinventions*. New York: Columbia University Press, 2016.

Burmeister, S. "Early Wagons in Eurasia: Disentangling an Enigmatic Innovation." From Stockhammer, P. and Maran, J. (eds), *Appropriating Innovations: Entangled Knowledge in Eurasia, 5000–1500 BCE*. Oxford: Oxbow Books, 2017.

Burmeister, S. "Innovation as a Possibility: Technological and Social Determinism in Their Dialectical Resolution." From Stefan Burmeister and Reinhard

Bernbeck (eds), *The Interplay of People and Technologies: Archaeological Case Studies on Innovation*. Berlin: Edition Topoi, 2017.

Candelo, E. *Marketing Innovations in the Automotive Industry: Meeting the Challenges of the Digital Age*. Cham, Switzerland: Springer, 2019.

Chondros, T. G., Milidonis, K. F., Rossi, C., and Zrnic, N. "The Evolution of the Double-Horse Chariots From the Bronze Age to the Hellenistic Times." *FME Transactions*, vol. 44 (2016): 229–236.

Cohen, M. M. "Forgotten Audiences in the Passion Pits: Drive-In Theatres and Changing Spectator Practices in Post-War America." *Film History*, vol. 6, no. 4 (Winter 1994): 470–486.

Cormier, B., and Bisley, L. (eds). *Cars: Accelerating the Modern World*. London: V&A Publishing, 2019.

Davison, B. "Super City: Los Angeles and the Birth of the Supermarket, 1914–1941." *California History*, vol. 93, no. 3 (Fall 2016): 9–27.

Dell, R. M., Moseley, P. T., and Rand, A. J. *Towards Sustainable Road Transport*. Waltham: Elsevier Academic Press, 2014.

Dickinson, H. W., and Titley, A. *Richard Trevithick: The Engineer and the Man*. Cambridge: Cambridge University Press, 2011.

Eckert, R., and Hilton, G. W. "The Jitneys." *The Journal of Law & Economics*, vol. 15, no. 2 (October 1972): 293–325.

Fogelson, R. M. *Downtown: Its Rise and Fall, 1880-1950*. New Haven: Yale University Press, 2003.

Fotsch, P. M. "The Building of a Superhighway Future at the New York World's Fair." *Cultural Critique*, no. 48 (Spring 2001): 65–97.

Gallagher, L. *The End of the Suburbs: Where the American Dream Is Moving*. New York: Portfolio/Penguin, 2014.

Gerbino, A. *François Blondel: Architecture, Erudition, and the Scientific Revolution*. London: Routledge, 2013.

Guroff, M. *Mechanical Horse: How the Bicycle Reshaped American Life*. Austin: University of Texas Press, 2018.

Hadland, T., Lessing, H.-E., Clayton, N., and Sanderson, G. W. *Bicycle Design: An Illustrated History*. Cambridge: MIT Press, 2016.

Halberstam, D. *The Fifties*. New York: Random House, 1994.

Hanchett, T. W. "U.S. Tax Policy and the Shopping-Center Boom of the 1950s and 1960s." *The American Historical Review*, vol. 101, no. 4 (October 1996): 1082–1110.

Harb, M., Xiao, Y., Circella, G. et al. "Projecting Travelers Into a World of Self-Driving Vehicles: Estimating Travel Behavior Implications via a Naturalistic Experiment." *Transportation*, vol. 45 (2018): 1671–1685.

Hardwick, J. M. *Mall Maker: Victor Gruen, Architect of an American Dream*. Philadelphia: University of Pennsylvania Press, 2010.

Herlihy, D. V. *Bicycle: The History*. New Haven: Yale University Press, 2004.

Hess, A. "The Origins of McDonald's Golden Arches." Journal of the Society of Architectural Historians, vol. 45, no. 1 (March 1986): 60–67.

Horváth, T., Svingor, E., and Molnár, M. "New Radiocarbon Dates for the Baden Culture." *Radiocarbon*, vol. 50 (2008): 447–458.

Jackson, K. T. "All the World's a Mall: Reflections on the Social and Economic Consequences of the American Shopping Center." *The American Historical Review*, vol. 101, no. 4 (October 1996): 1111–1121.

Jackson, L. *Dirty Old London: The Victorian Fight Against Filth*. New Haven: Yale University Press, 2014.

Jacobs, J. *The Death and Life of Great American Cities*. New York: Random House, 1961.

Jakle, J. A., and Sculle, K. A. *Fast Food: Roadside Restaurants in The Automobile Age*. Baltimore: Johns Hopkins Univ. Press, 2002.

Kostof, S., and Castillo, G. *The City Assembled: The Elements of Urban Form Through History*. New York: Thames & Hudson, 2014.

Kostof, S., and Tobias, R. *The City Shaped: Urban Patterns and Meanings Through History*. New York: Bulfinch Press, 2012.

Ladd, B. *Autophobia: Love and Hate in the Automotive Age*. Chicago: University of Chicago Press, 2011.

Larsen, L. H. "Nineteenth-Century Street Sanitation: A Study of Filth and Frustration." *The Wisconsin Magazine of History*, vol. 52, no. 3 (Spring 1969): 239–247.

Lipski, P. W. "The Introduction of 'Automobile' into American English." *American Speech*, vol. 39, no. 3 (October 1964): 176–187.

Longstreth, R. "The Drive-In, the Supermarket, and the Transformation of Commercial Space in Los Angeles, 1914-1941." *Modernism/Modernity*, vol. 7 (January 2000): 194–196.

Luther, R. "Drive-In Theaters: Rags to Riches in Five Years." *Hollywood Quarterly*, vol. 5, no. 4 (Summer 1951): 401–411.

Maggs, C. *Great Britain's Railways: A New History*. Stroud: Amberley Publishing, 2018.

Marshall, C. "The Obsolescent Auto." *Michigan Quarterly Review*, vol. 19, no. 4 (Fall 1980): 750–753.

McCarthy, T. "The Coming Wonder? Foresight and Early Concerns about the Automobile." *Environmental History*, vol. 6, no. 1 (January 2001): 46–74.

McShane, C. "The Origins and Globalization of Traffic Control Signals." *Journal of Urban History*, vol. 25, no. 3 (March 1999): 379–404.

McShane, C. *Down the Asphalt Path: The Automobile and the American City*. New York: Columbia University Press, 1994.

Milne-Smith, A. "Shattered Minds: Madmen on the Railways, 1860-80." *Journal of Victorian Culture*, vol. 21, no. 1 (2016): 21–39.

Morgunova, N. L., and Turetskij, M. A. "Archaeological and Natural Scientific Studies of Pit-Grave Culture Barrows in The Volga-Ural Interfluve." *Estonian Journal of Archaeology*, vol. 20, no. 2 (2016): 128–149.

Mumford, E. P. *Designing the Modern City: Urbanism Since 1850*. New Haven: Yale University Press, 2018.

Norton, P. D. *Fighting Traffic: The Dawn of the Motor Age in the American City.* Cambridge: MIT Press, 2011.

O'Connell, S. *The Car and British Society: Class, Gender and Motoring, 1896–1939.* Manchester: Manchester University Press, 1998.

Painter, D. S. "Oil and the American Century." *The Journal of American History,* vol. 99, no. 1 (June 2012): 24–39.

Parpola, A. "Proto-Indo-European Speakers of the Late Tripolye Culture as the Inventors of Wheeled Vehicles: Linguistic and Archaeological Considerations of the PIE Homeland Problem." From Jones-Bley, K., Huld, M. E., Della Volpe, A., Dexter M. R. (eds), *Proceedings of the 19th Annual UCLA Indo-European Conference.* Washington, D.C.: Institute for the Study of Man, 2008.

Peiss, K. "Charity Girls and City Pleasures." *OAH Magazine of History,* vol. 18, no. 4 (July 2004): 14–16.

Piggott, S. *The Earliest Wheeled Transport. From the Atlantic Coast to the Caspian Sea.* London: Thames and Hudson, 1983

Poehler, E., Van Roggen, J., and Crowther, B. "The Iron Streets of Pompeii." *American Journal of Archaeology,* vol. 123, no. 2 (2019): 237–262.

Poehler, E. "Romans on the Right: The Art and Archaeology of Traffic." *Athanor,* vol. 21 (2003): 7–15.

Poehler, E. *The Traffic Systems of Pompeii.* New York: Oxford University Press, 2017.

Reid, C. *Roads Were Not Built For Cars.* Washington, D.C.: Island Press, 2015.

Rhodes, R. *Energy: A Human History.* New York: Simon & Schuster, 2019.

Schlich, T. "Trauma Surgery and Traffic Policy in Germany in the 1930s: A Case Study in the Coevolution of Modern Surgery and Society." *Bulletin of the History of Medicine,* vol. 80, no. 1 (Spring 2006): 73–94.

Schlosser, E. *Fast Food Nation: What the All-American Meal is Doing to the World.* London: Penguin, 2007.

Schwantes, C. A. "The West Adapts the Automobile: Technology, Unemployment, and the Jitney Phenomenon of 1914–1917." *Western Historical Quarterly*, vol. 16, no. 3 (July 1985): 307–326.

Shelton, T. "Automobile Utopias and Traditional Urban Infrastructure: Visions of the Coming Conflict, 1925–1940." *Traditional Dwellings and Settlements Review*, vol. 22, no. 2 (Spring 2011): 63–76.

Shishlina, N., Kovalev, D. S., and Ibragimova, E. "Catacomb Culture Wagons of the Eurasian Steppes." *Antiquity*, vol. 88, no. 340 (2014): 378–394.

Slater, C. "General Motors and the Demise of Streetcars." *Transportation Quarterly*, vol. 51, no. 3 (Summer 1997): 45–66.

Sloan, A. P. *My Years with General Motors*. Garden City, NY: Doubleday, 1972.

Sorin, G. S. *Driving While Black: African American Travel and the Road to Civil Rights*. New York: Liveright Publishing, 2020.

Standage, T. "Reinventing Wheels: A Special Report on Autonomous Vehicles." *Economist*, March 3, 2018.

Tarr, J. A. *The Search for the Ultimate Sink: Urban Pollution in Historical Perspective*. Akron, OH: University of Akron Press, 1996.

Tarr, L. *The History of the Carriage*. London: Vision Press, 1969.

Tedlow, R.S. "The Struggle for Dominance in the Automobile Market: The Early Years of Ford and General Motors." *Business and Economic History*, second series, vol. 17 (1988): 49–62.

Thompson, F. M. L. *Victorian England: The Horse-Drawn Society. An Inaugural Lecture*. London: Bedford College, 1970.

Tilburg, C. V. "Traffic Policy and Circulation in Roman Cities." *Acta Classica* vol. 54 (2011): 149–171.

Townsend, C. "Year Without a Summer." *Paris Review*, October 26, 2016.

Trevithick, F. *The Life of Richard Trevithick: With an Account of His Inventions*. London: E. and F. Spon, 1872.

Volti, R. *Cars and Culture: The Life Story of a Technology*. Westport, CT: Greenwood Press, 2004.

Vuchic, V. R. *Urban Transit Systems and Technology*. Hoboken: John Wiley & Sons, 2010.

Weaver, R. C. "The Suburbanization of America." Paper presented to the Commission on Civil Rights, Washington, D.C., December 1975.

Weiland, J. H. "The Adolescent and the Automobile." *Chicago Review*, vol. 9, no. 3 (Fall 1955): 61–64.

Wells, C. W. "The Road to the Model T: Culture, Road Conditions, and Innovation at the Dawn of the American Motor Age." *Technology and Culture*, vol. 48, no. 3 (July 2007): 497–523.

Williamson, J. "Retrofitting Suburbia: A Pedagogical Perspective." Paper in *Proceedings of 97th ACSA Annual Meeting*. Portland: ACSA Press, 2009.

Wrigley, R. *The Flâneur Abroad: Historical and International Perspectives*. Newcastle upon Tyne: Cambridge Scholars Publishing, 2014.

Zimmerman, M. M. "The Supermarket and the Changing Retail Structure." *Journal of Marketing*, vol. 5, no. 4 (April 1941): 402–409.

IMAGE CREDITS

INDEX

Note: page numbers in *italics* refer to figures.

A NOTE ON THE AUTHOR

TOM STANDAGE is deputy editor at the *Economist*, and editor of its future-gazing annual, *The World Ahead*. Standage is the author of seven books, including the *New York Times* bestsellers *A History of the World in 6 Glasses* and *An Edible History of Humanity*, and *The Victorian Internet*, described by the *Wall Street Journal* as a "dot-com cult classic." Standage studied engineering and computer science at the University of Oxford and has written for many other publications, including the *New York Times* and *Wired*. He lives in London with his wife and children. Visit his website at www.tomstandage.com.